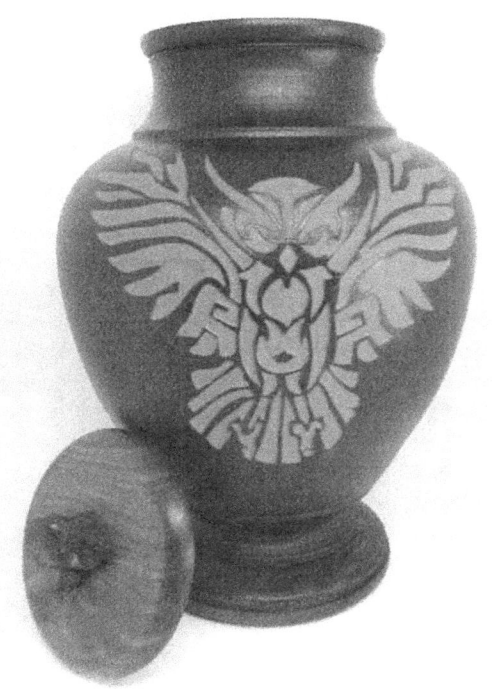

"CLAYSLINGER" — TOOTALLSPOTTERY
First artist to use a tattoo machine on ceramics!

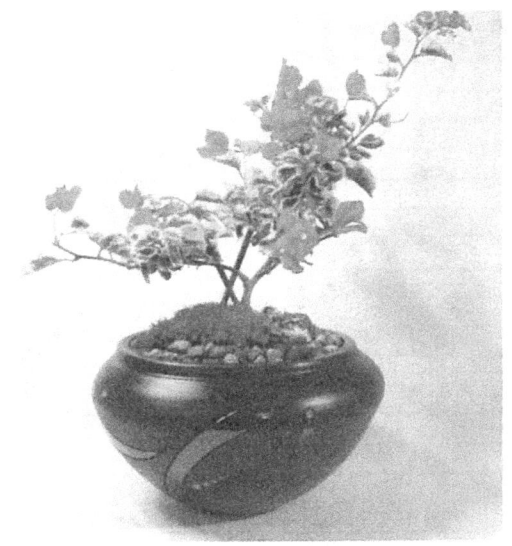

I0481191

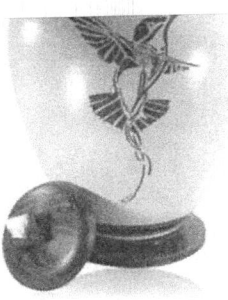

Artist Biography

Matthew S. Kennedy is a self-taught ceramic artist with an international reputation, whose professional career has spanned more than 20+ years as a ceramic artist. He is the first artist to use a tattoo machine as a carving tool on ceramics. His art work is featured in many offline and online galleries. In recent years, Matthew has developed strong relationships within the art community, consultants, television and movie artists and stylists, corporate representatives and interior designers who wish to provide their clients with extraordinary beautiful works of art. His art mediums are ceramic, and enameling, making unique use of vibrant pigments and colors for each piece of art work. The Ceramic Tattoo inspired collection is his most recent works. Matthew hand carves each design element for every piece. Visit the Website: www.ceramictattooart.com

Matthew also gives 10% of all sales proceeds to his charity:
http://www.homelessresourcesca.org

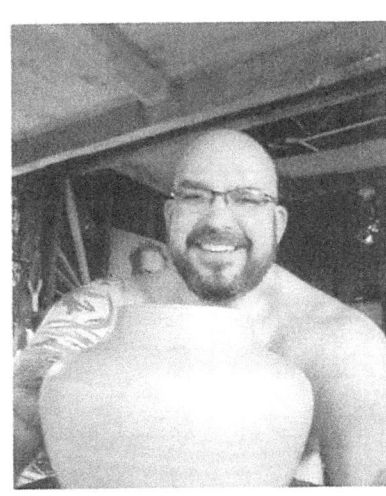

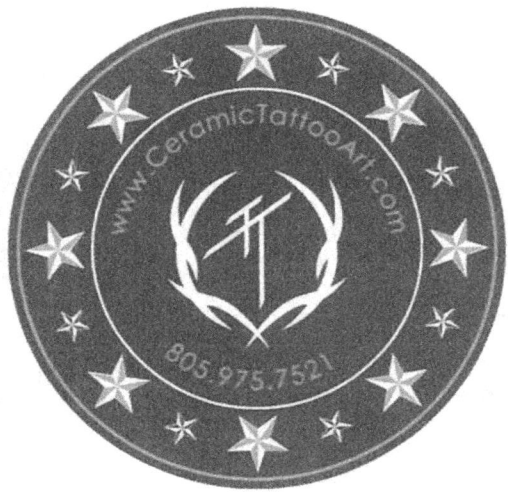

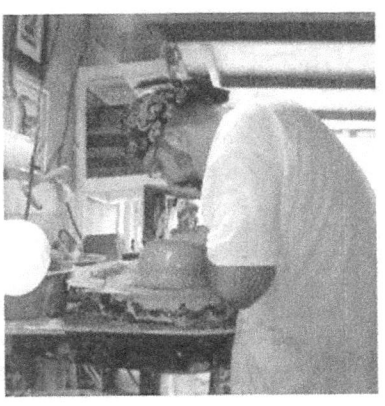

California Homeless Resources

www.homelessresourcesca.org

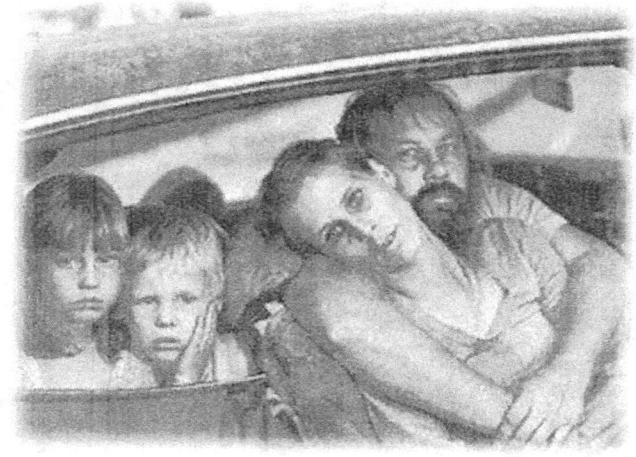

Many of our homeless not only go without adequate shelter, but without adequate warm clothing as well. Help us keep the less fortunate as warm as possible! ☺

What do we do?

We <u>inform</u> the people in California who are just about to be homeless or are already homeless. We also are providing a list of resources in every City in California. We want to help people "connect the dots" and be able to access the resources that are available as quickly as possible.

Contact Information:
Matt Kennedy
E-mail: tootallspottery@gmail.com
Website: www. homelessresourcesca.org
Ceramic Tattoo Art Website: www.ceramictattooart.com

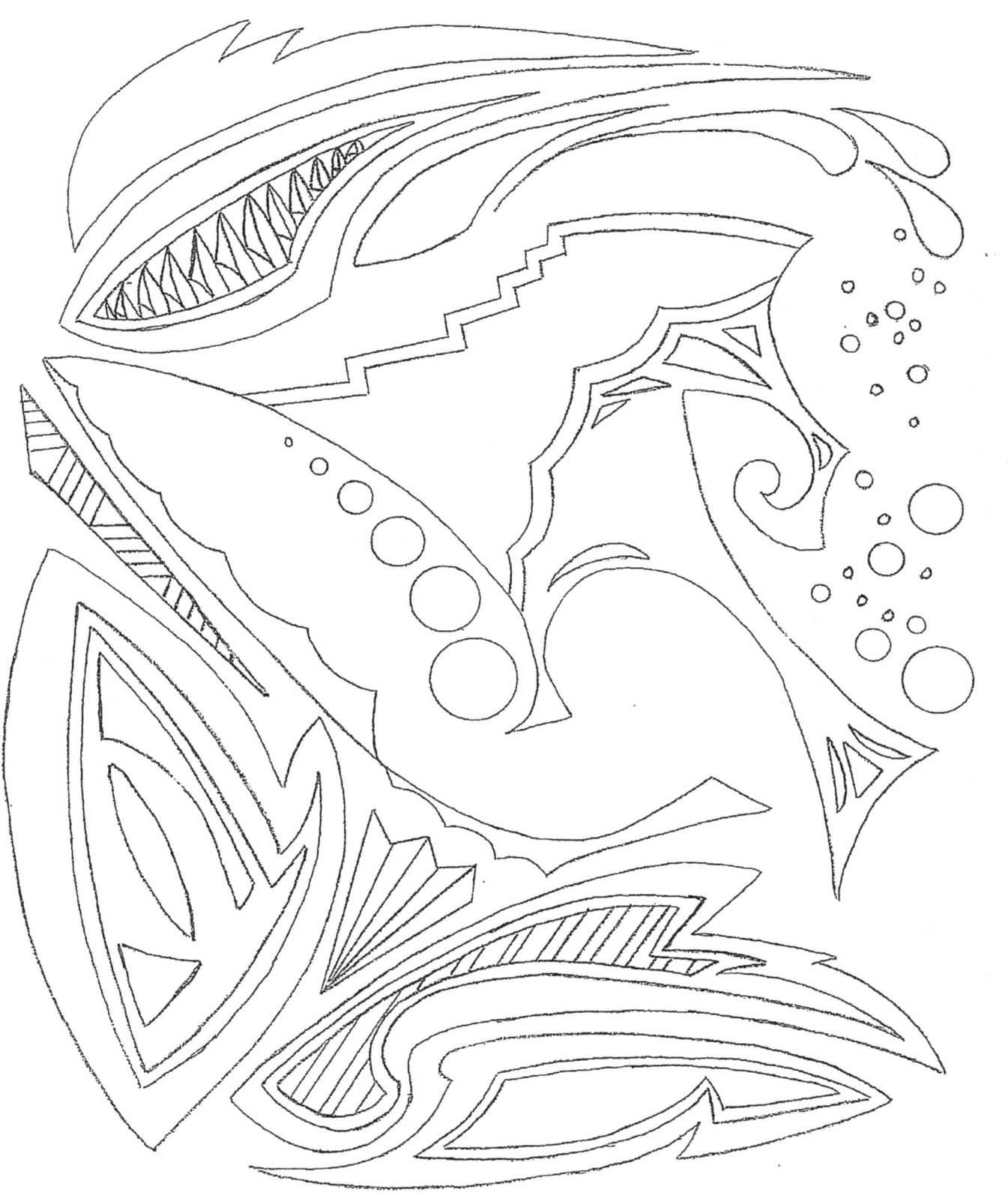

Learn how to be happy with what you have while you pursue all that you want.

Jim Rohn

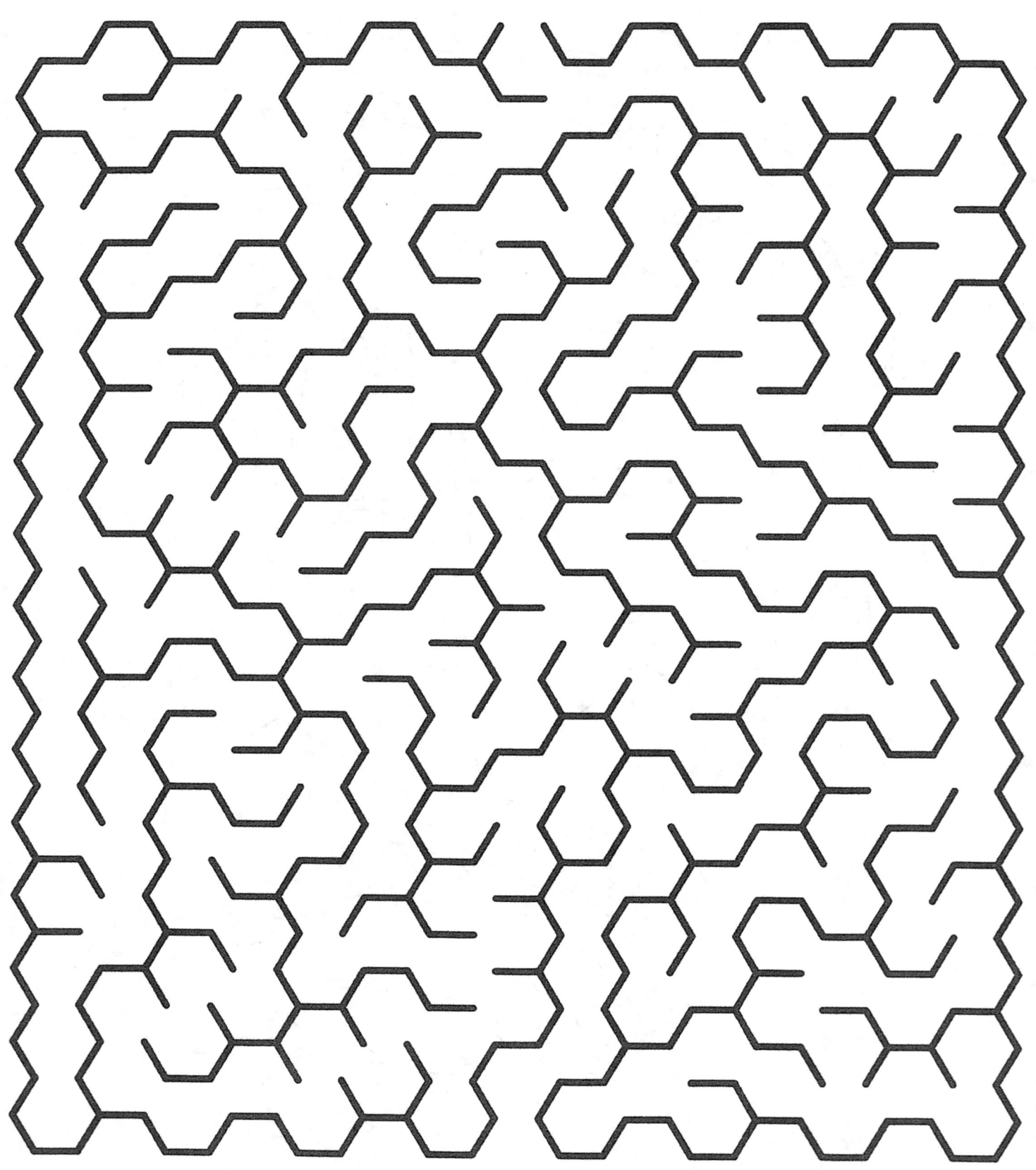

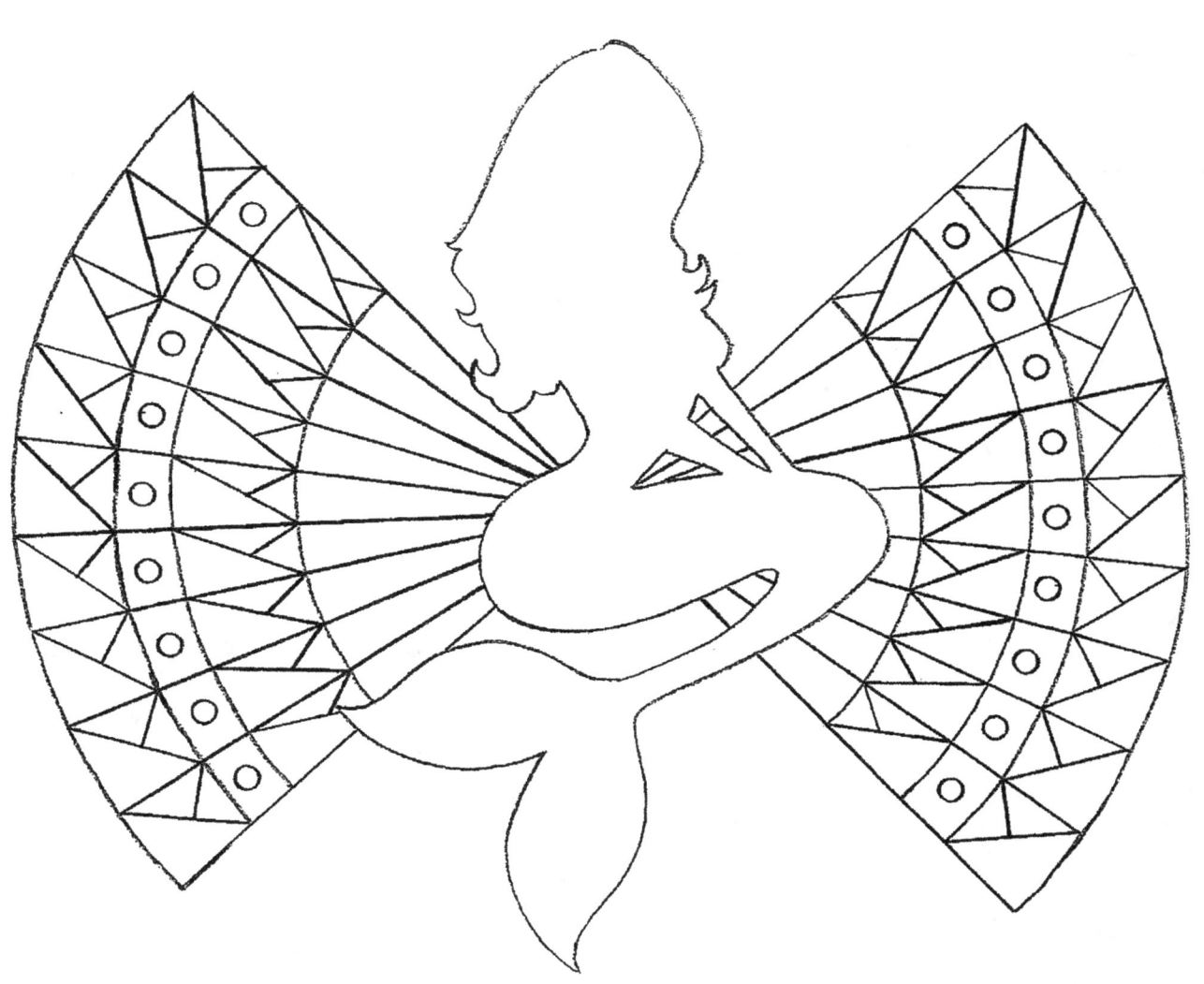

Being cool is being your own self, not doing something that someone else is telling you to do.

Vanessa Hudgens

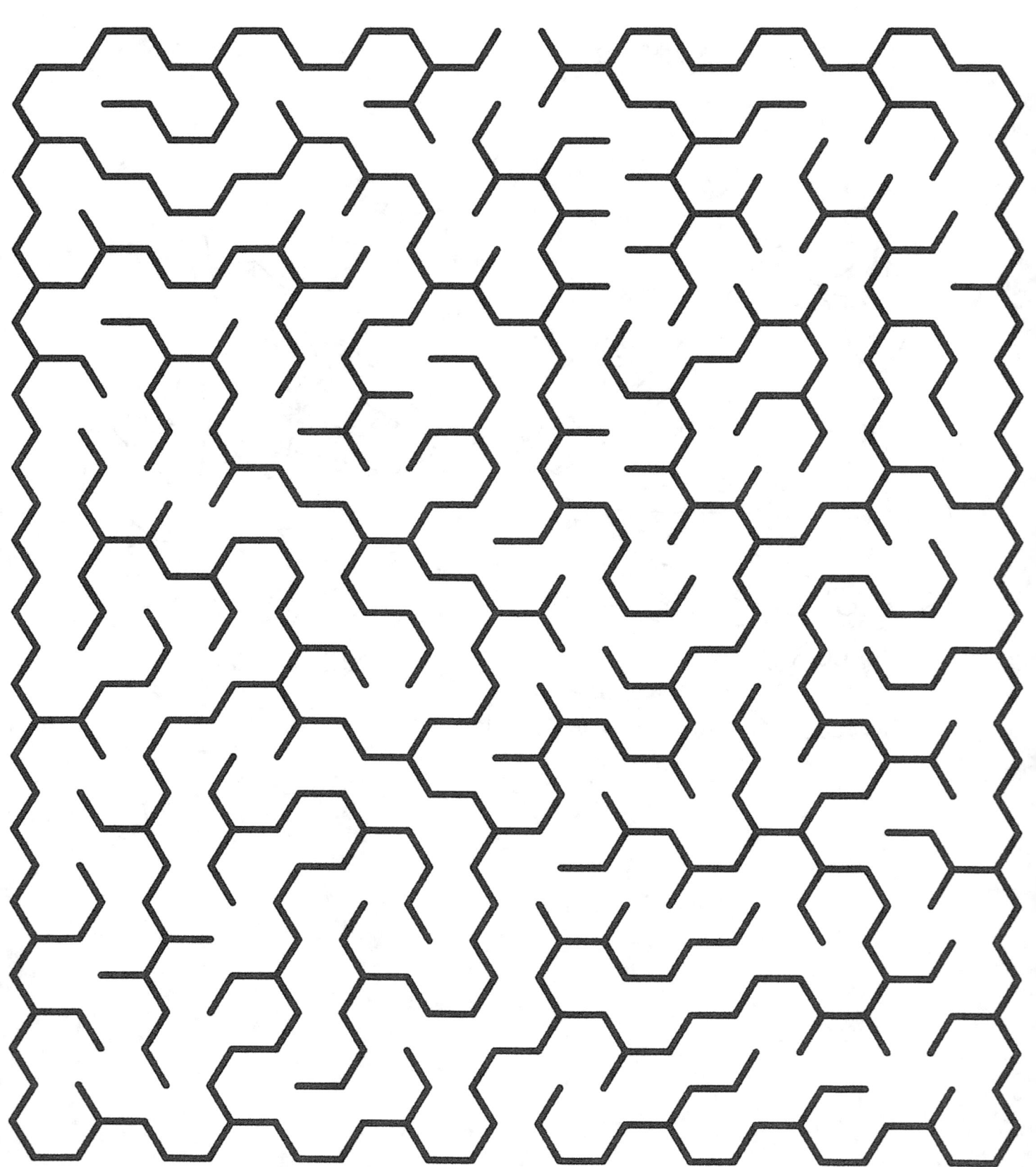

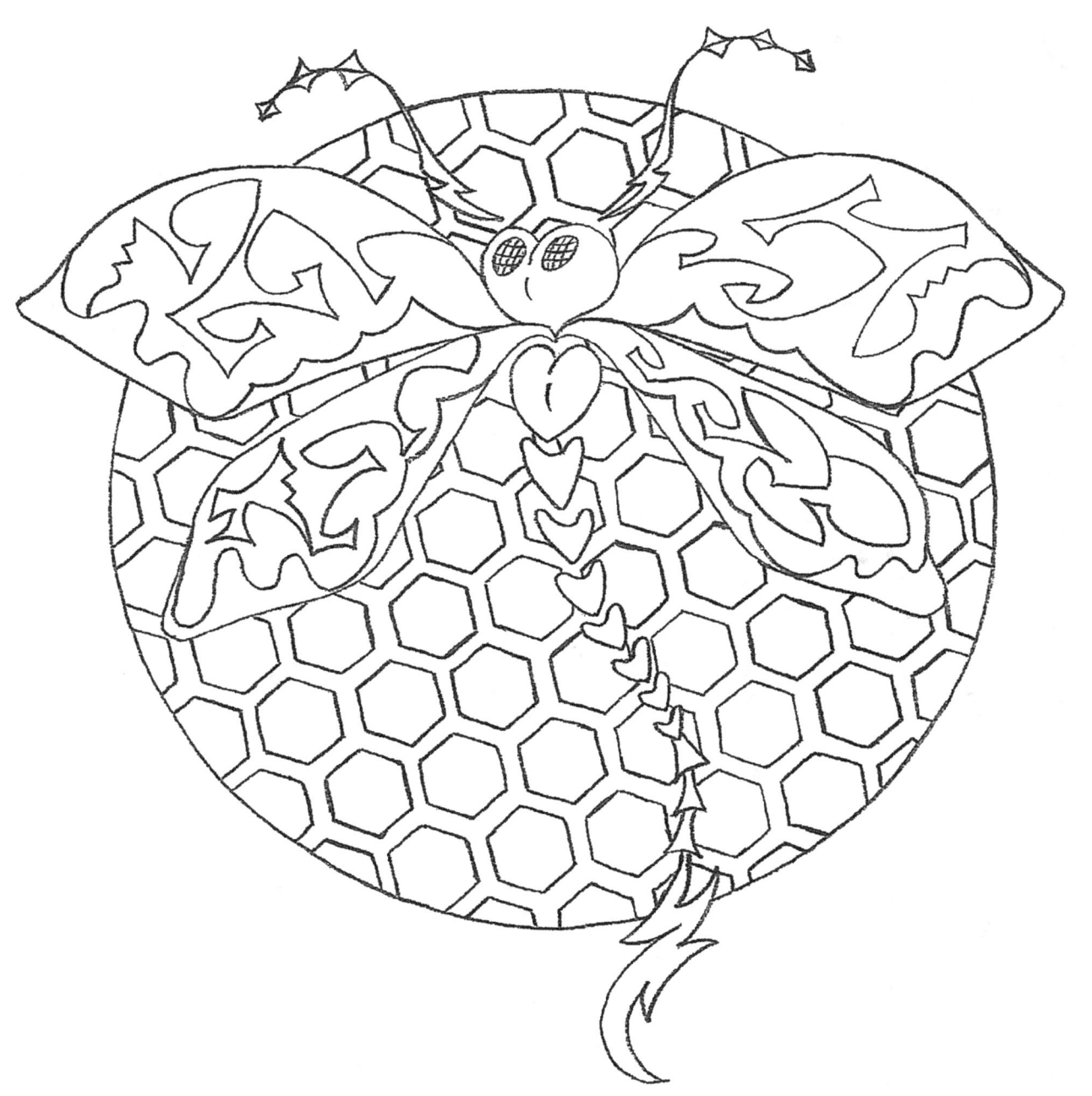

Art, freedom and creativity will change society faster than politics.

Victor Pinchuk

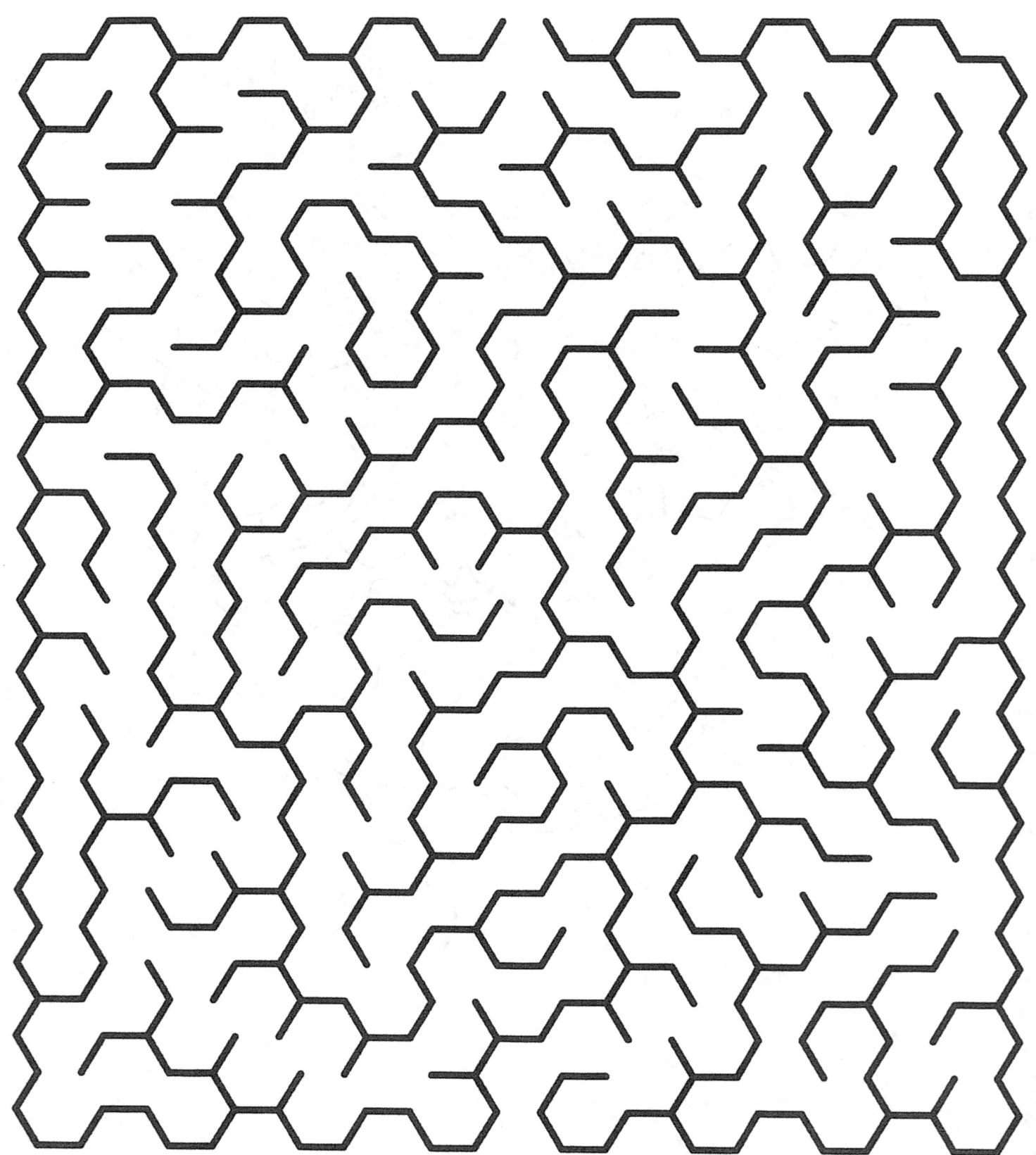

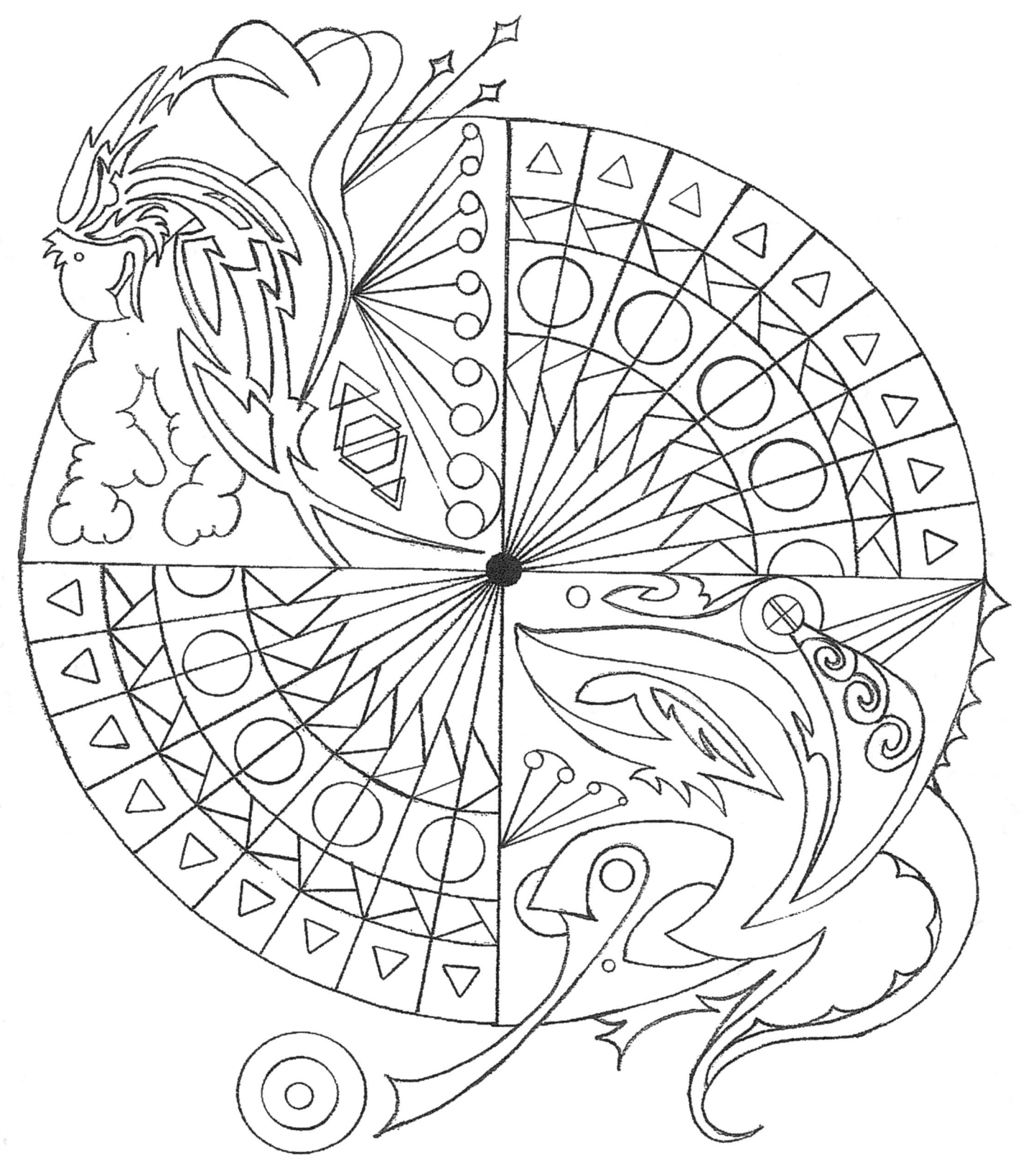

There is only one happiness in this life, to love and be loved.

George Sand

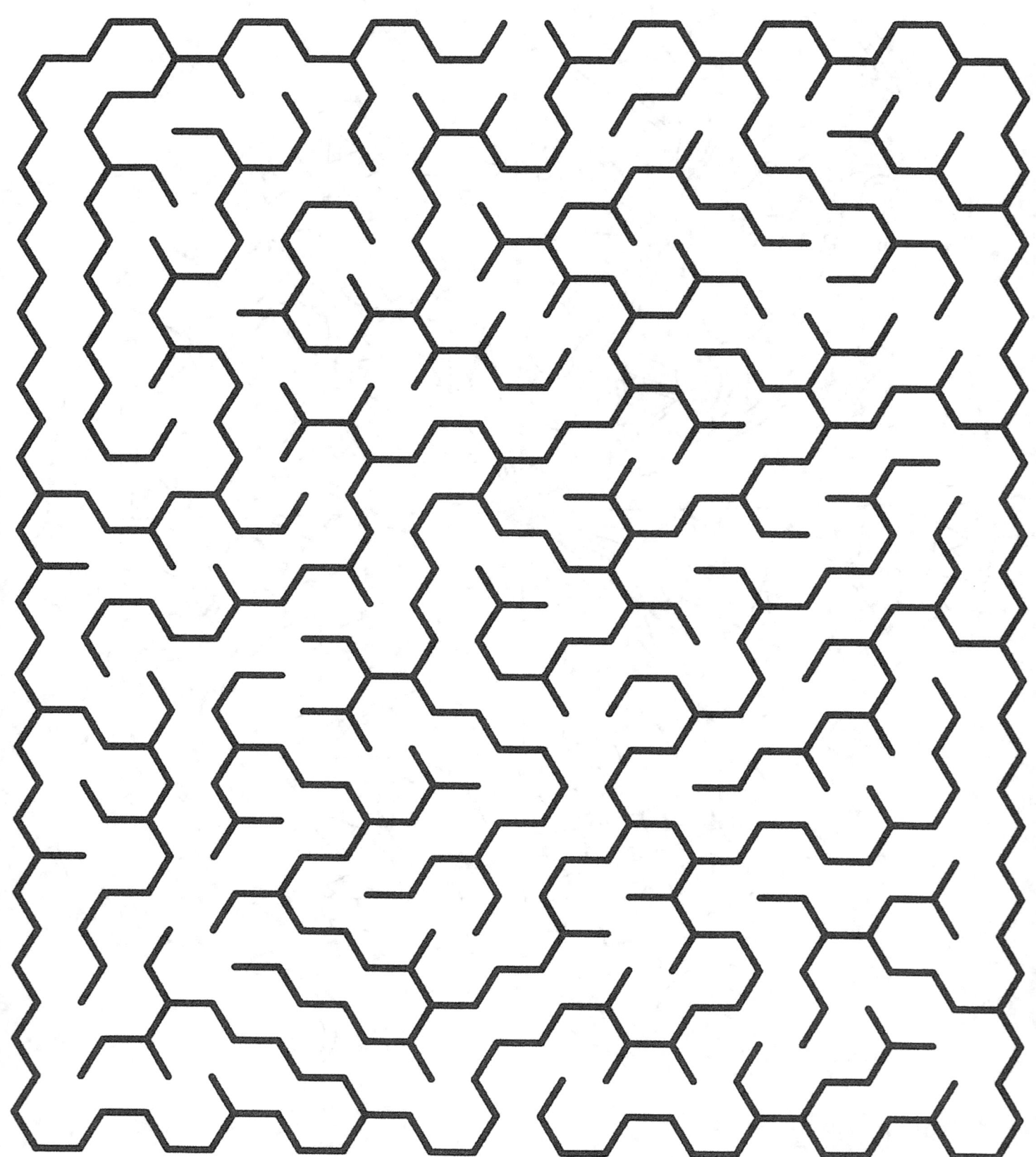

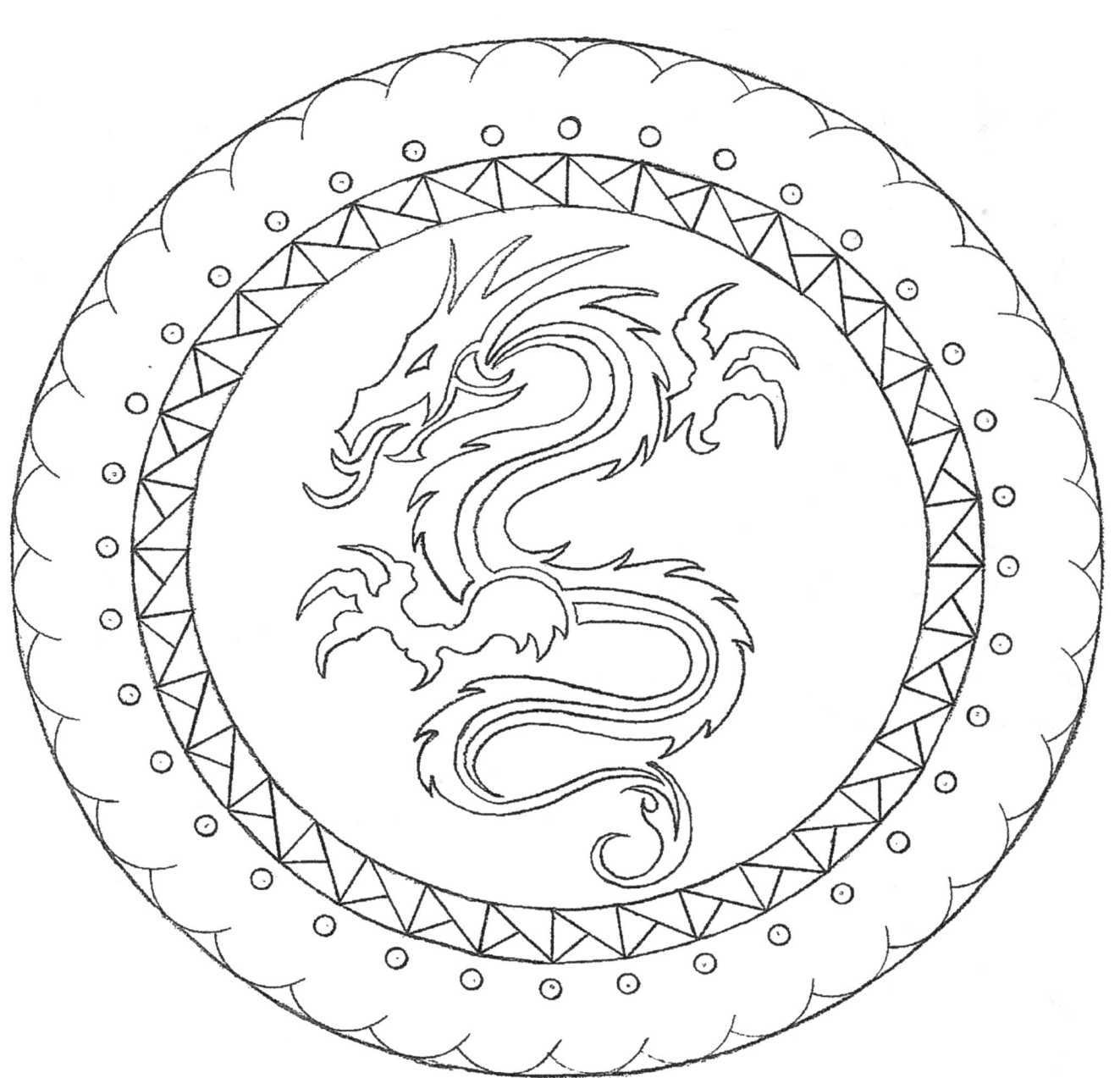

It's all about quality of life and finding a happy balance between work and friends and family.

Philip Green

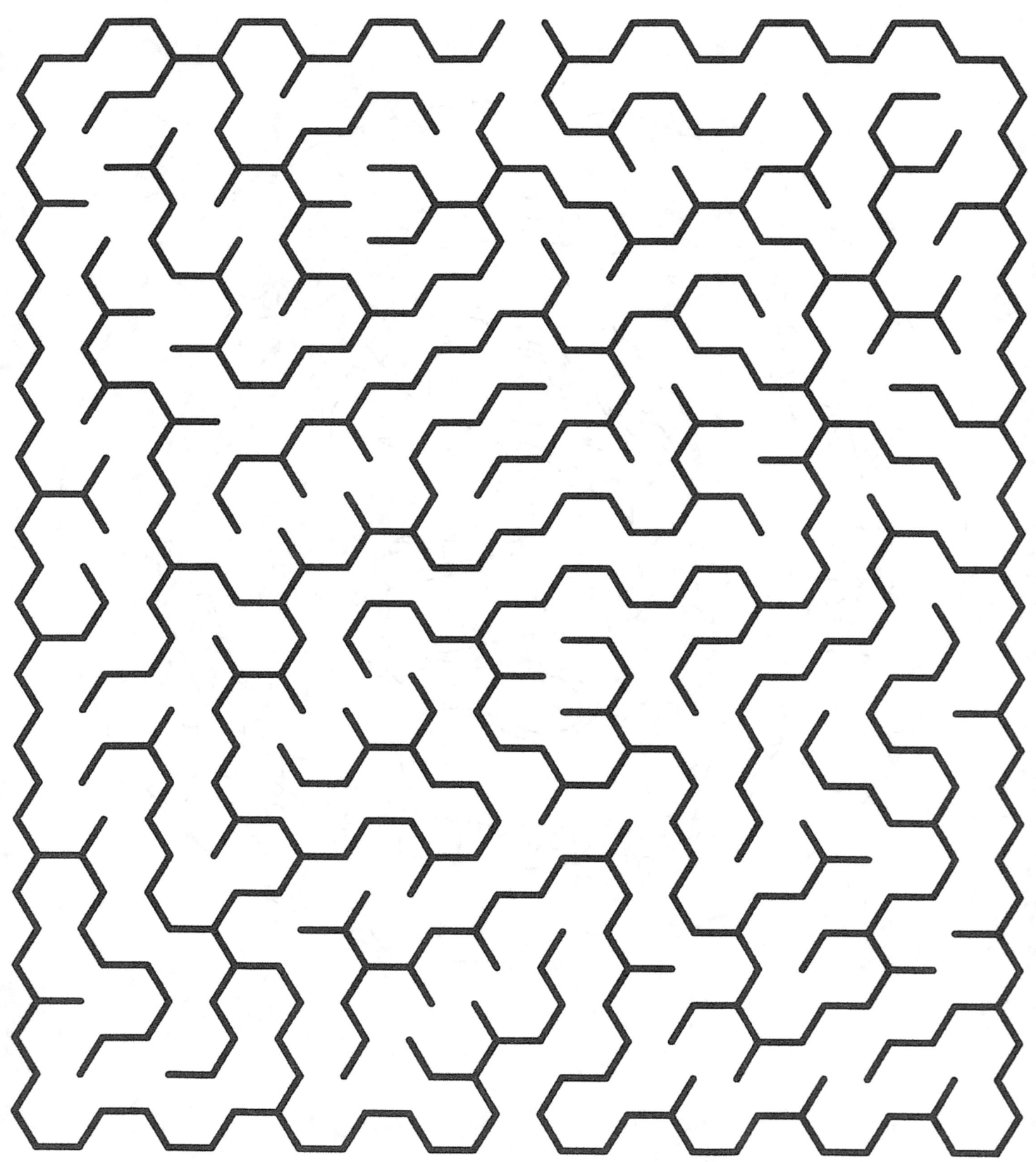

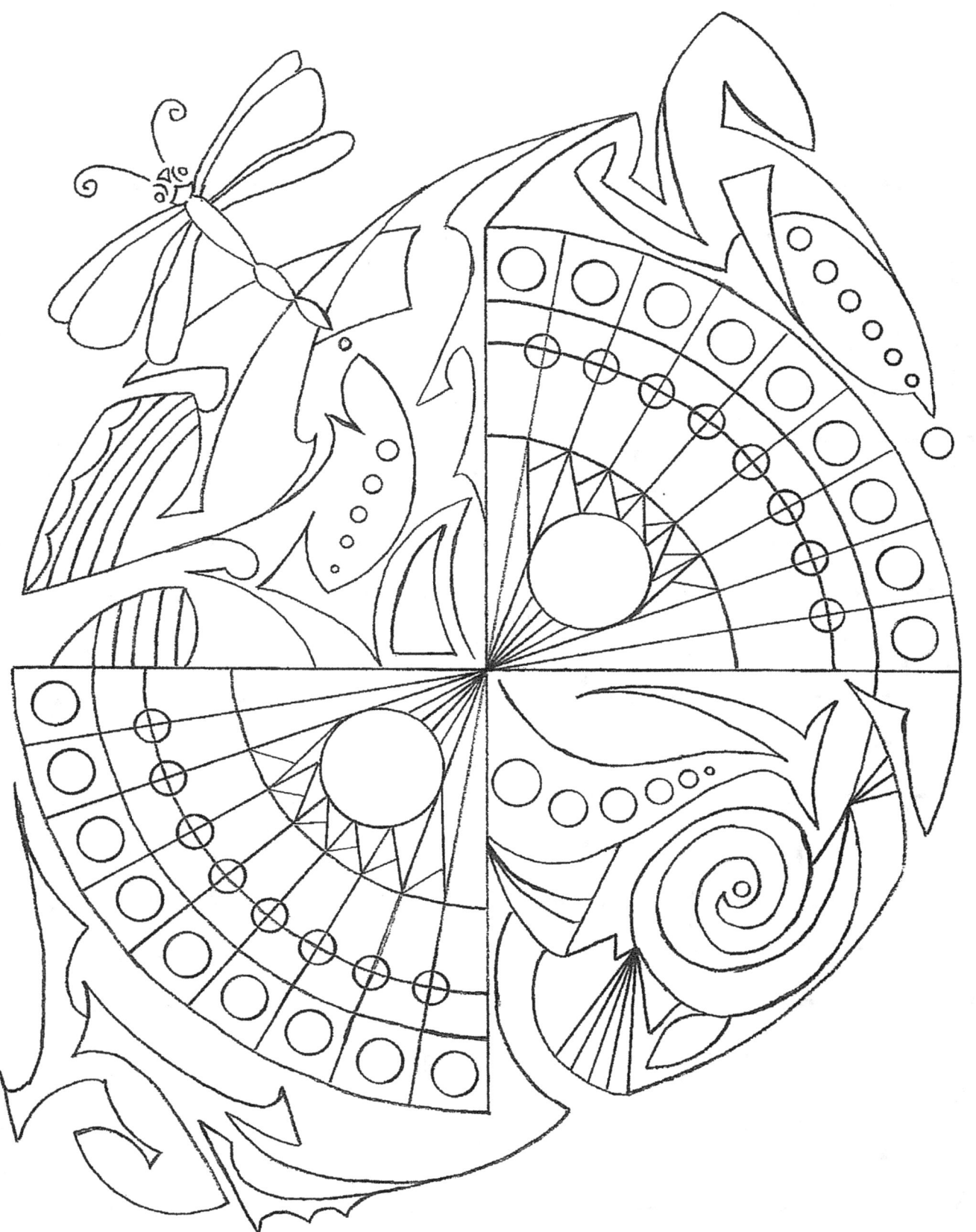

Do not take life too seriously. You will never get out of it alive.

Elbert Hubbard

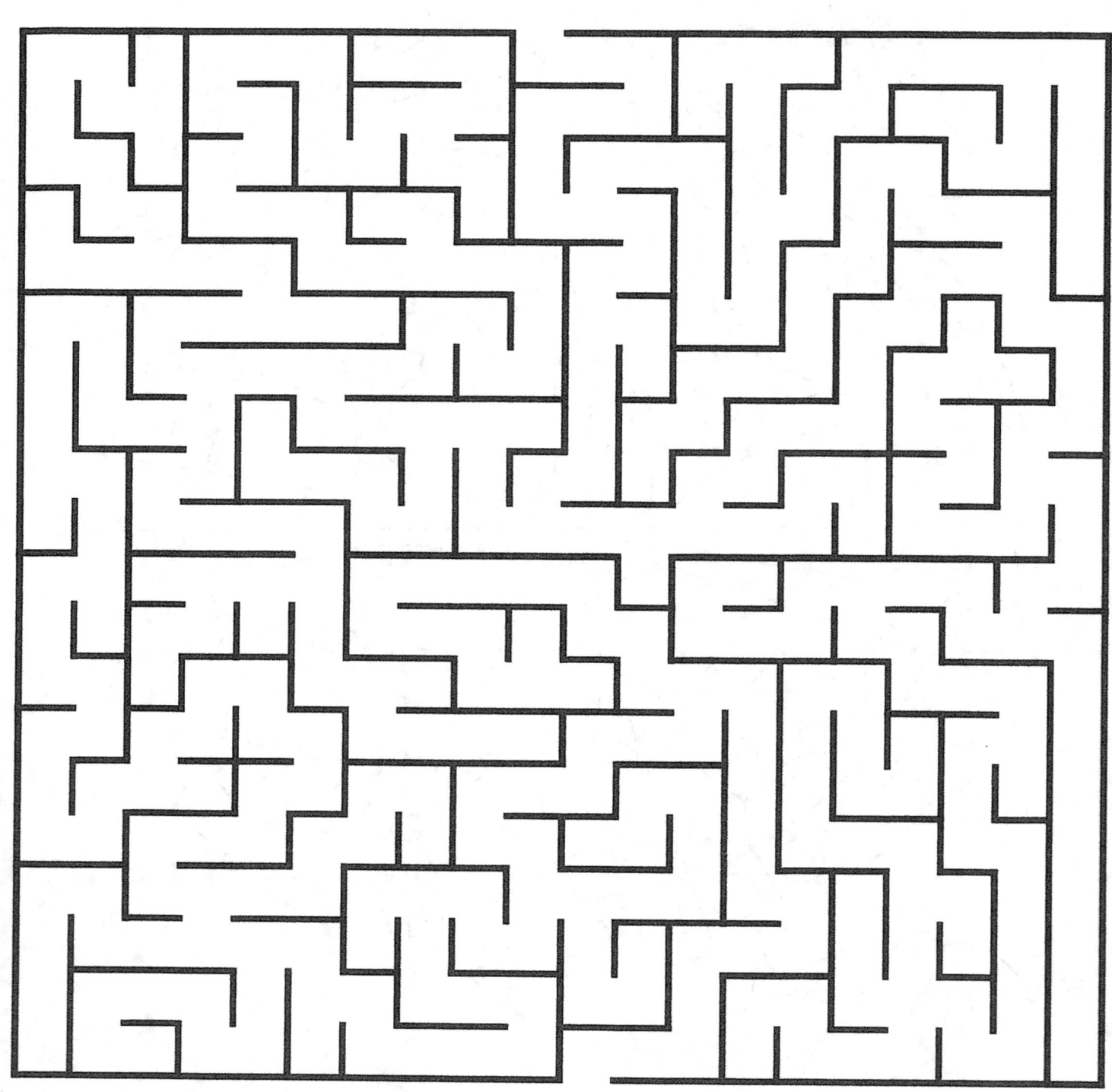

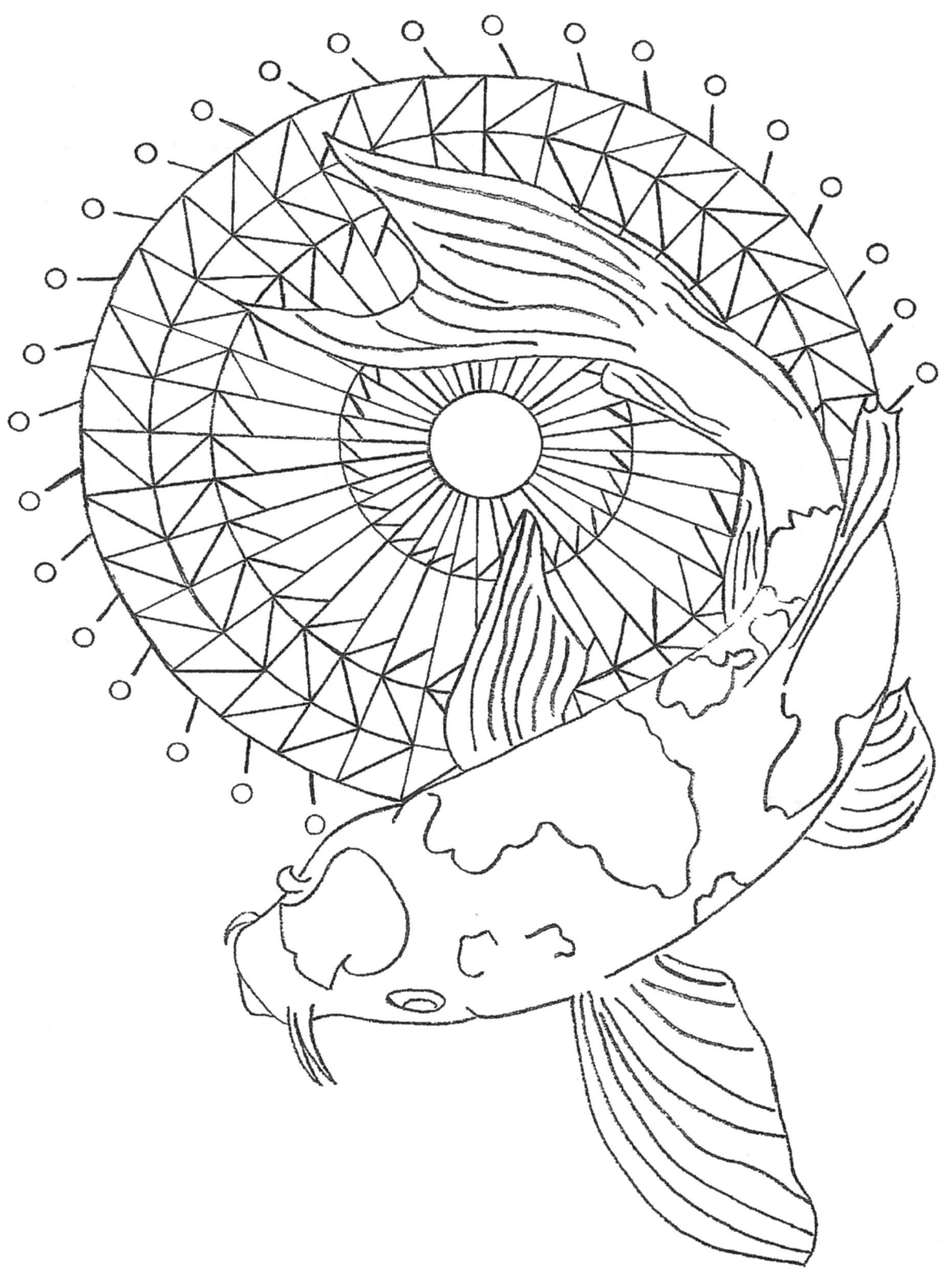

There are two great days in a person's life - the day we are born and the day we discover why.

William Barclay

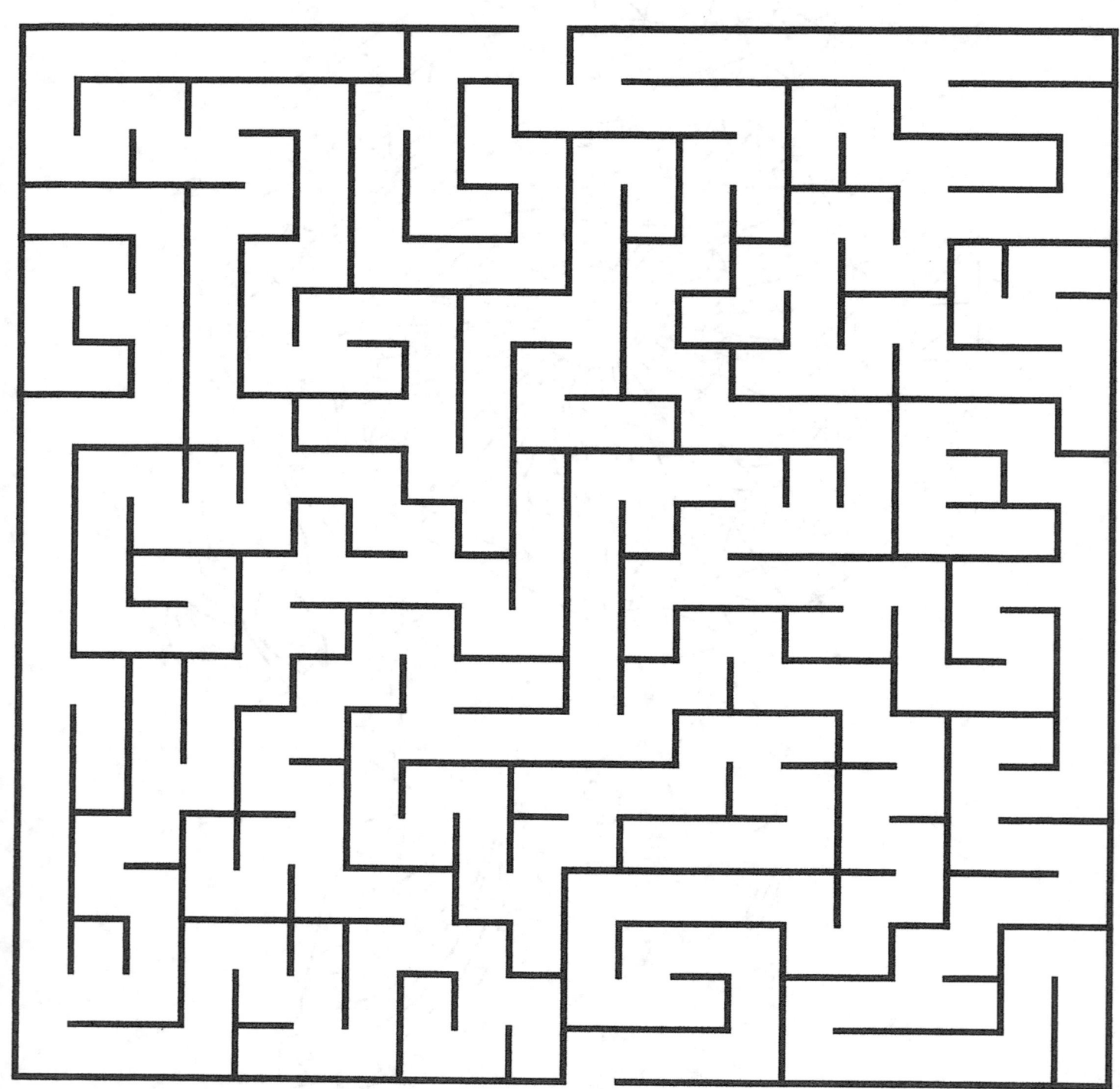

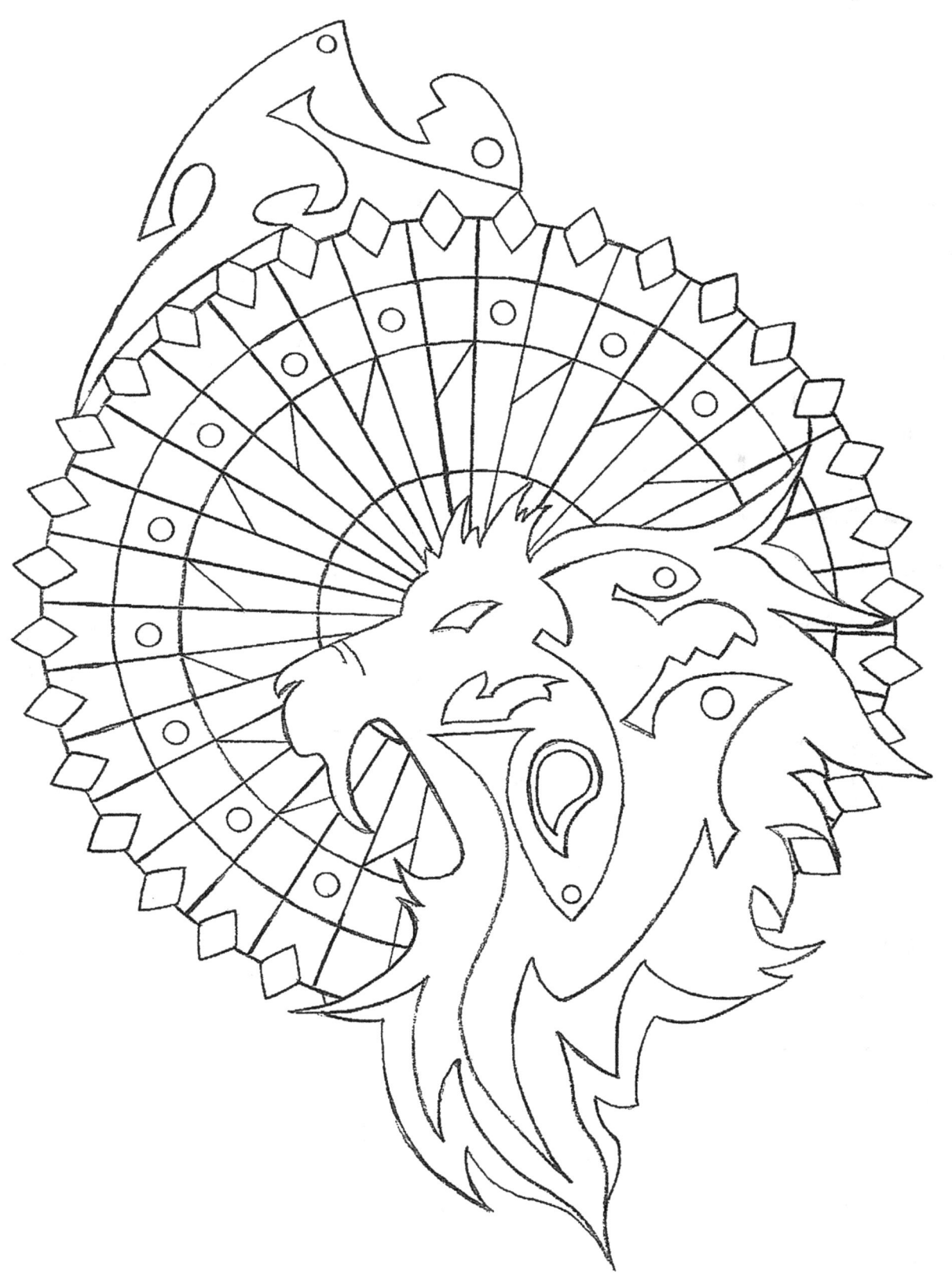

The biggest adventure you can take is to live the life of your dreams.

Oprah Winfrey

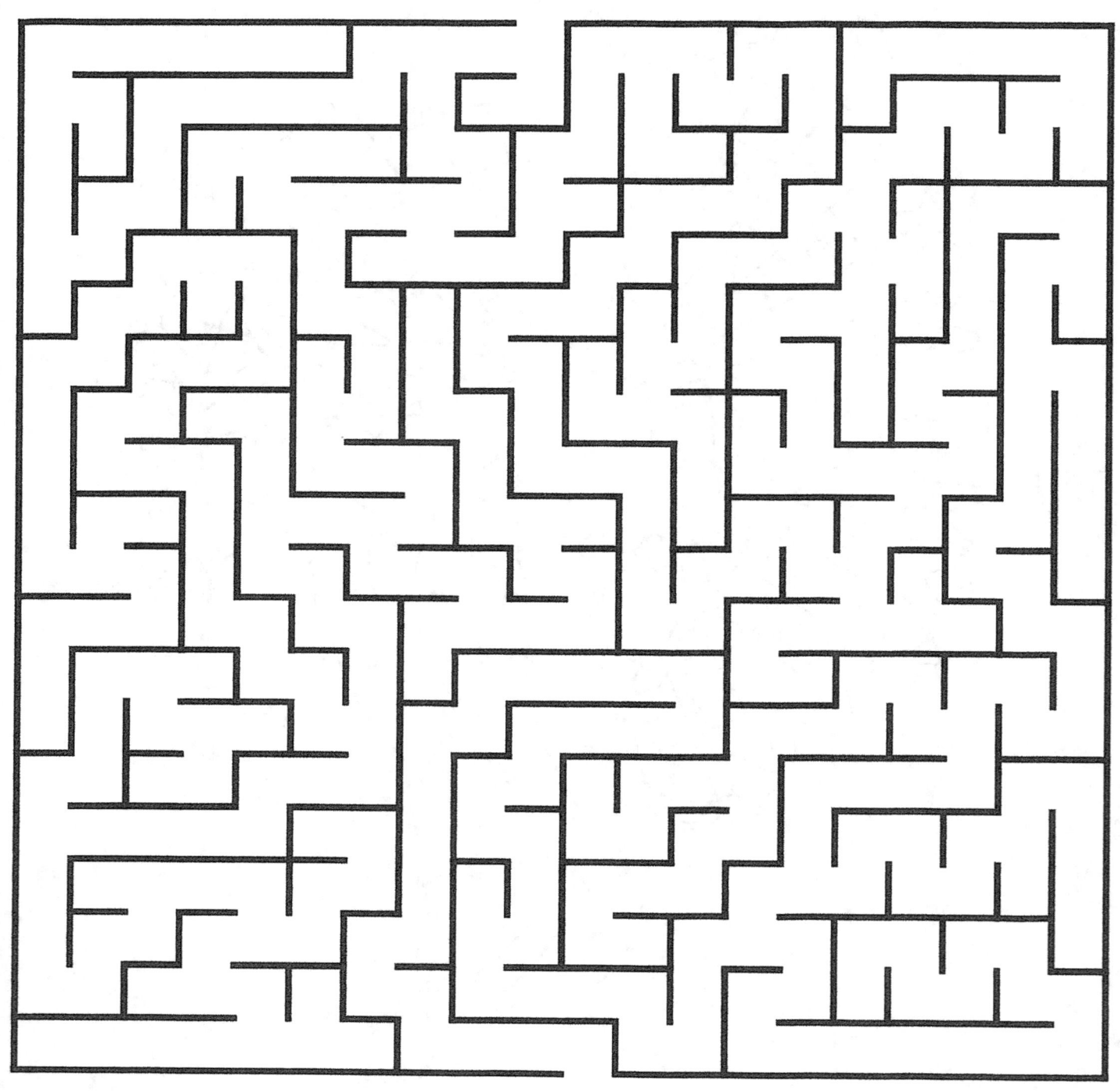

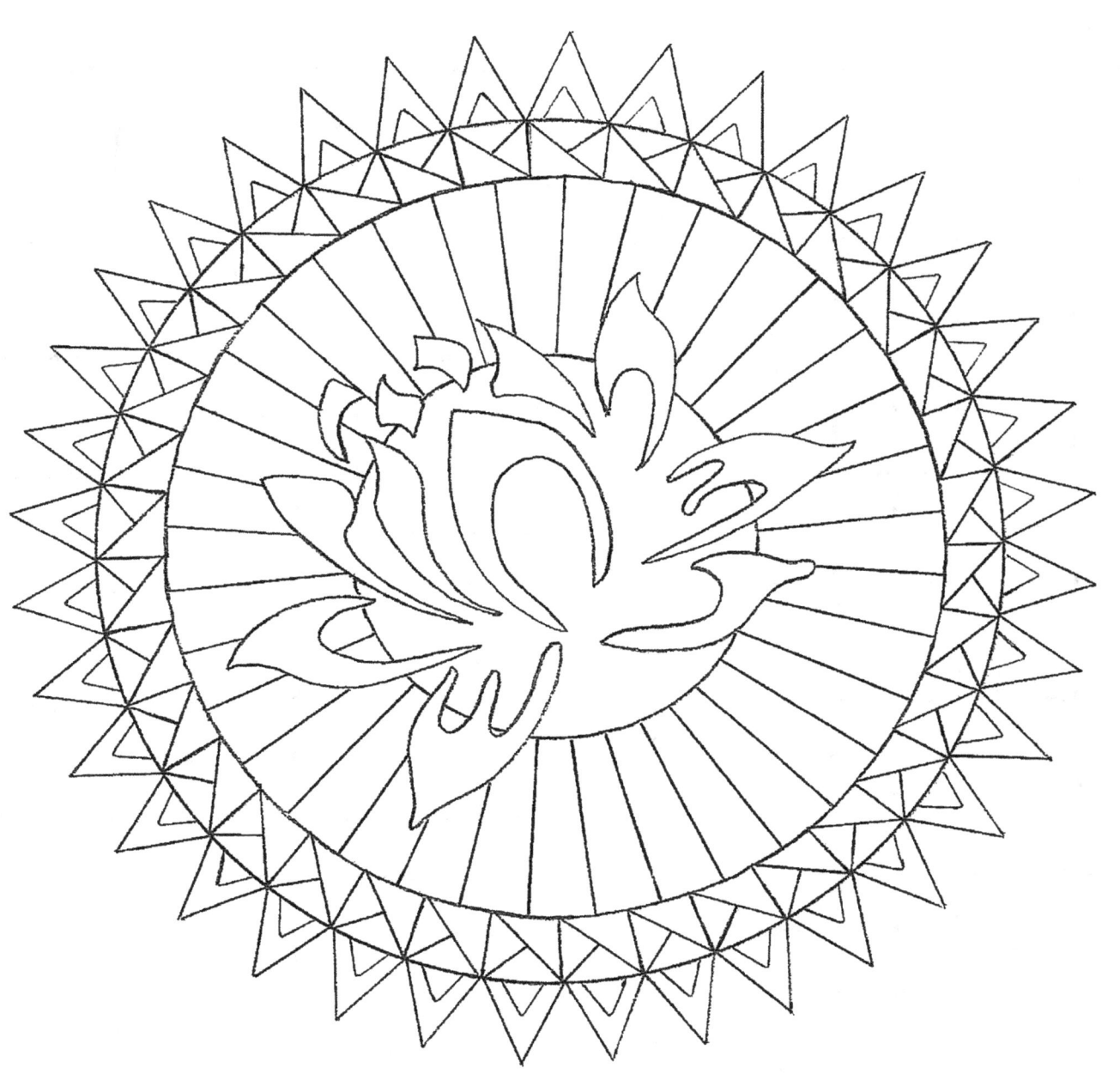

If you love life, don't waste time, for time is what life is made up of.

Bruce Lee

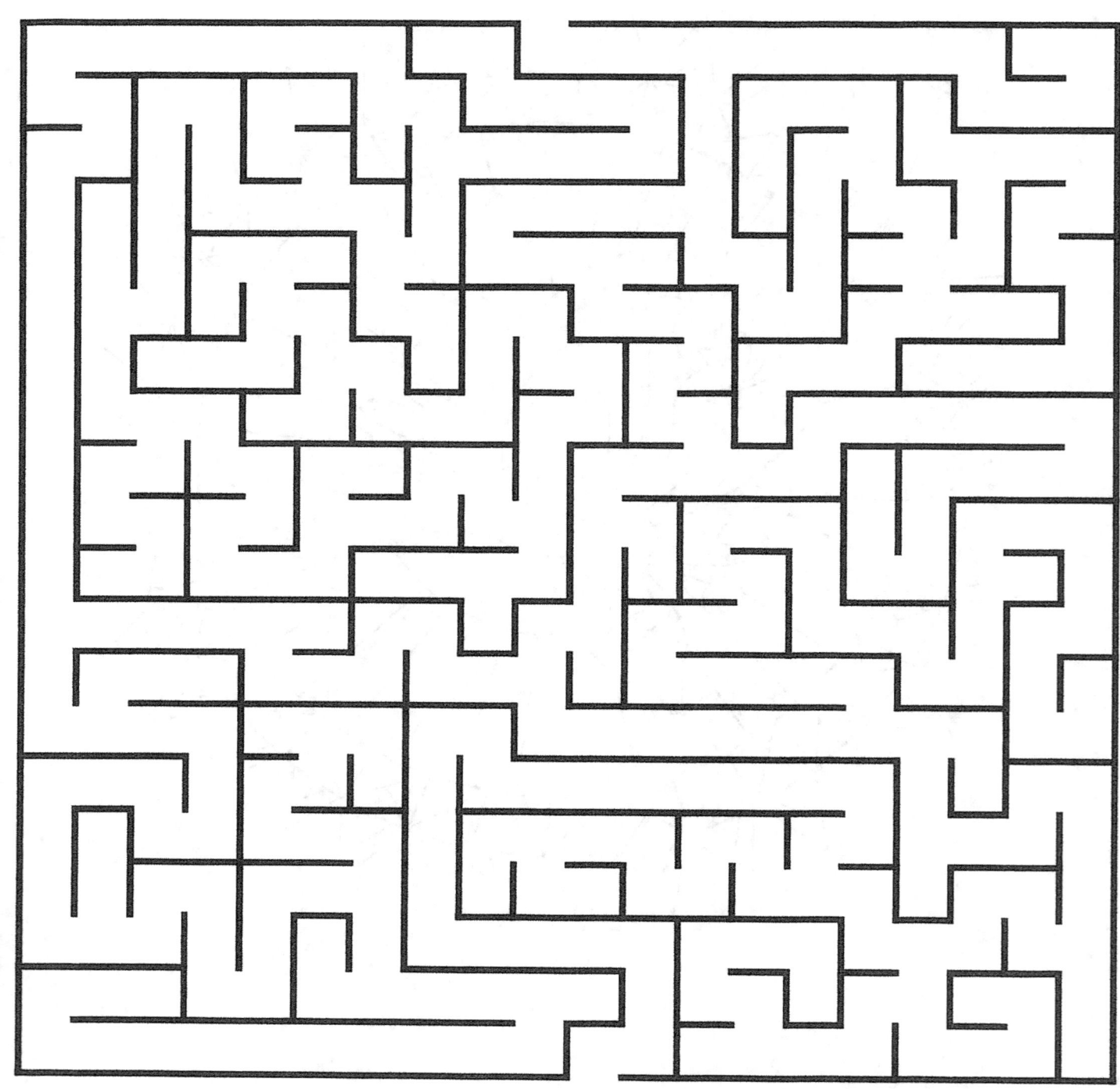

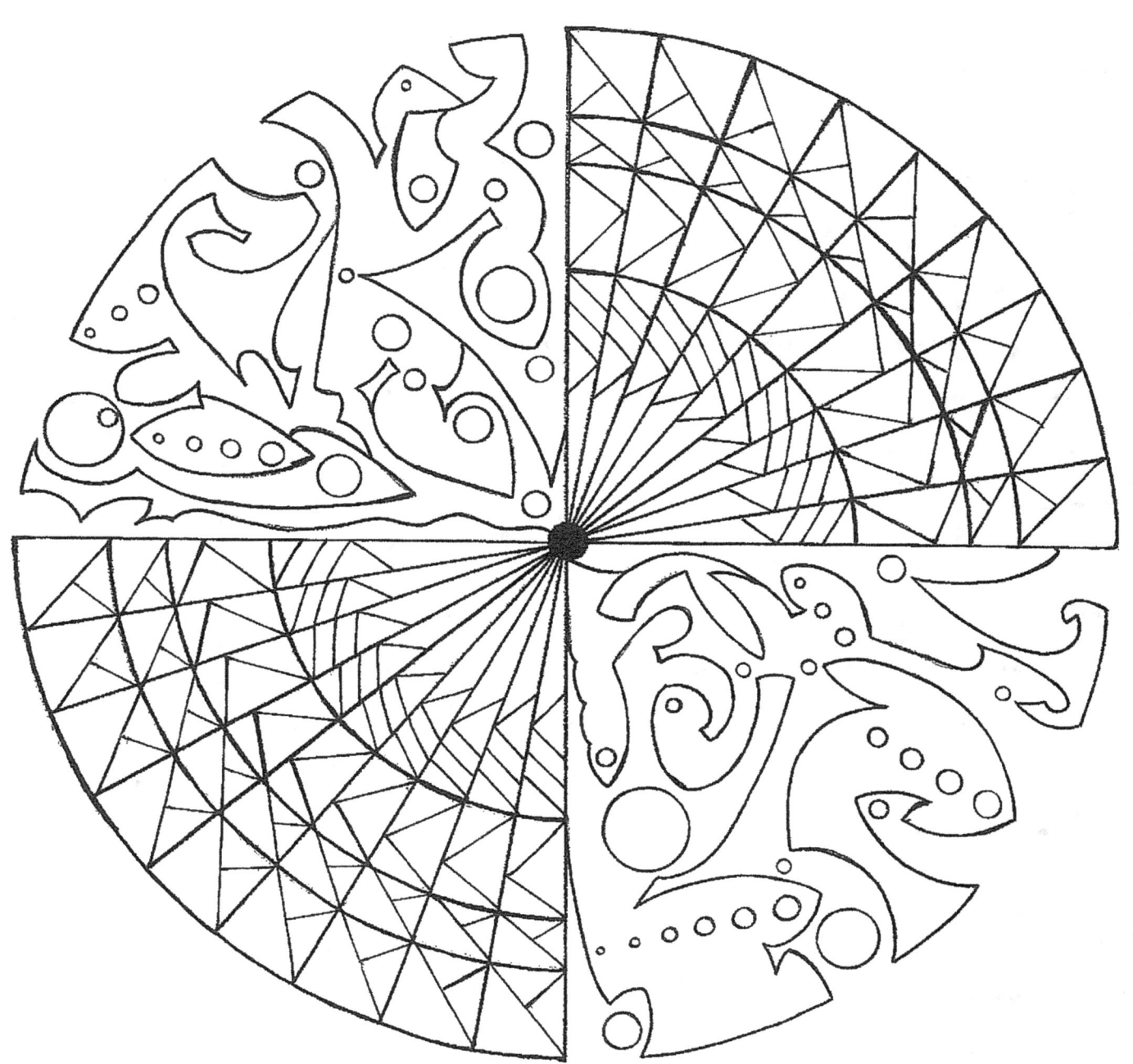

God gave us the gift of life; it is up to us to give ourselves the gift of living well.

Voltaire

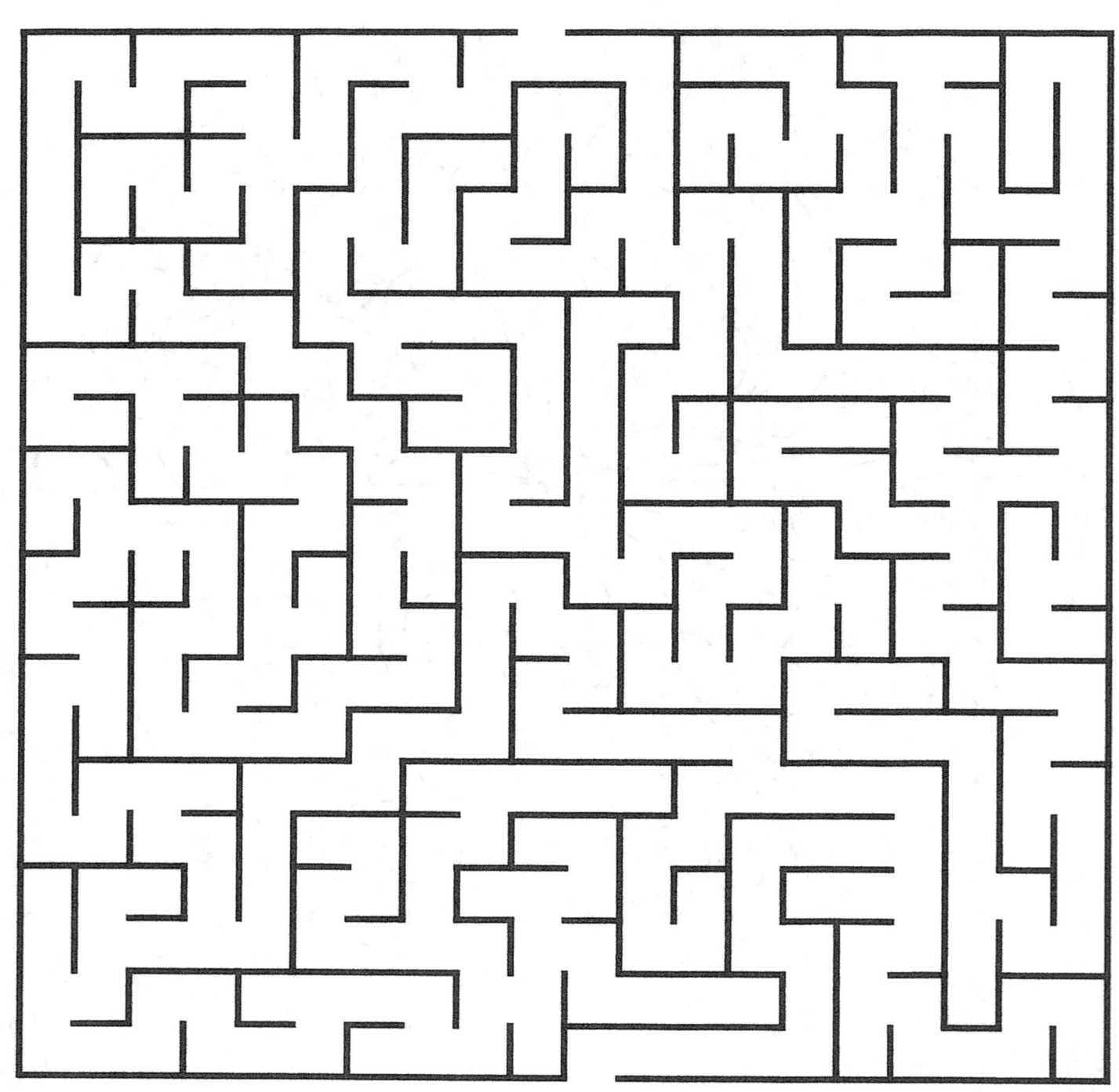

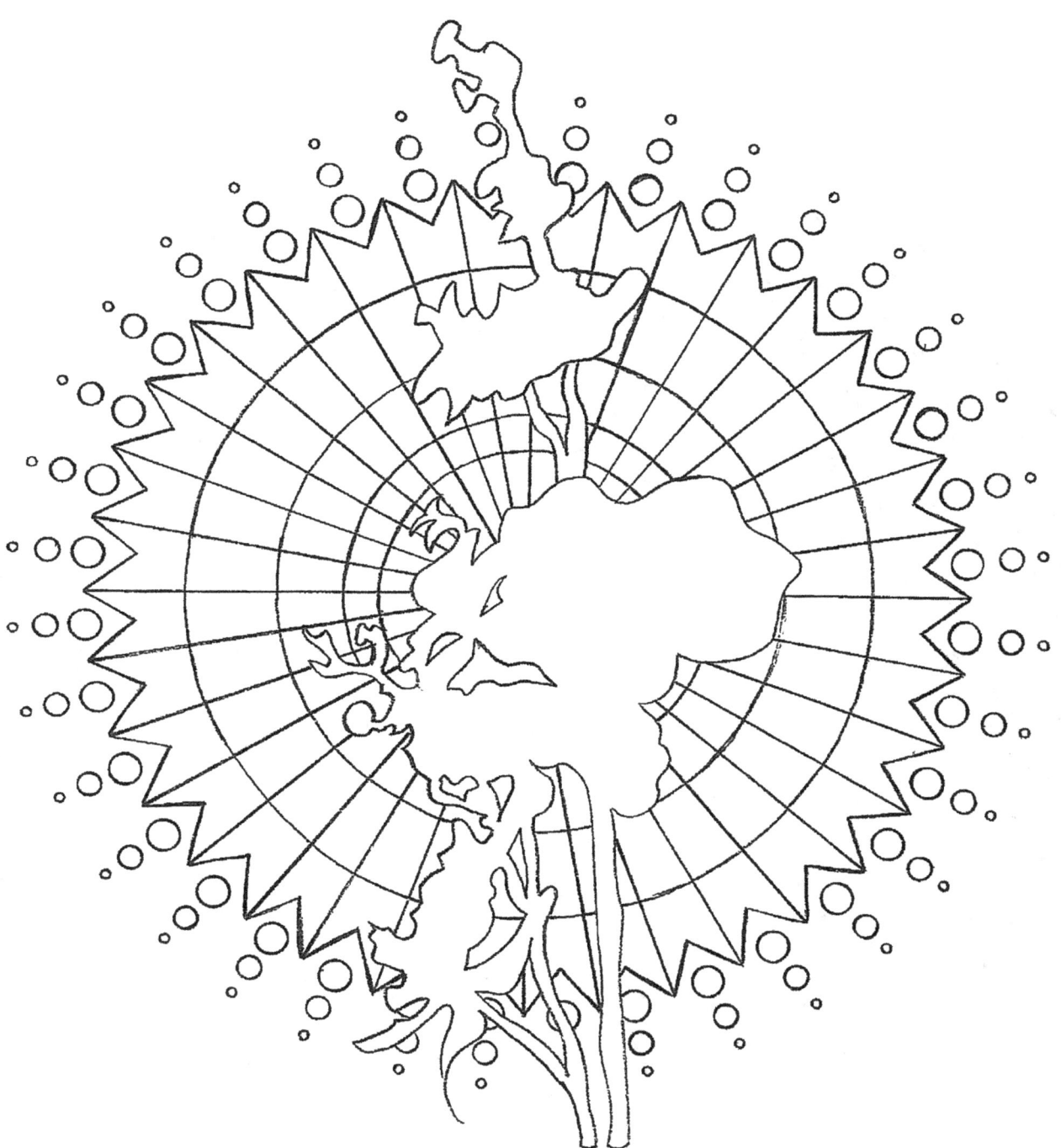

Successful people ask better questions, and as a result, they get better answers.

Tony Robbins

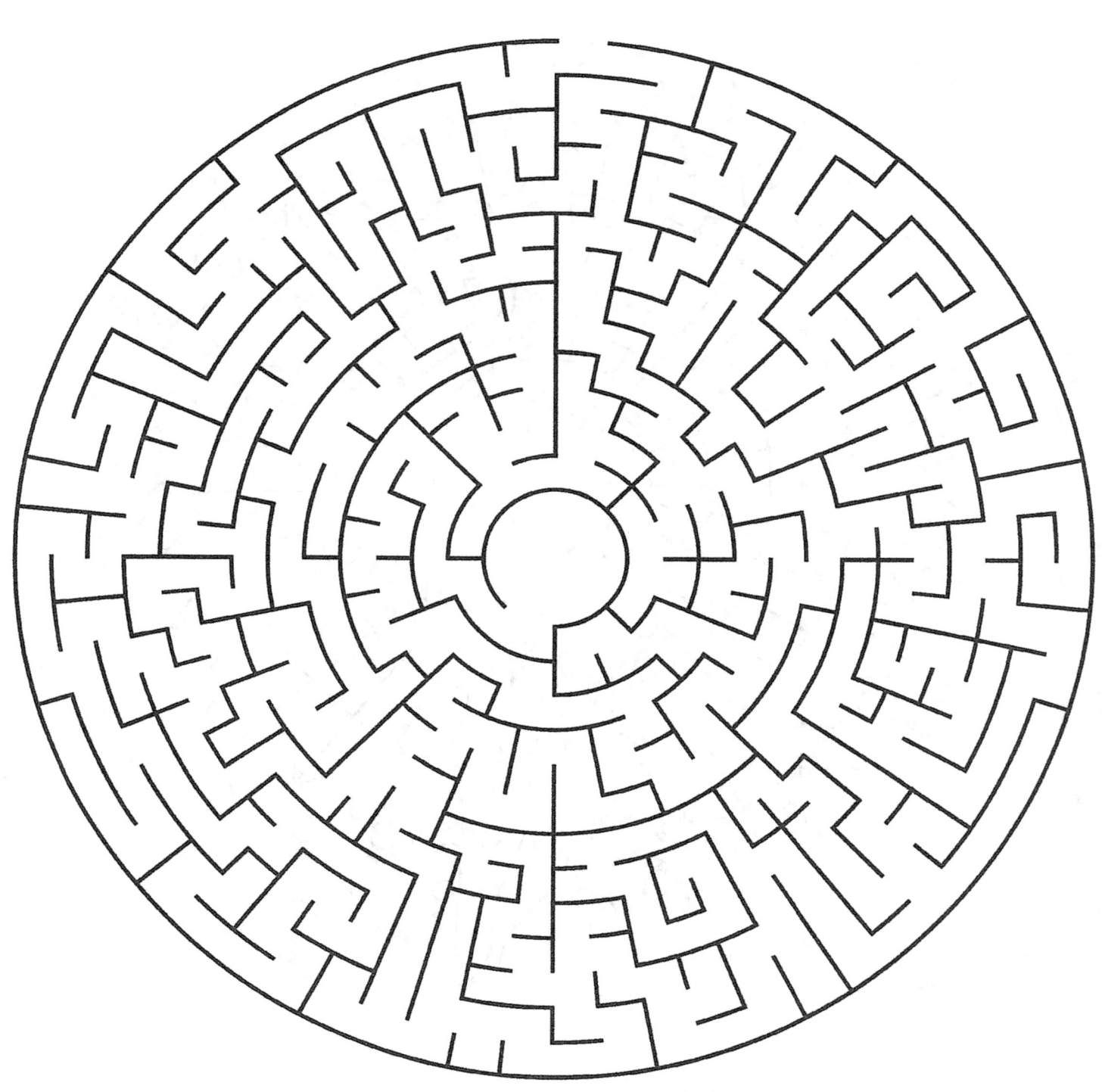

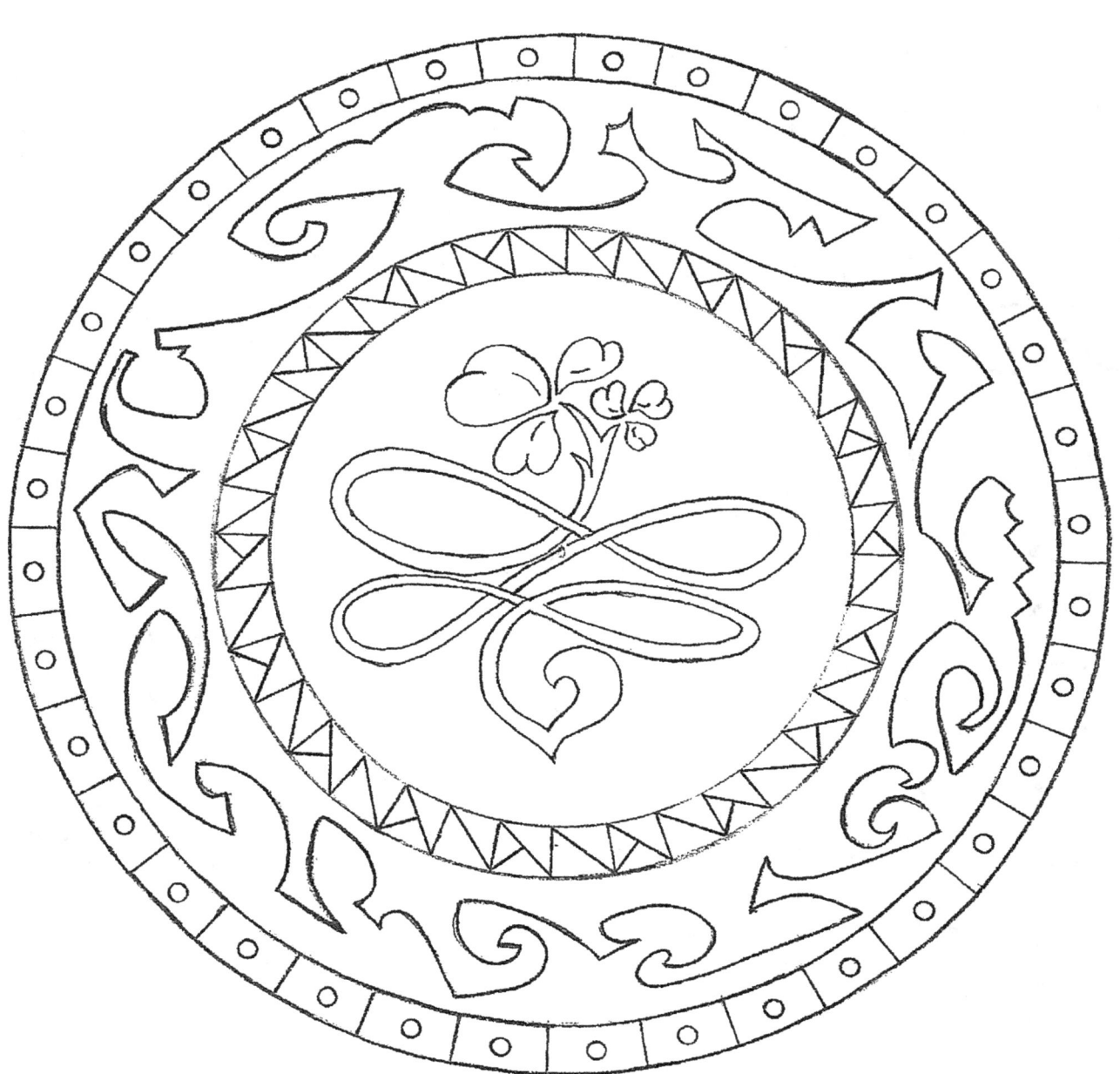

Clouds come floating into my life, no longer to carry rain or usher storm, but to add color to my sunset sky.

Rabindranath Tagore

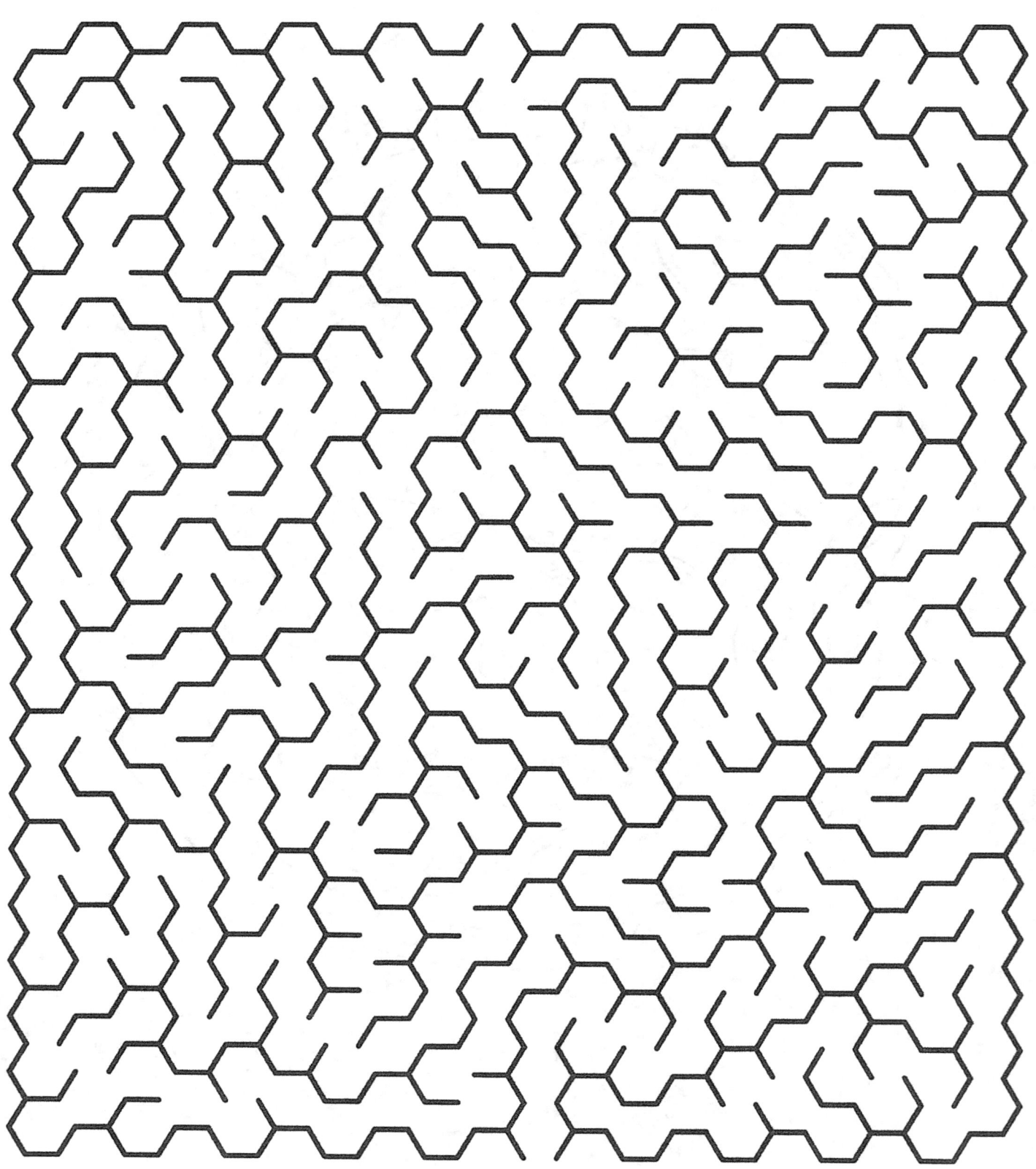

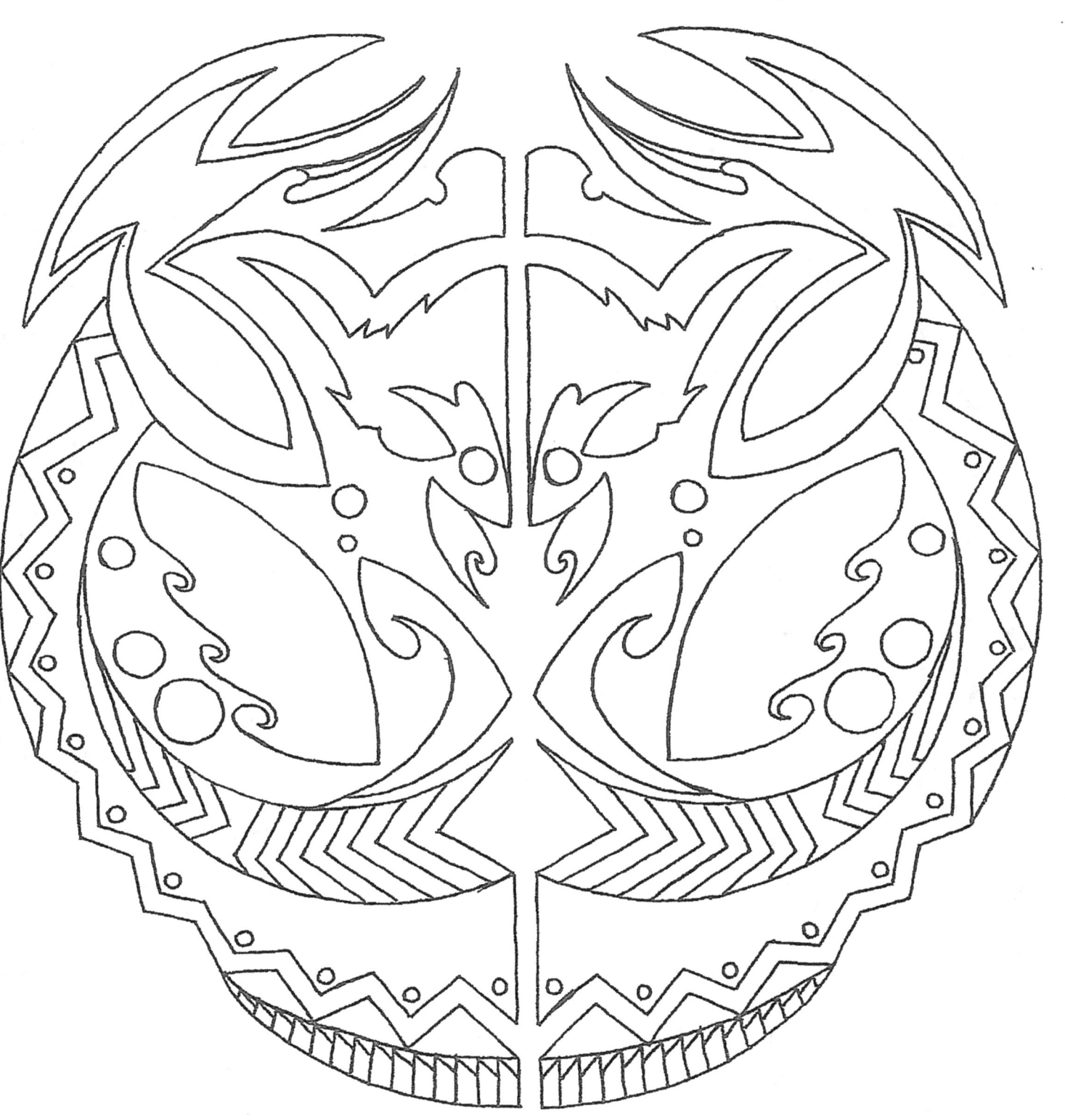

Lighten up, just enjoy life, smile more, laugh more, and don't get so worked up about things.

Kenneth Branagh

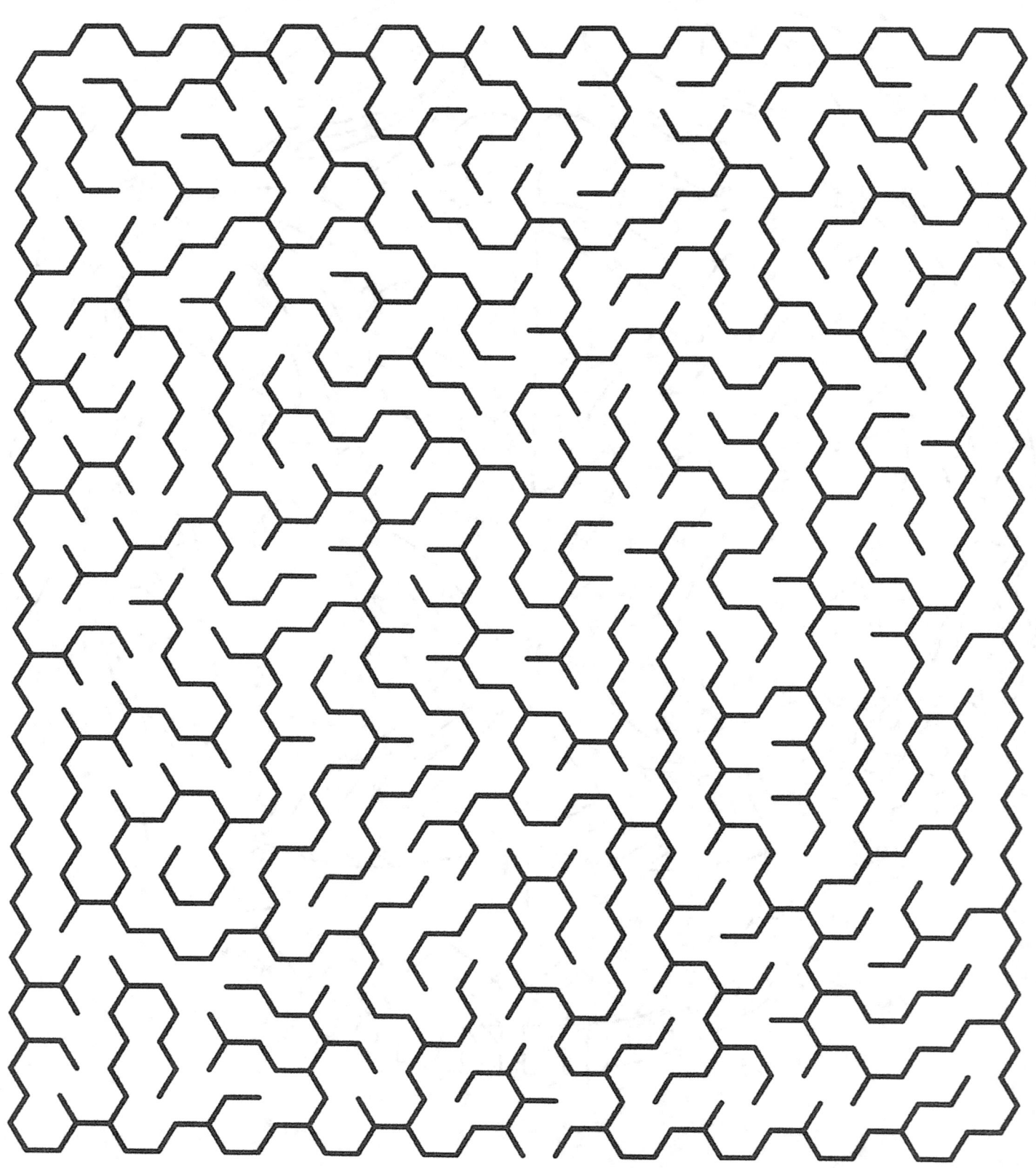

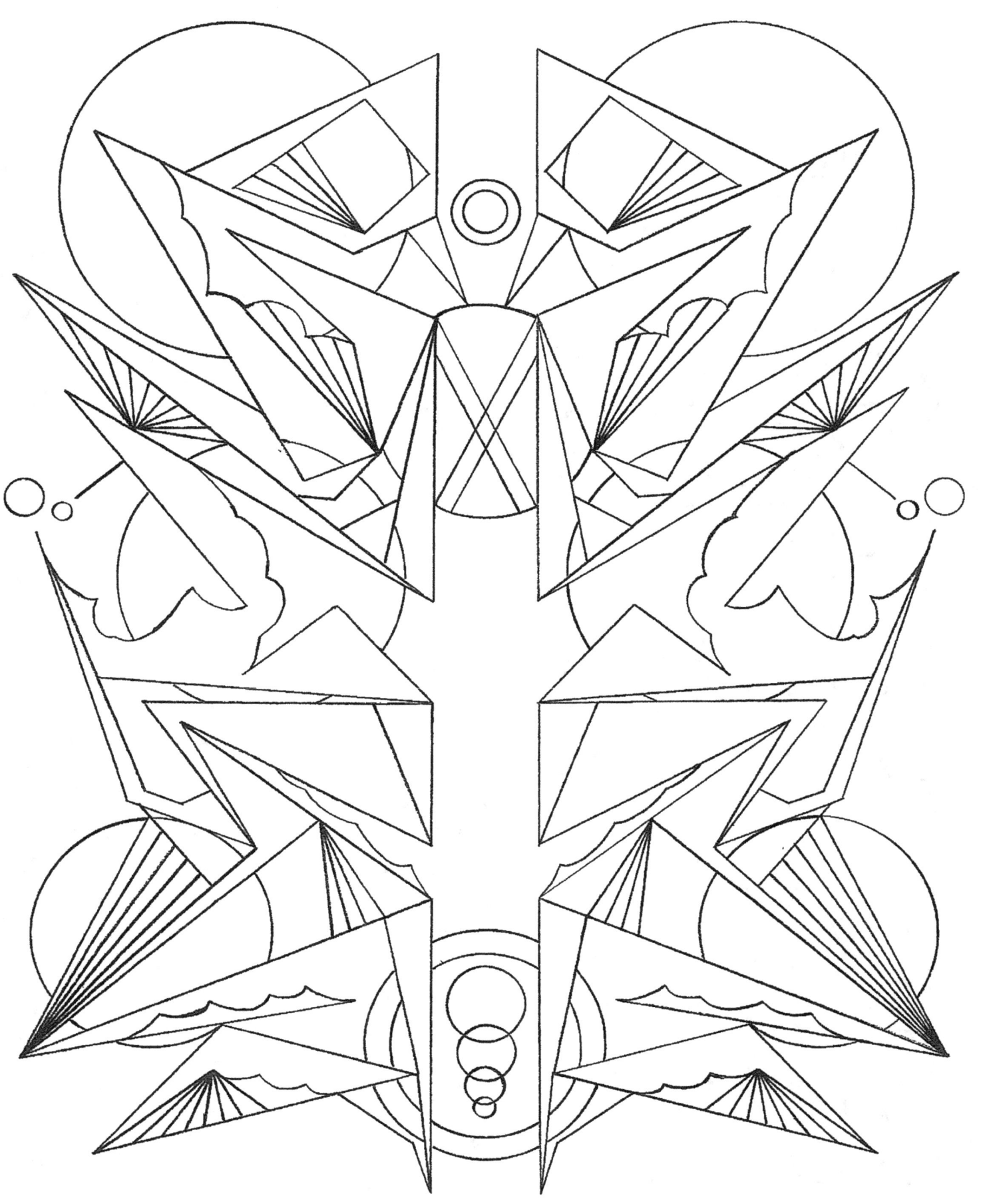

The good life is one inspired by love and guided by knowledge.

Bertrand Russell

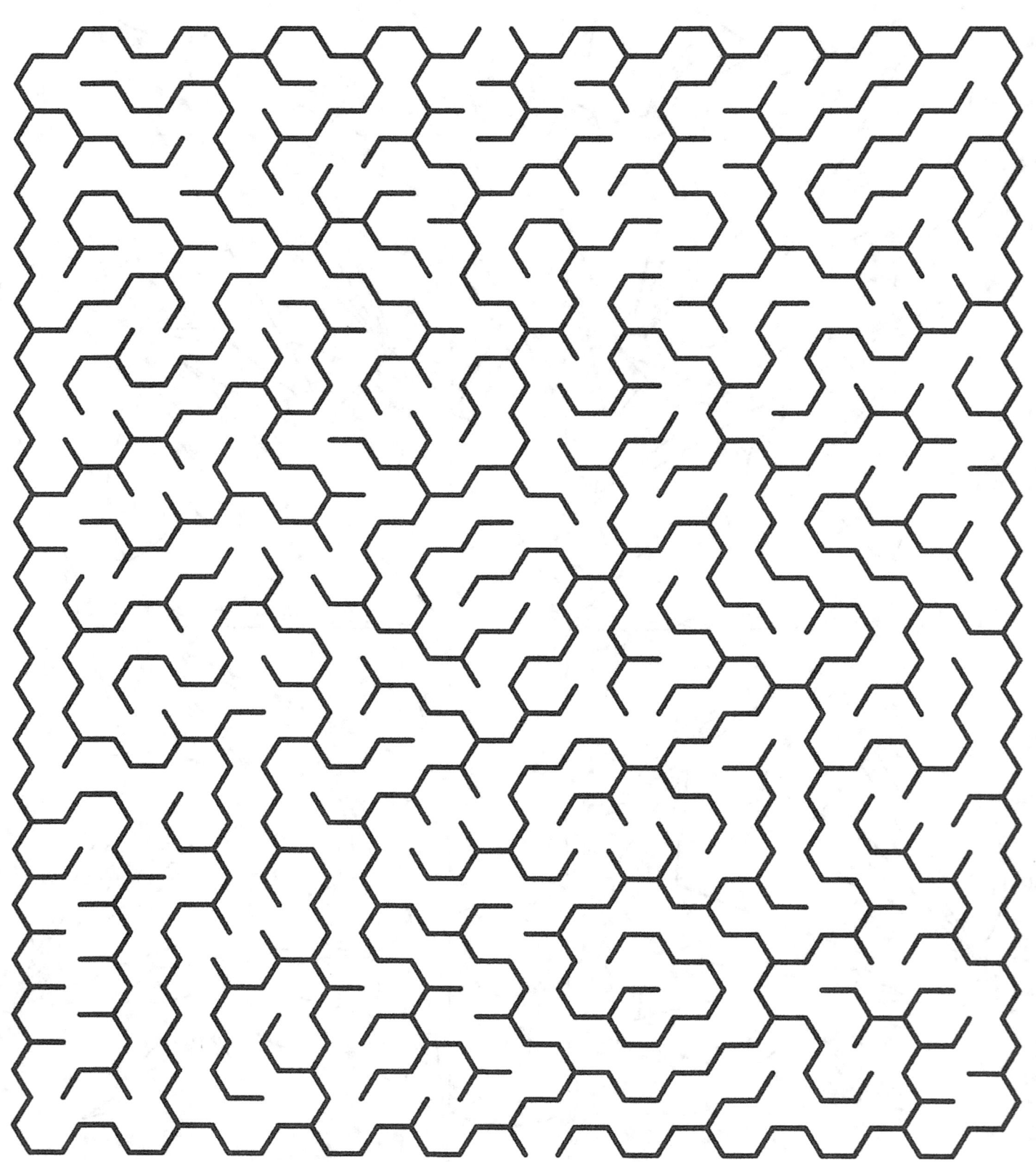

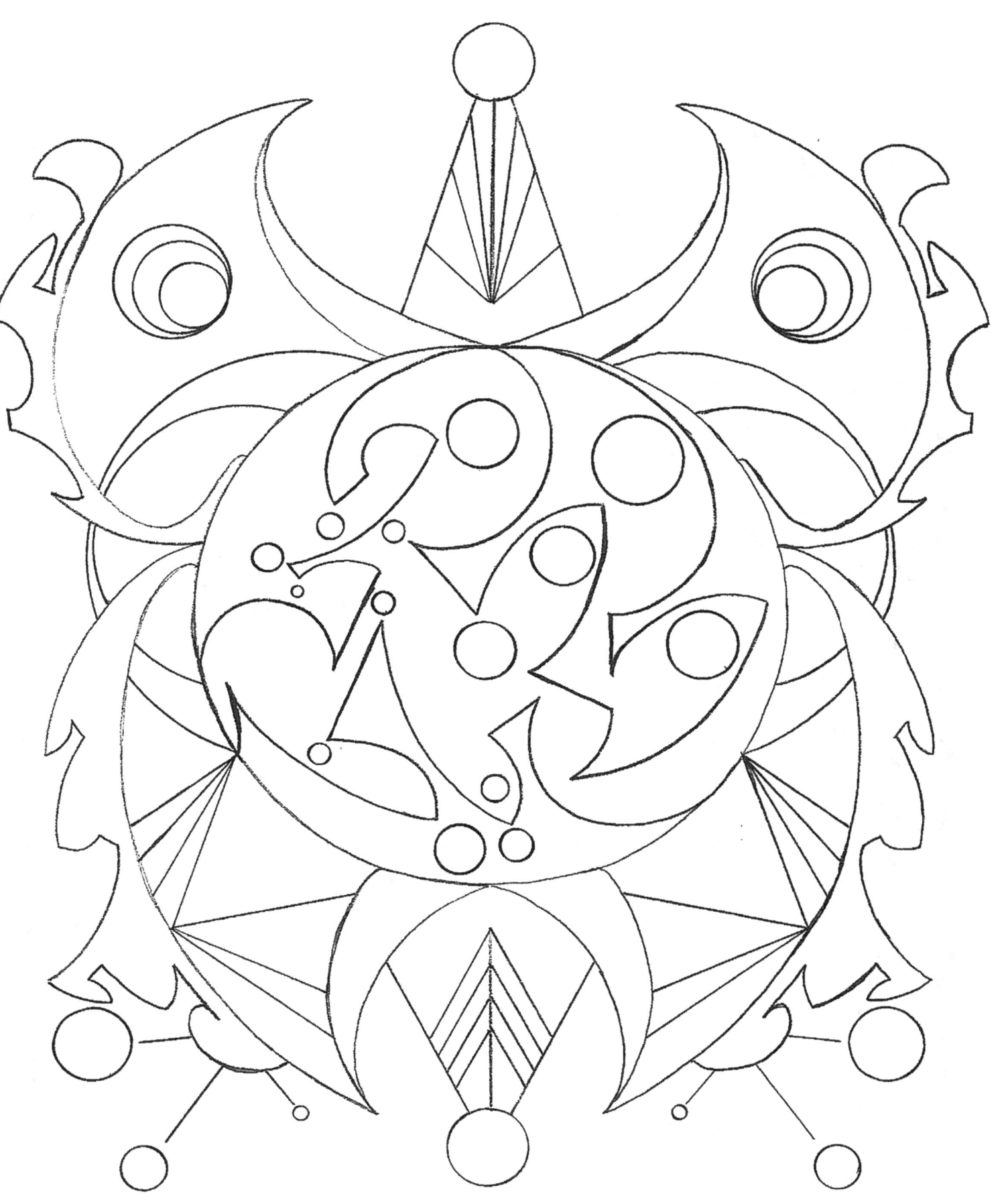

Love yourself. It is important to stay positive because beauty comes from the inside out.

Jenn Proske

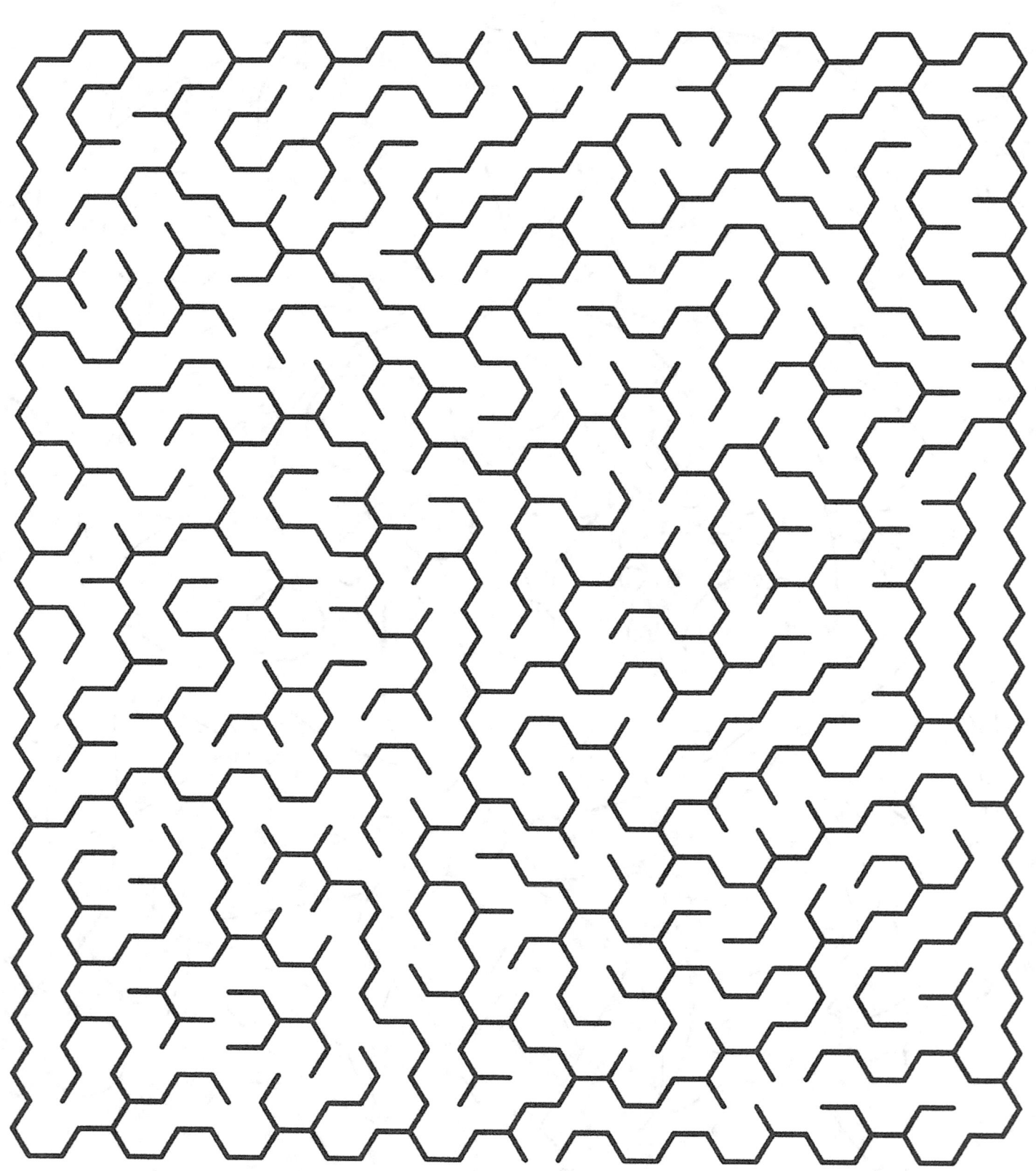

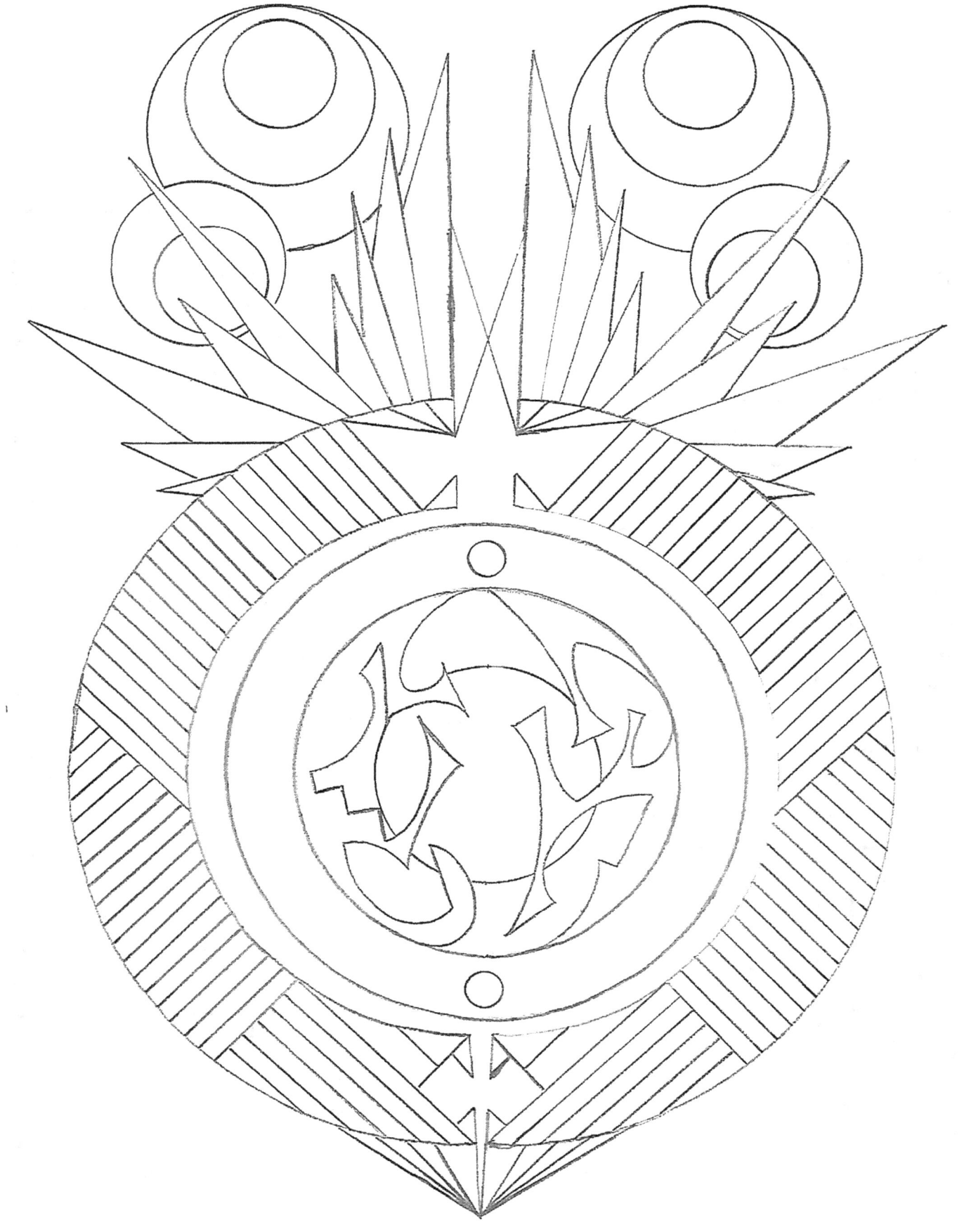

Sometimes the heart sees what is invisible to the eye.

H. Jackson Brown, Jr.

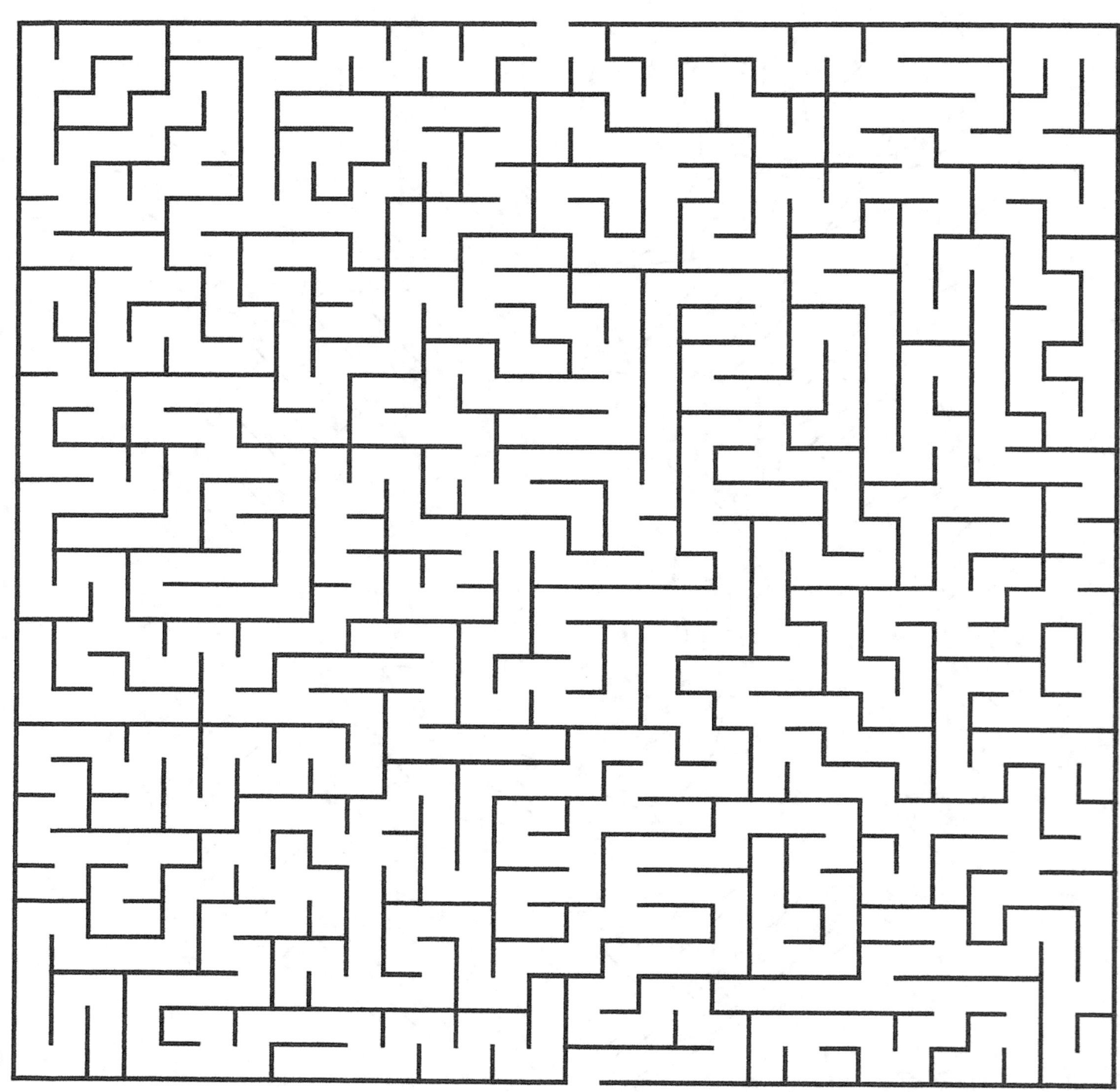

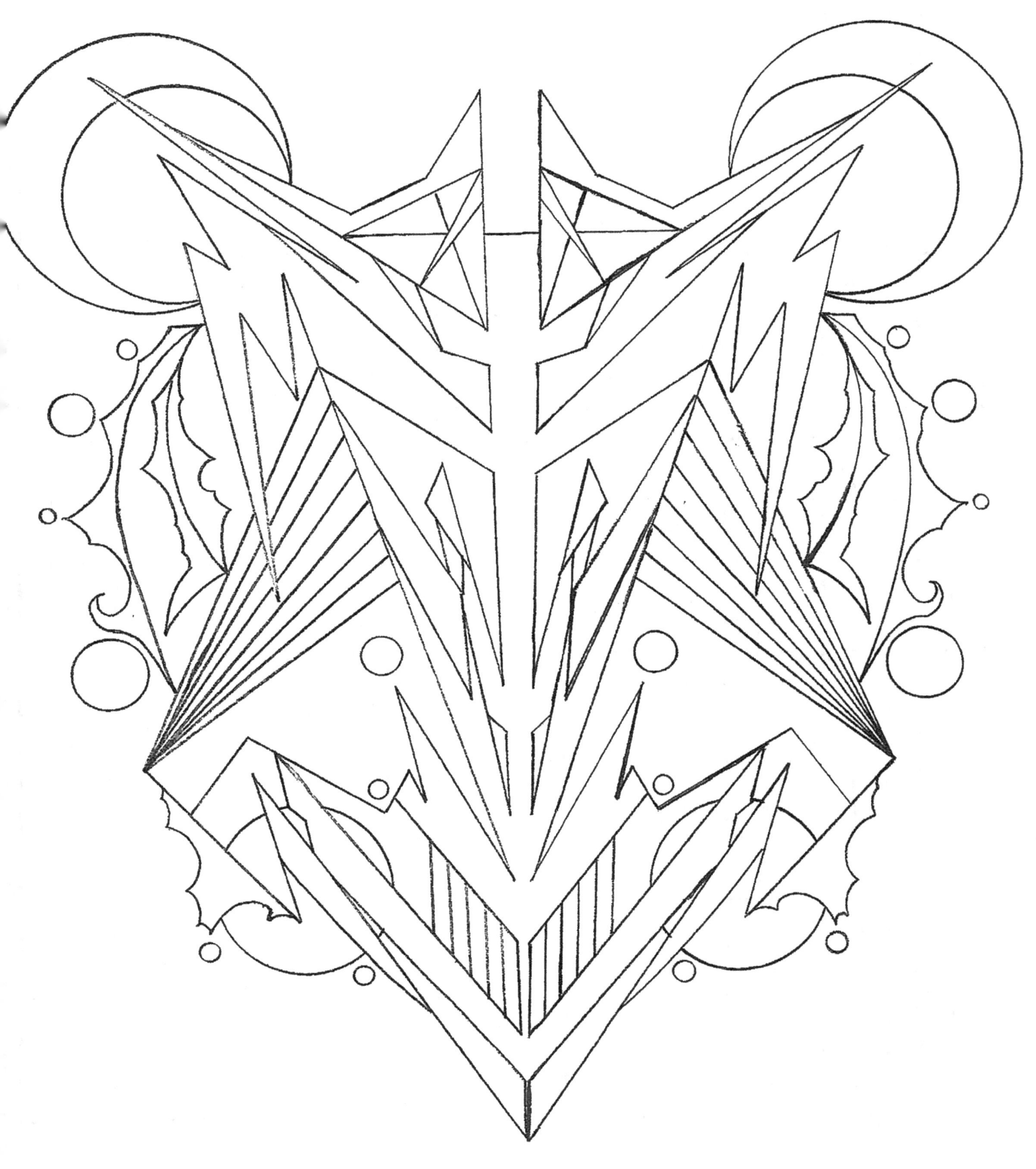

Being deeply loved by someone gives you strength, while loving someone deeply gives you courage.

Lao Tzu

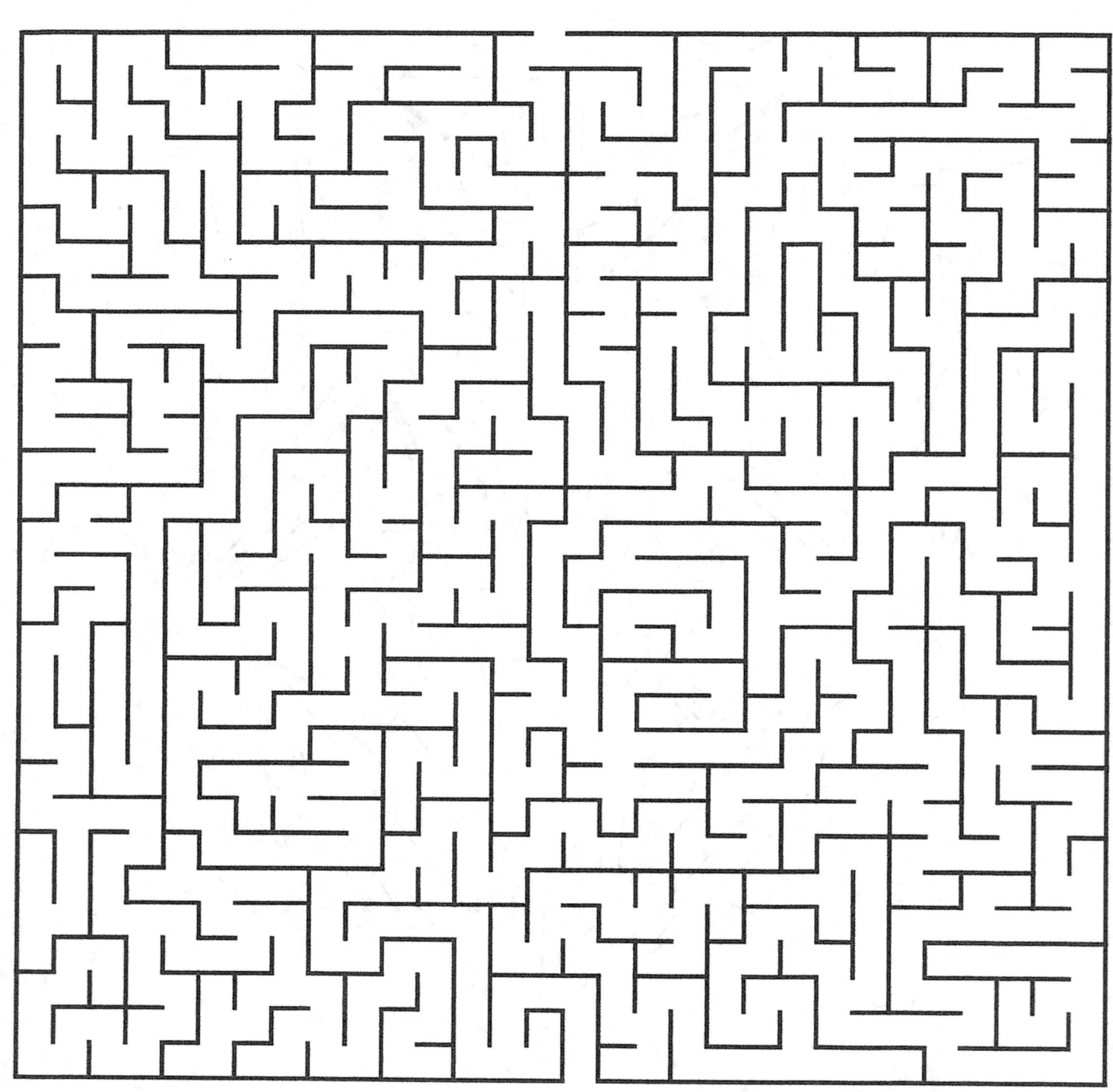

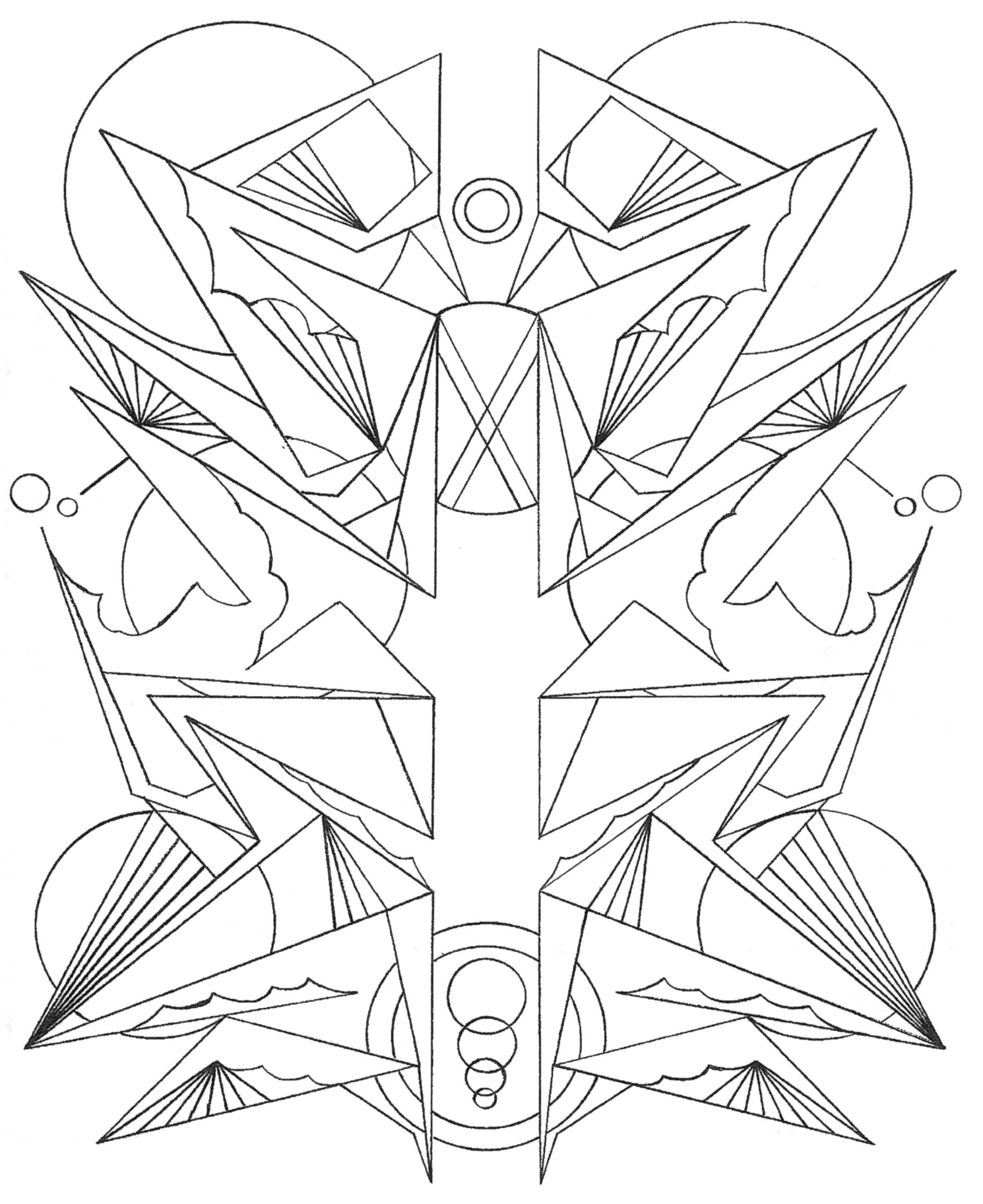

We're born alone, we live alone, we die alone. Only through our love and friendship can we create the illusion for the moment that we're not alone.

Orson Welles

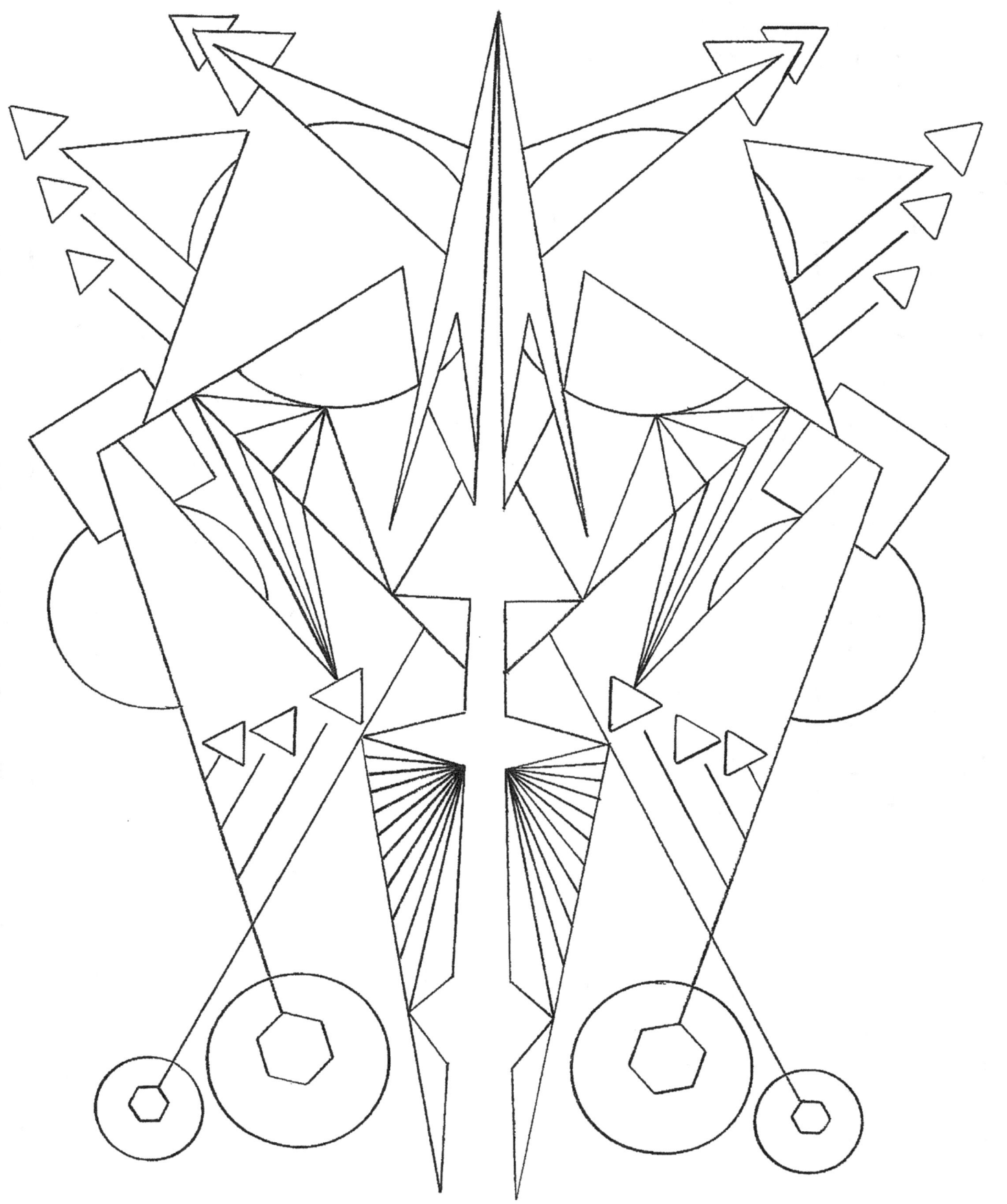

Your work is going to fill a large part of your life, and the only way to be truly satisfied is to do what you believe is great work. And the only way to do great work is to love what you do. If you haven't found it yet, keep looking. Don't settle. As with all matters of the heart, you'll know when you find it.

Steve Jobs

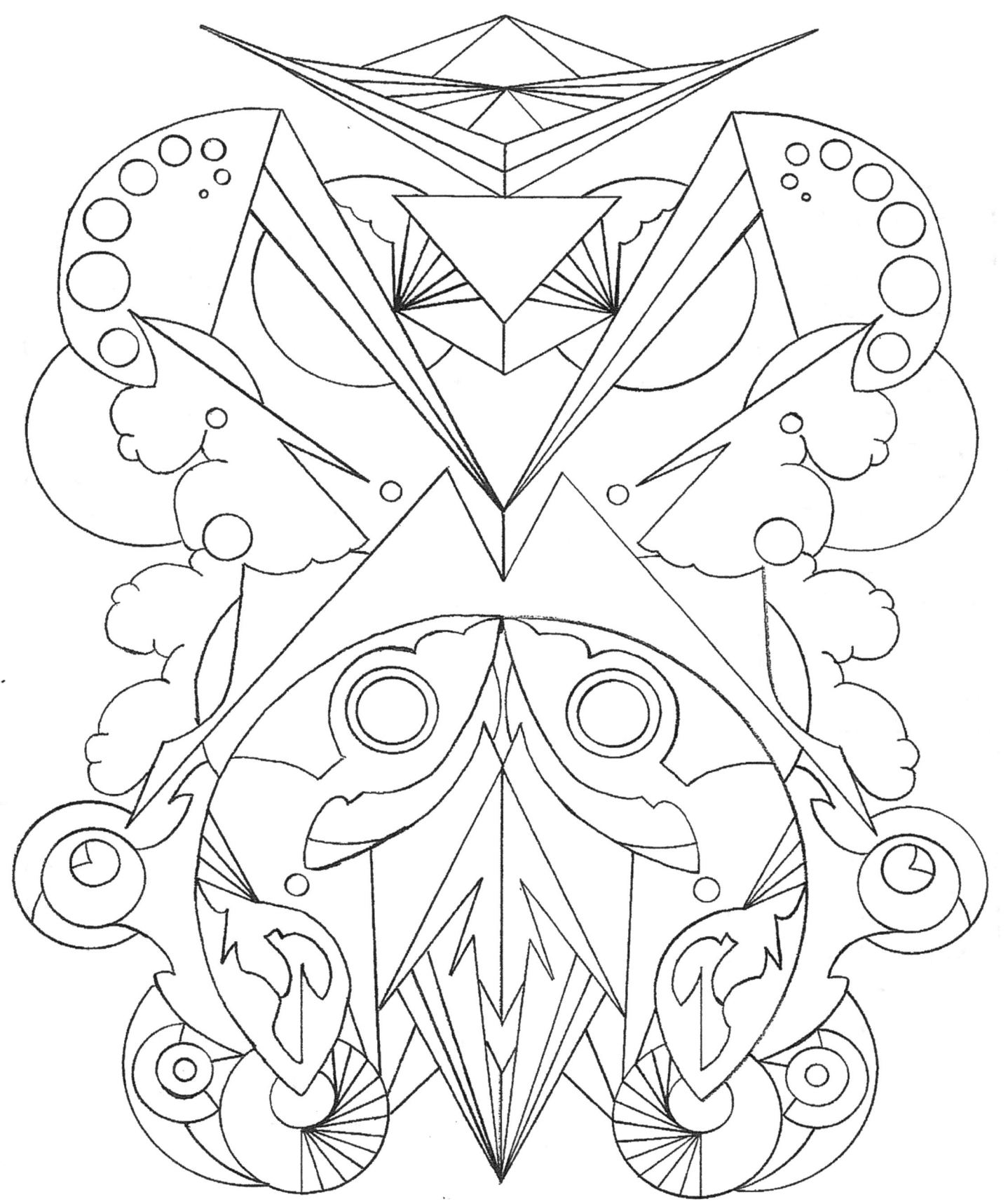

Let us always meet each other with smile, for the smile is the beginning of love.

Mother Teresa

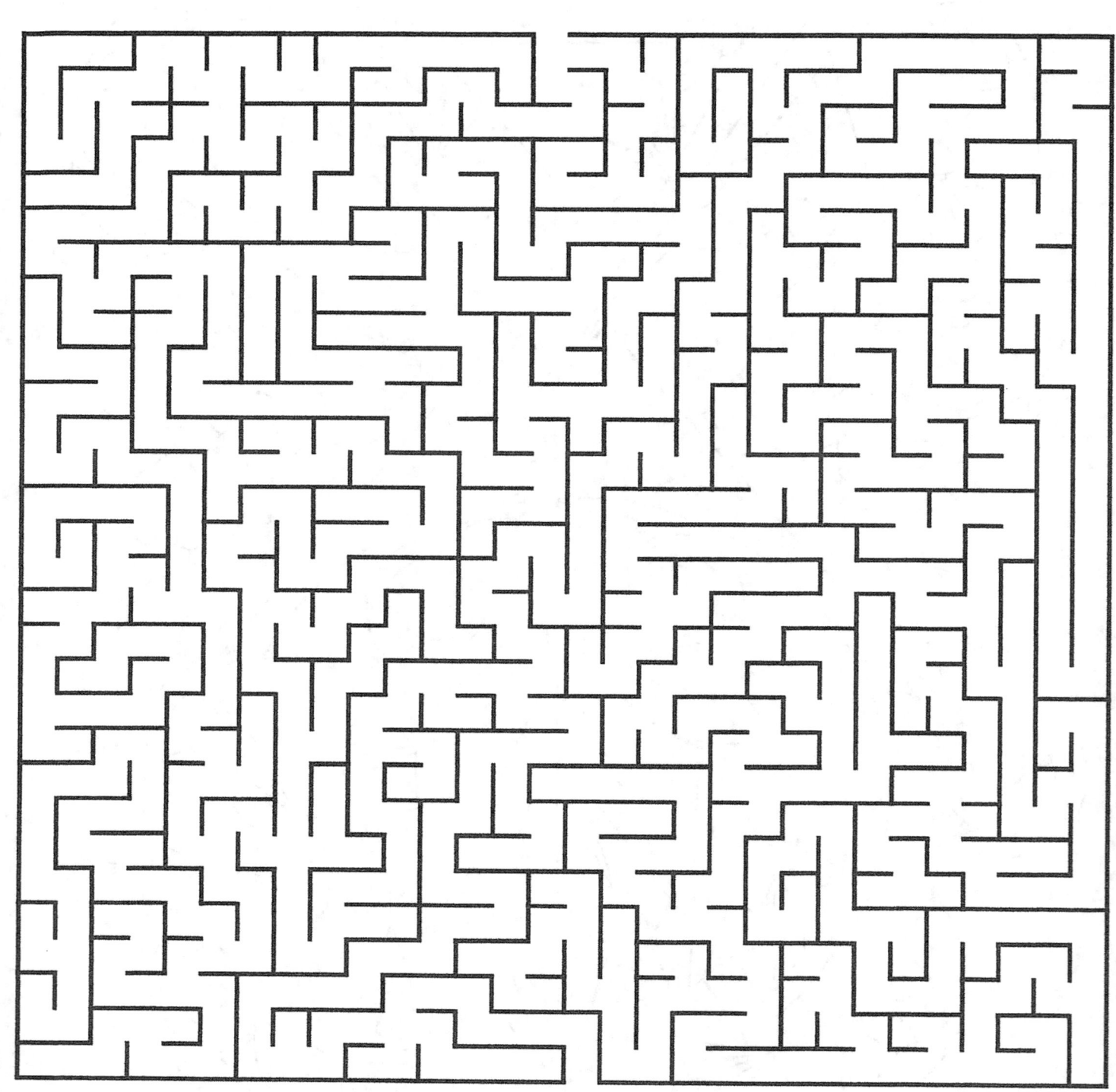

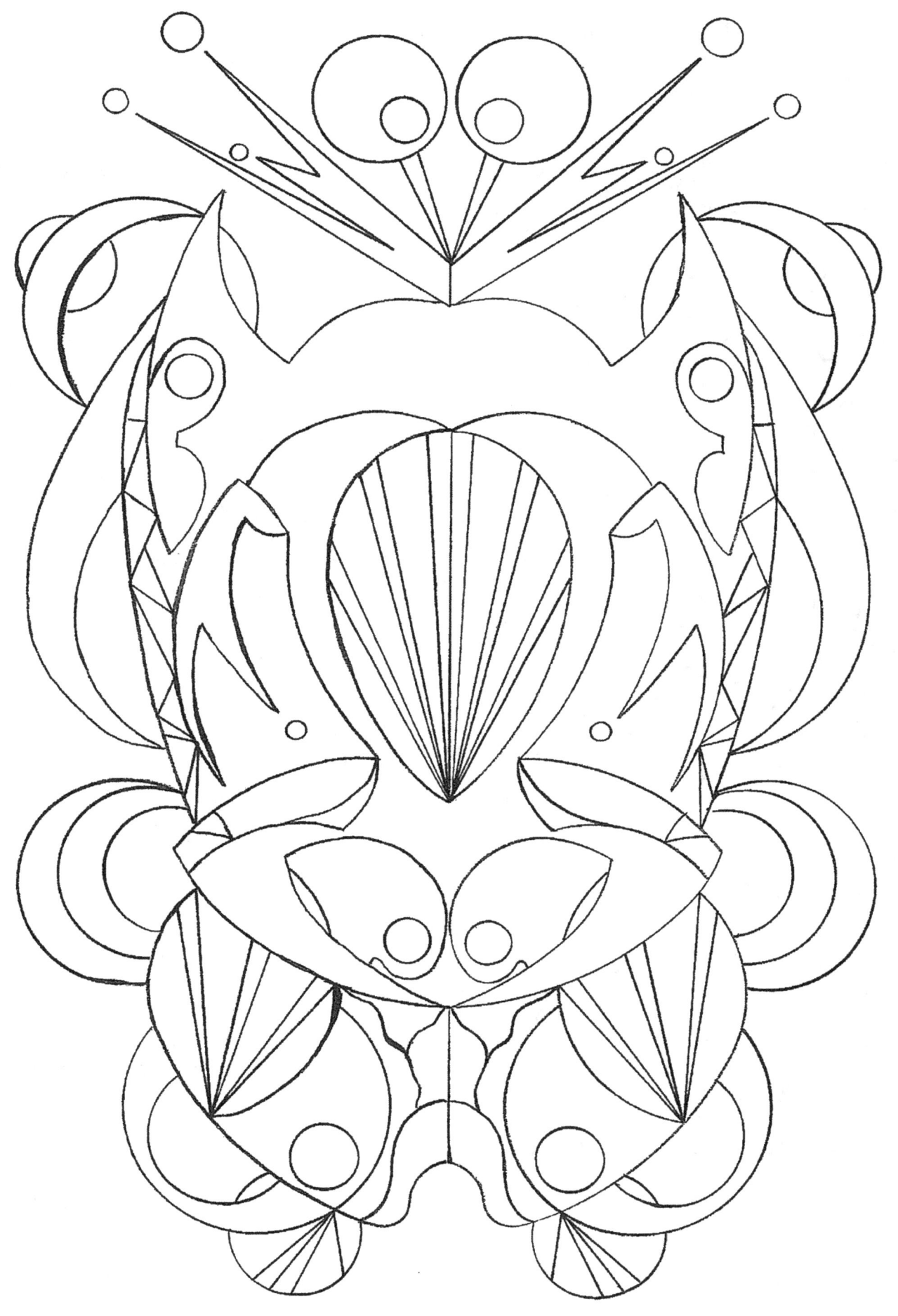

The greatest healing therapy is friendship and love.

Hubert H. Humphrey

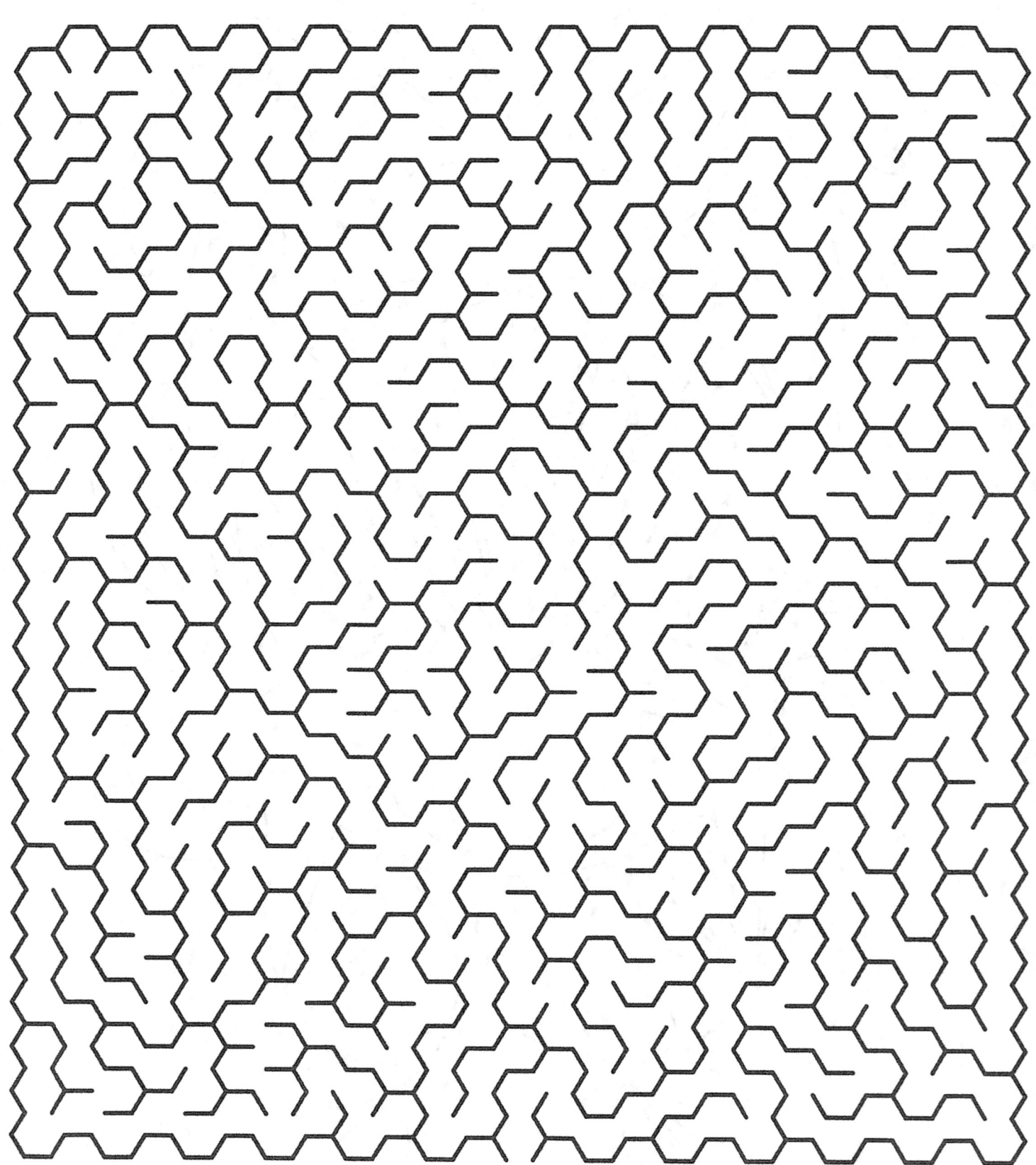

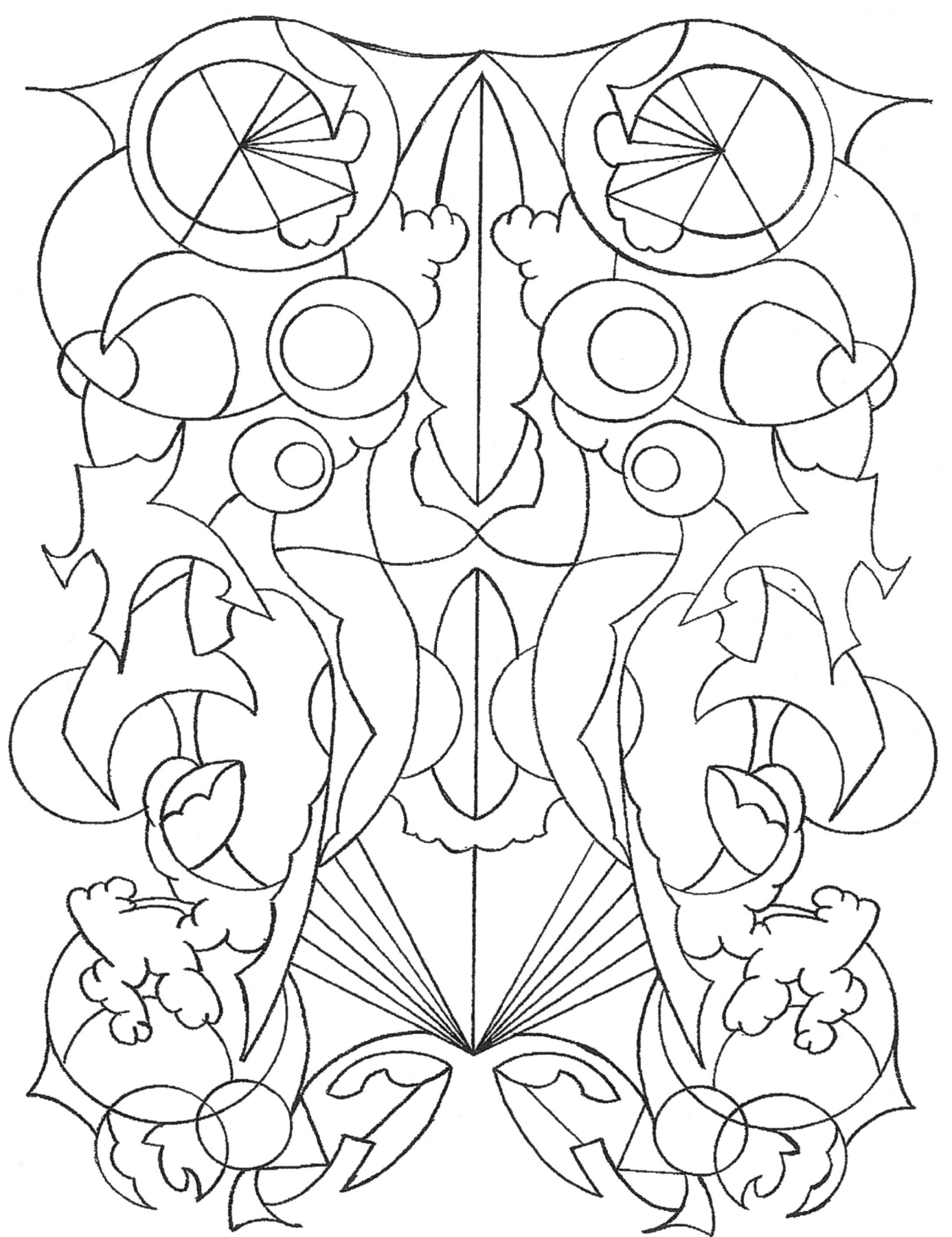

Study nature, love nature, stay close to nature. It will never fail you.

Frank Lloyd Wright

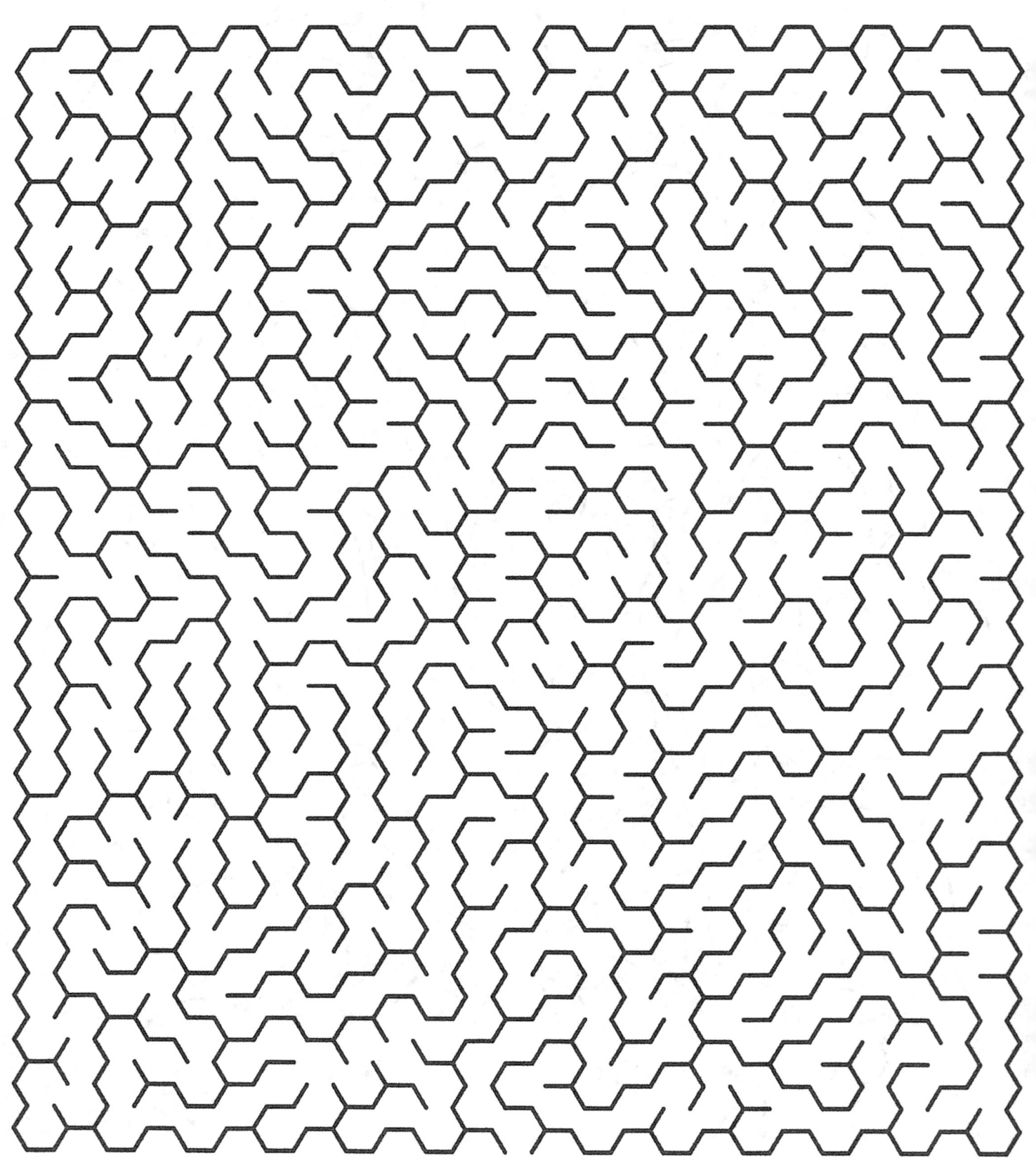

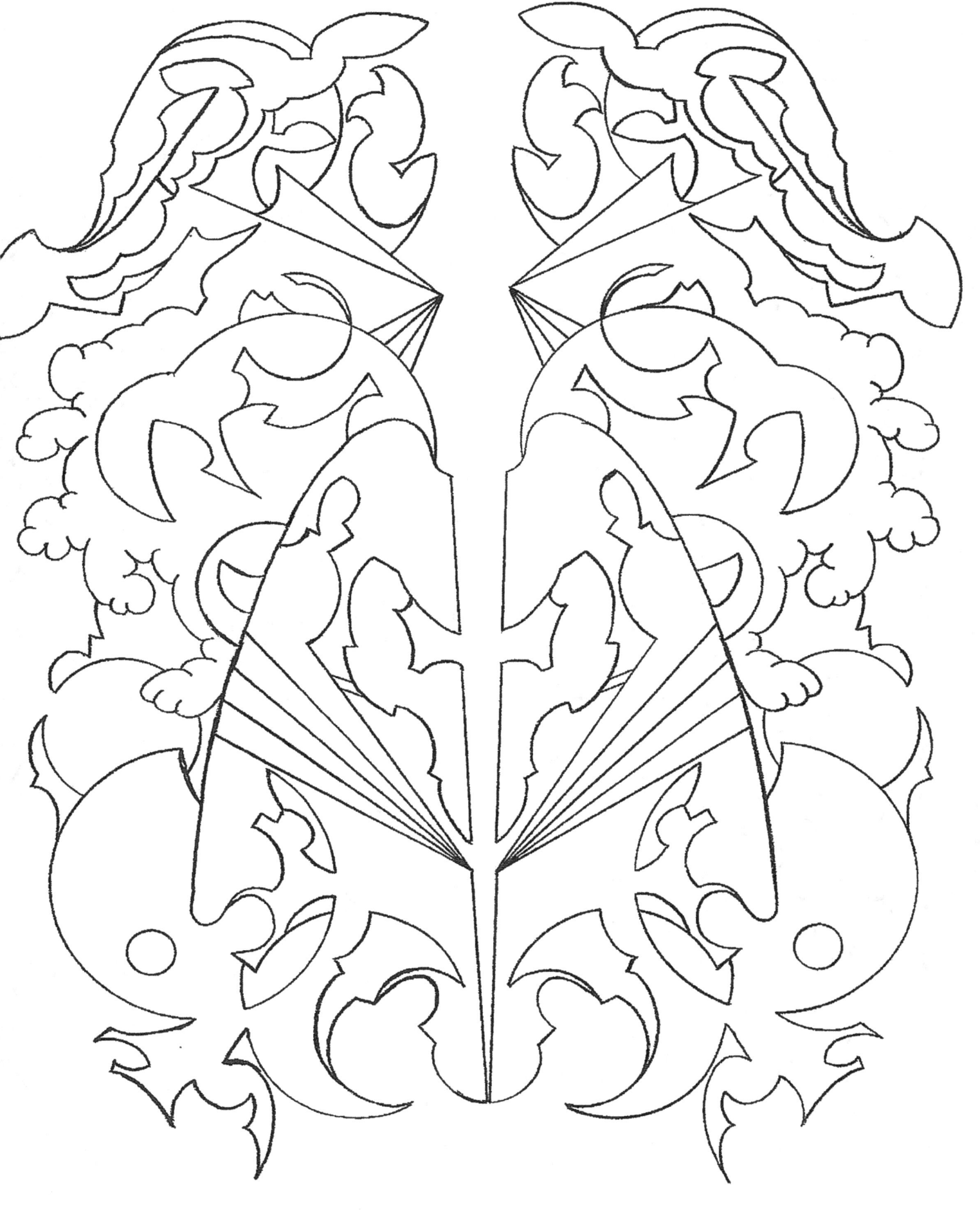

It is not what we get. But who we become, what we contribute... that gives meaning to our lives.

Tony Robbins

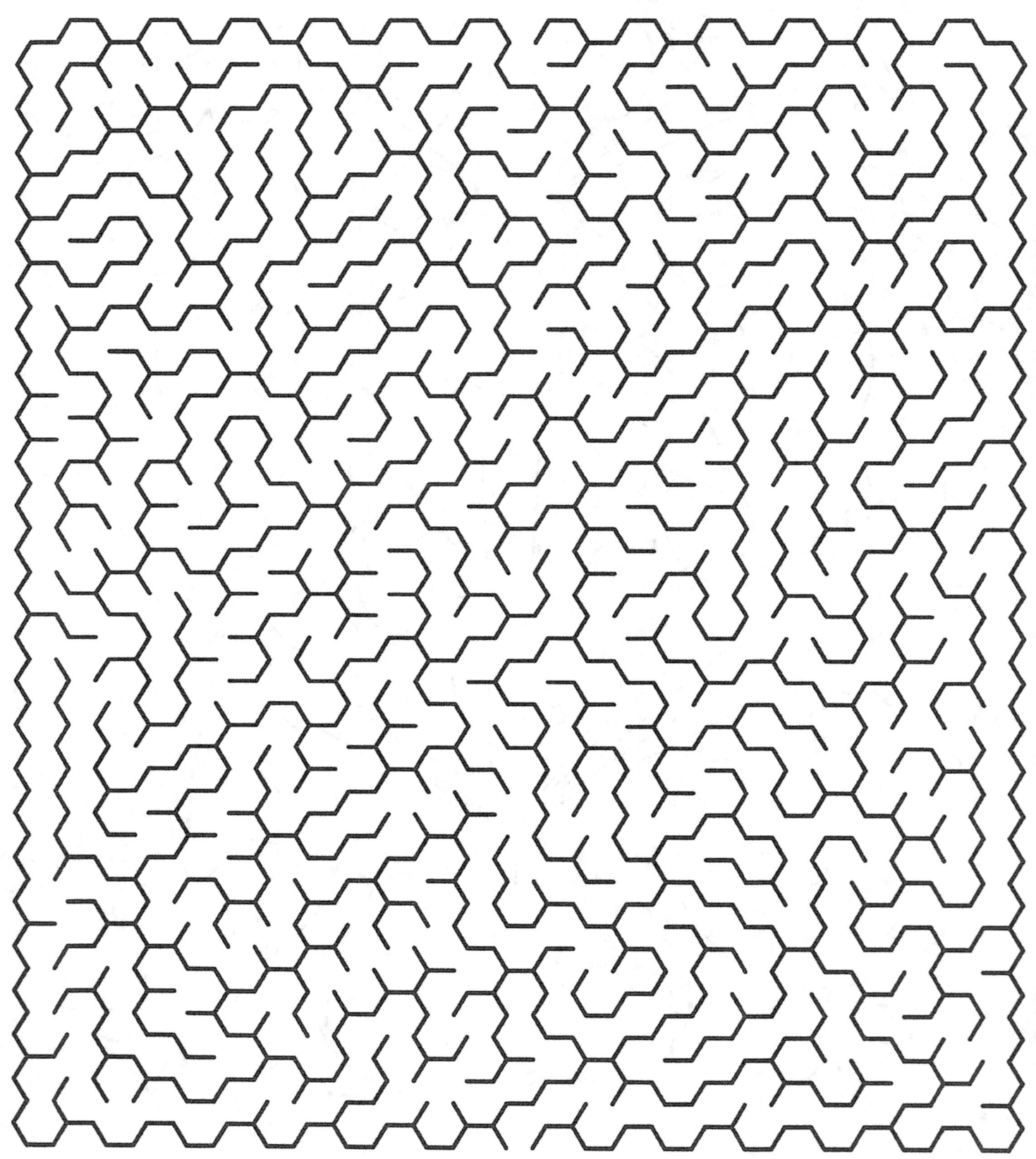

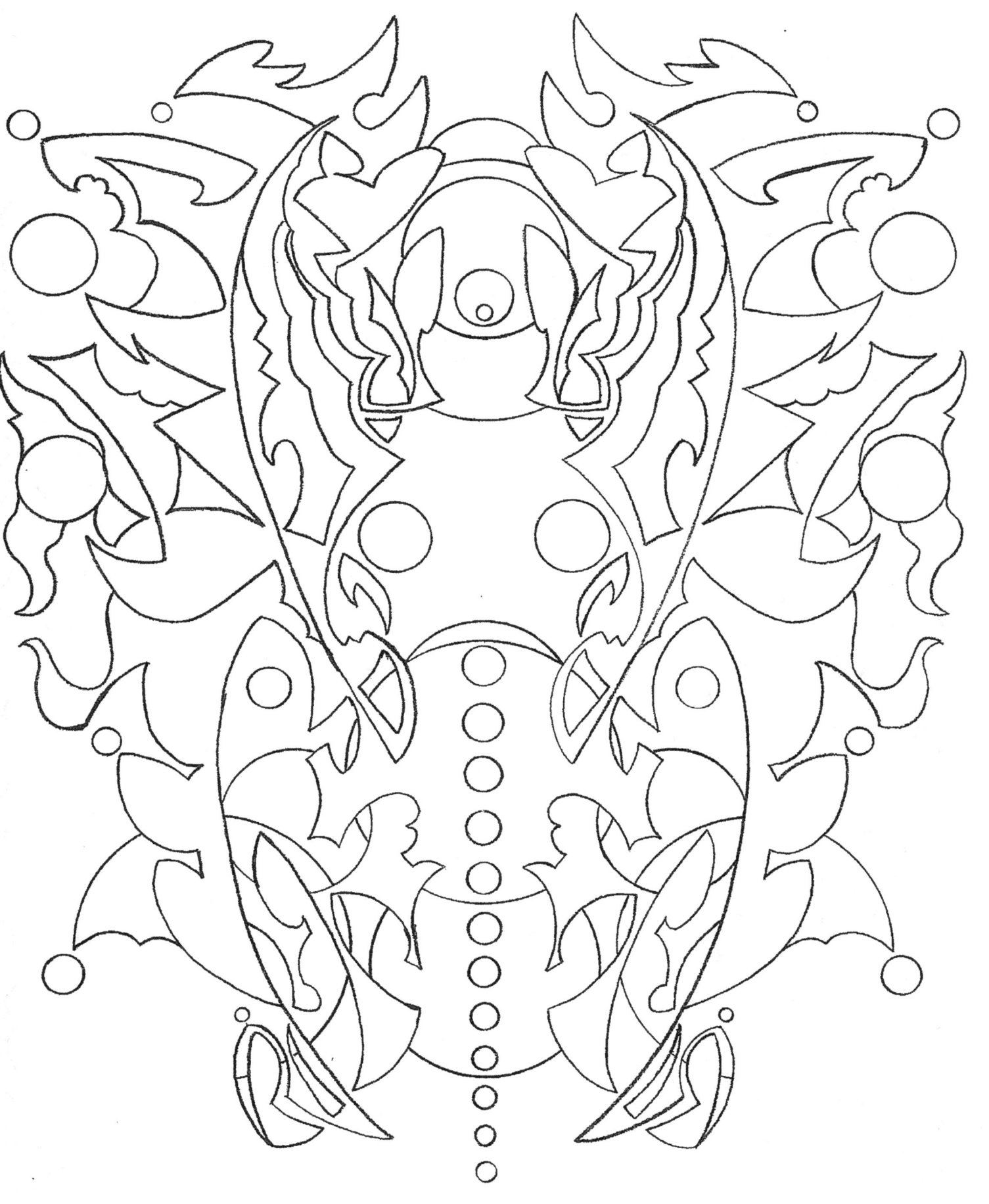

I have decided to stick with love. Hate is too great a burden to bear.

Martin Luther King, Jr.

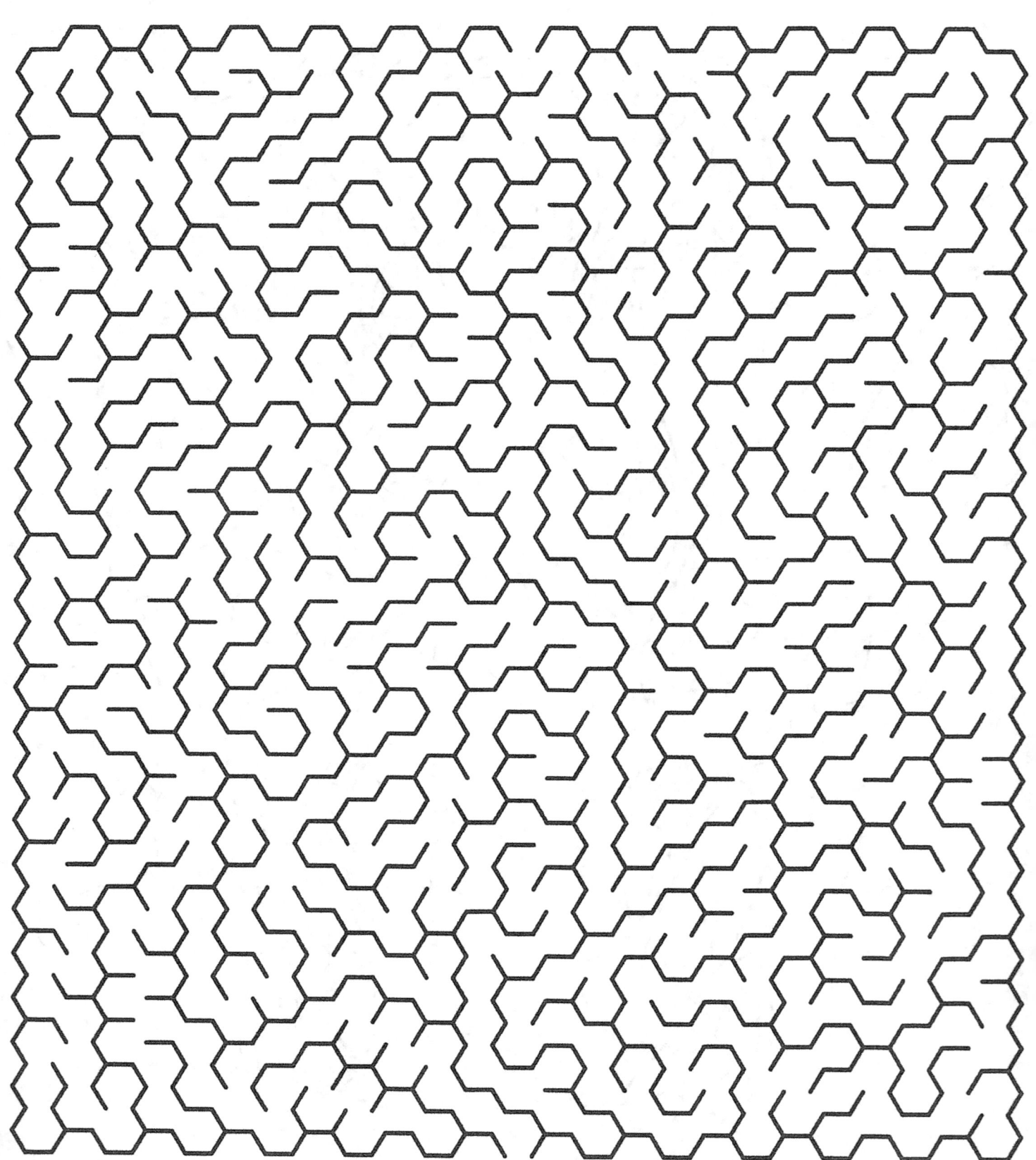

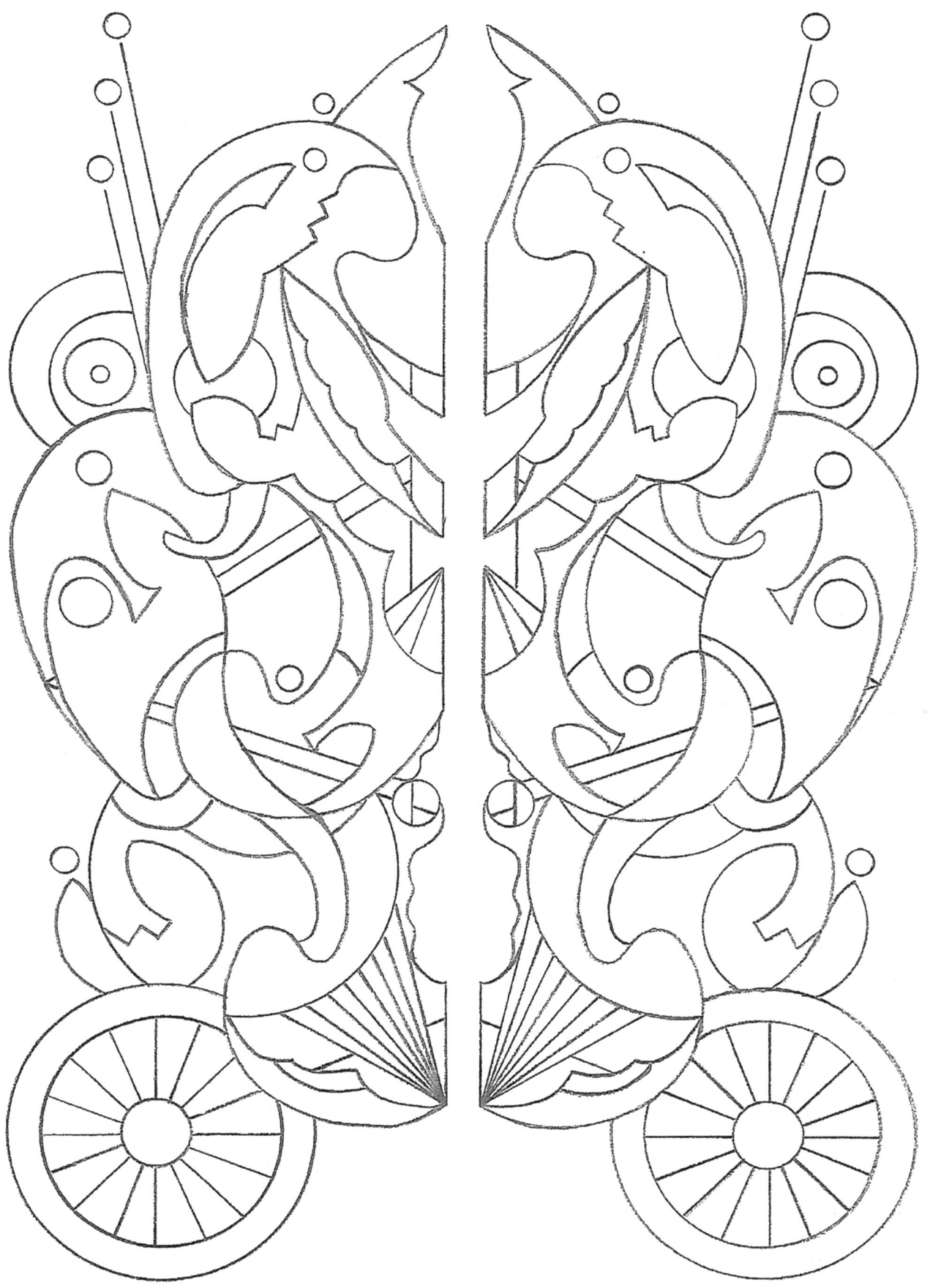

Life is 10% what happens to you and 90% how you react to it.

Charles R. Swindoll

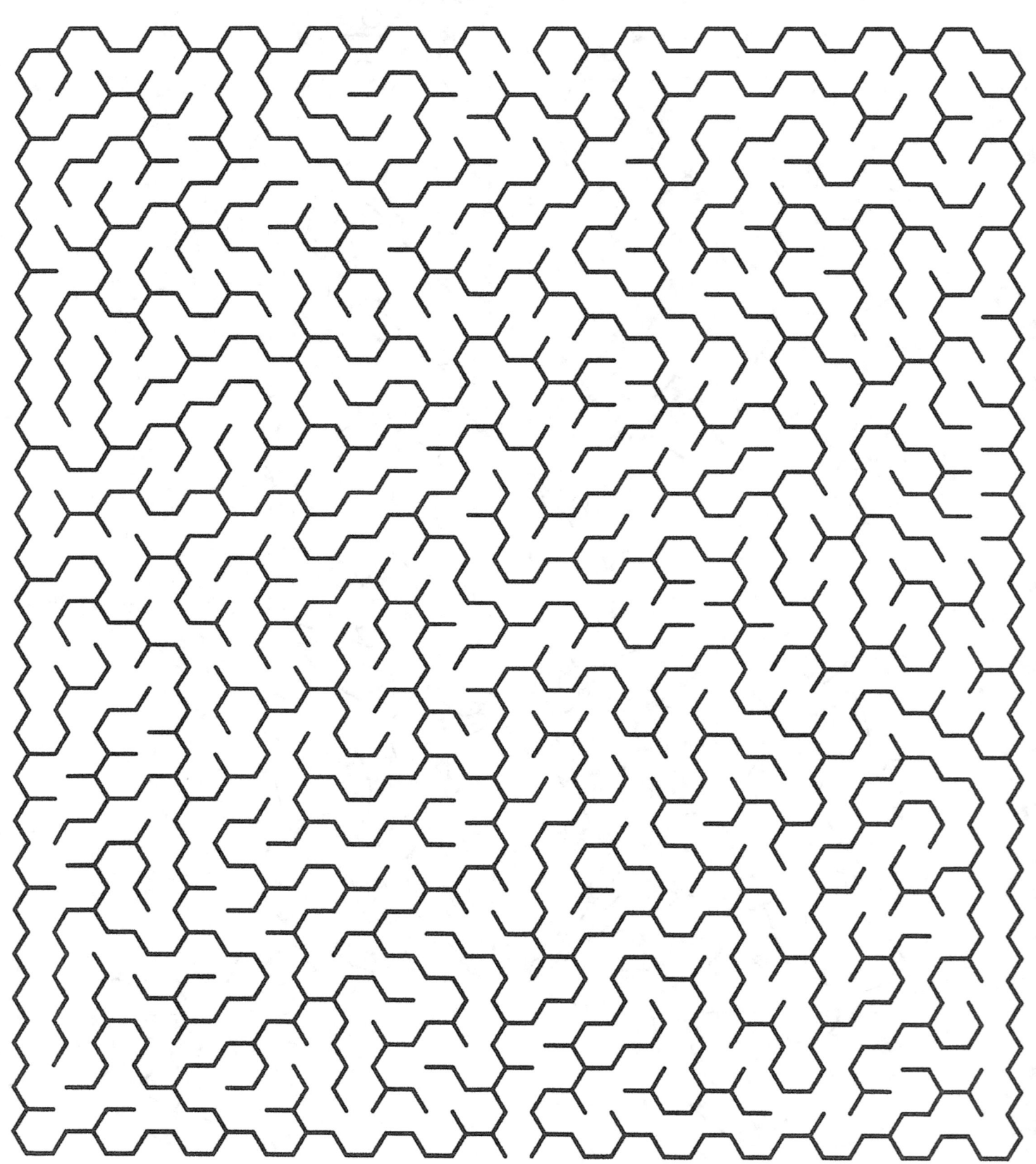

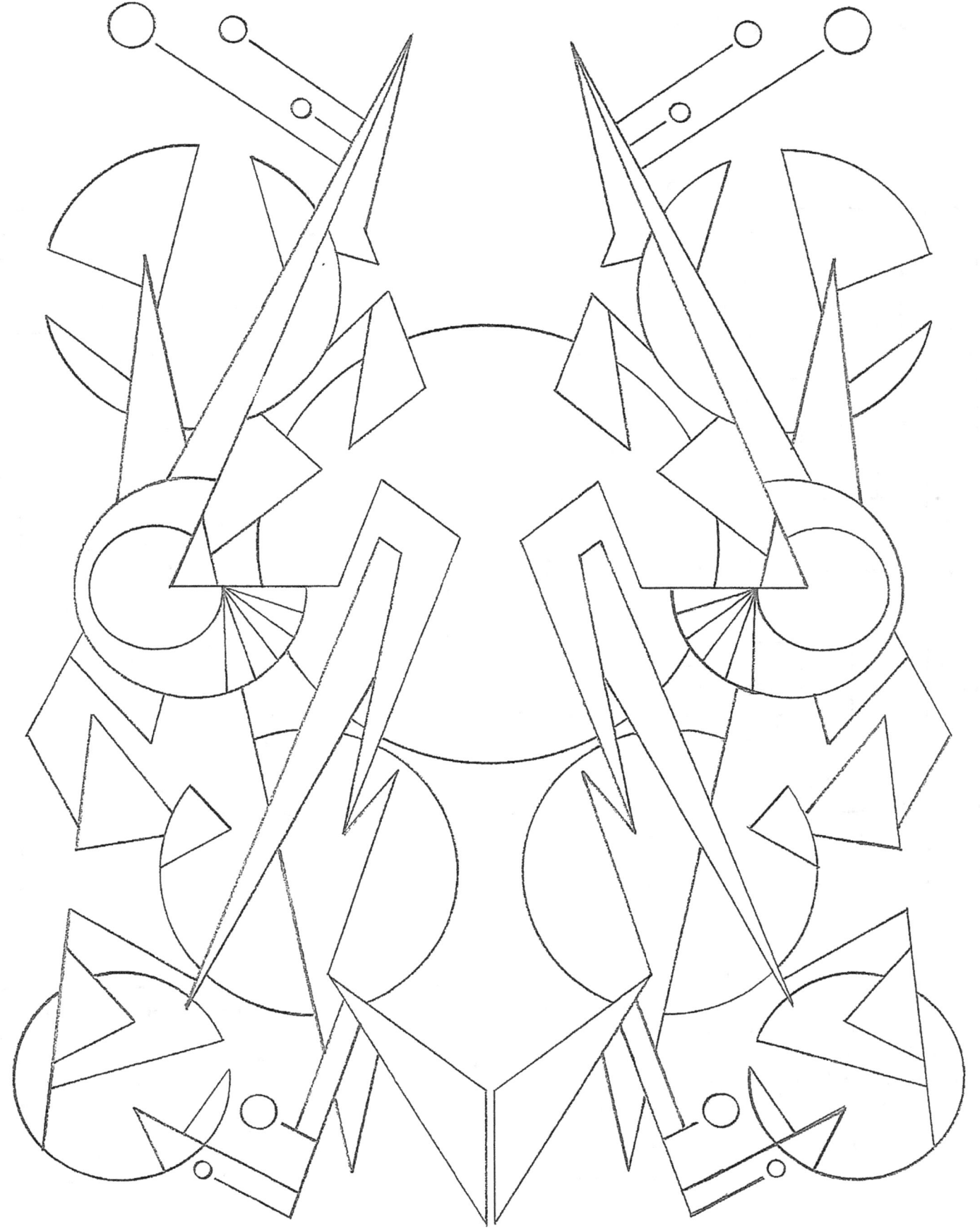

Optimism is the faith that leads to achievement. Nothing can be done without hope and confidence.

Helen Keller

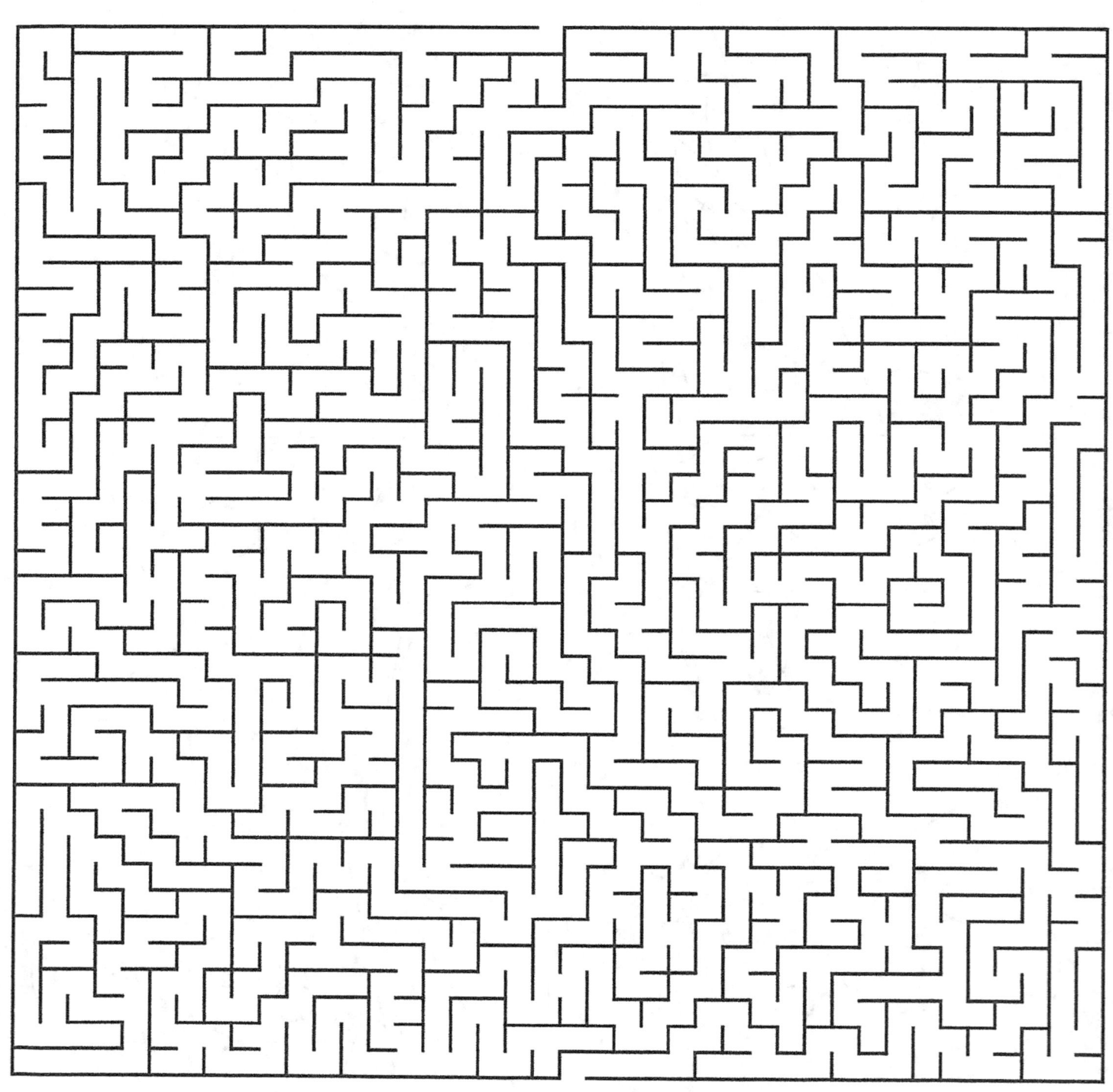

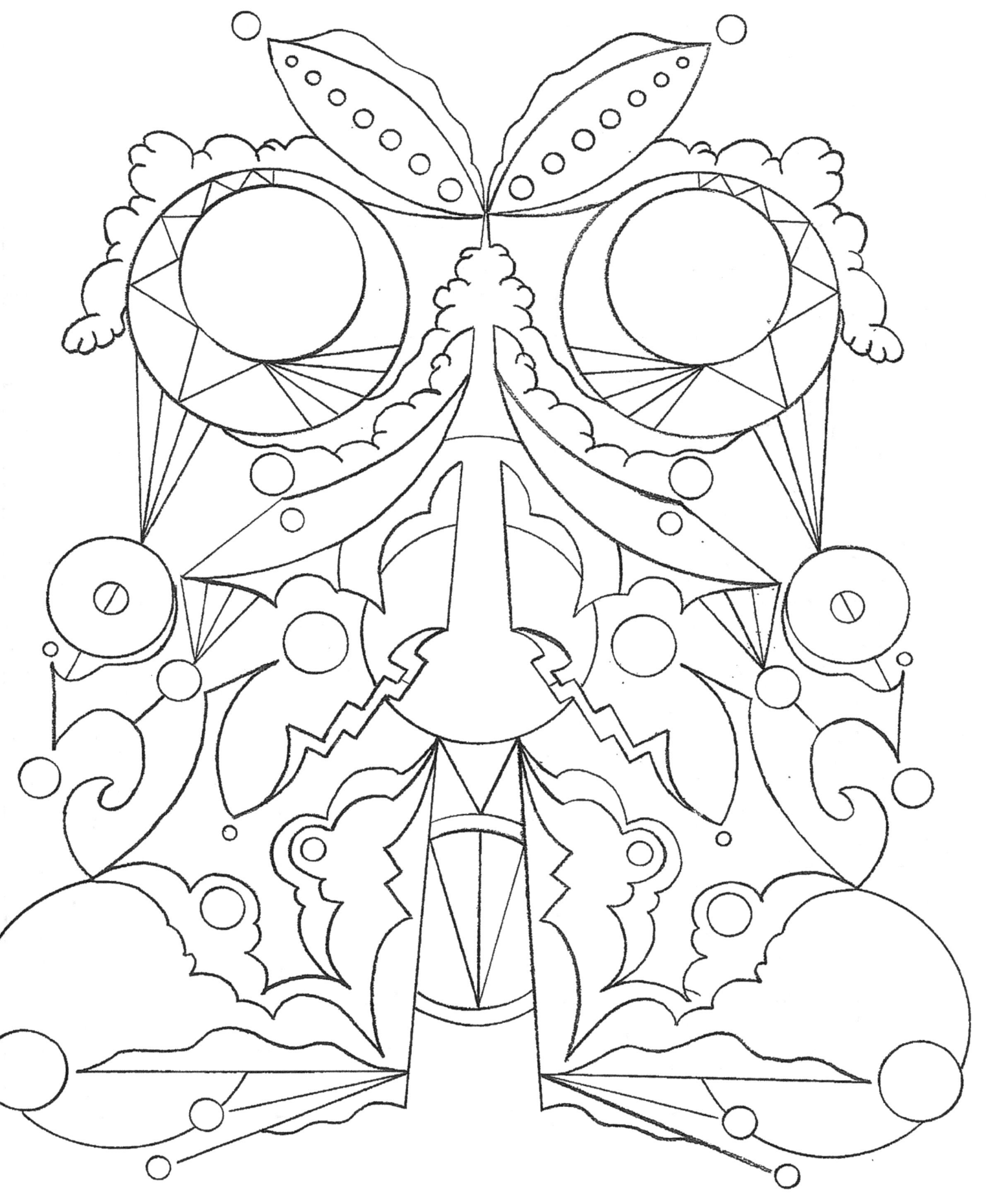

People are not lazy. They simply have impotent goals – that is, goals that do not inspire them.

Tony Robbins

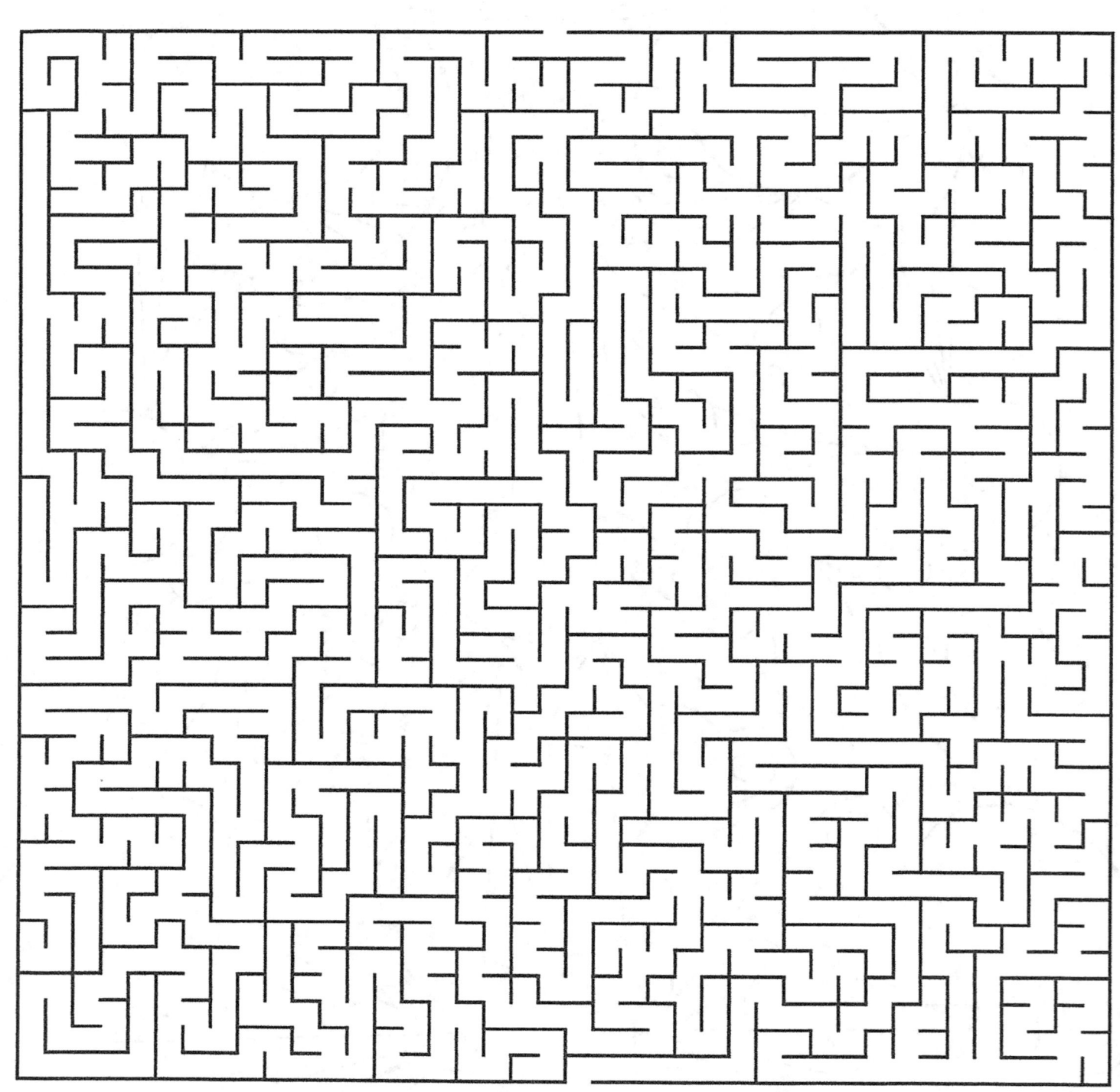

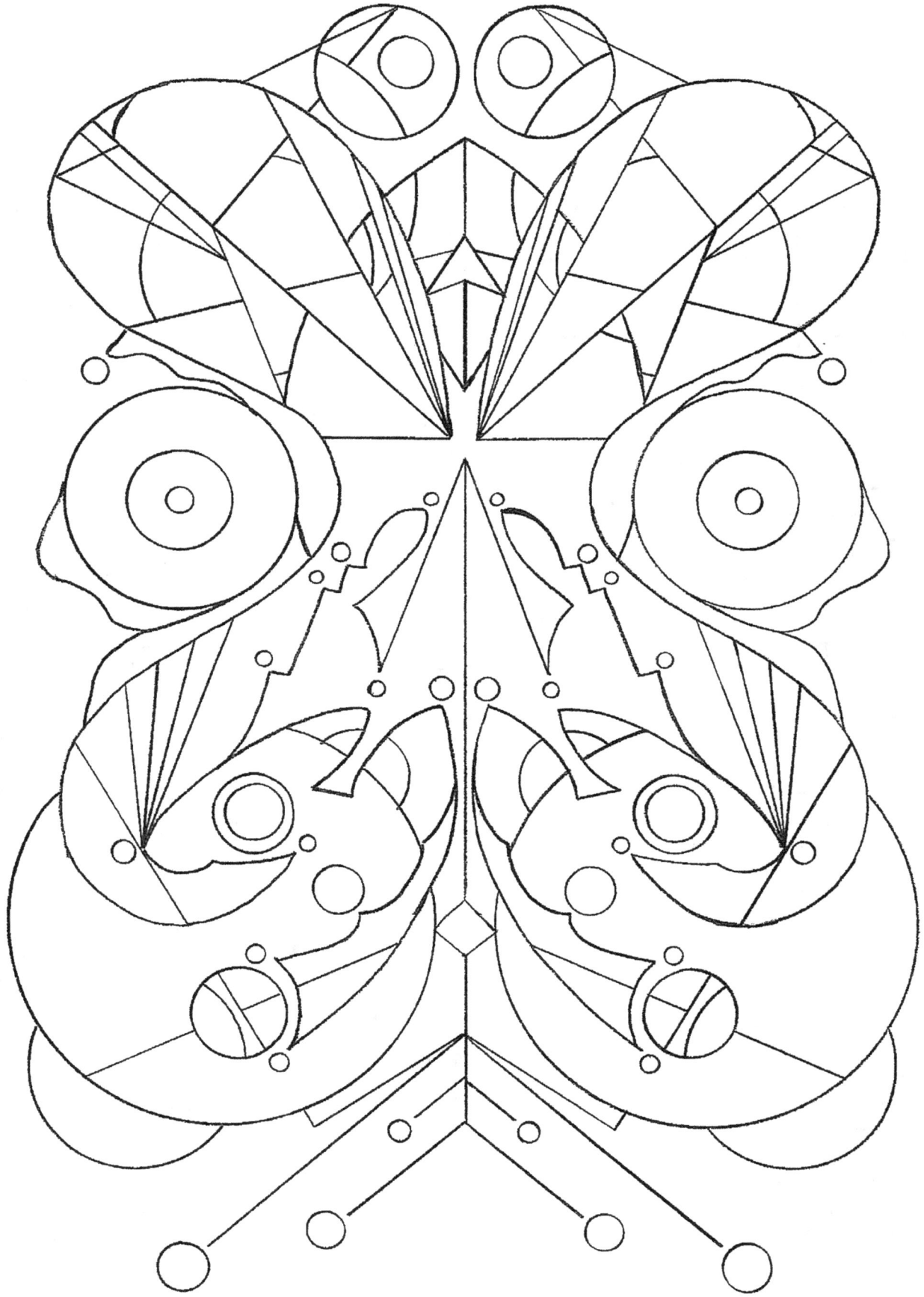

Good, better, best. Never let it rest. 'Til your good is better and your better is best.

St. Jerome

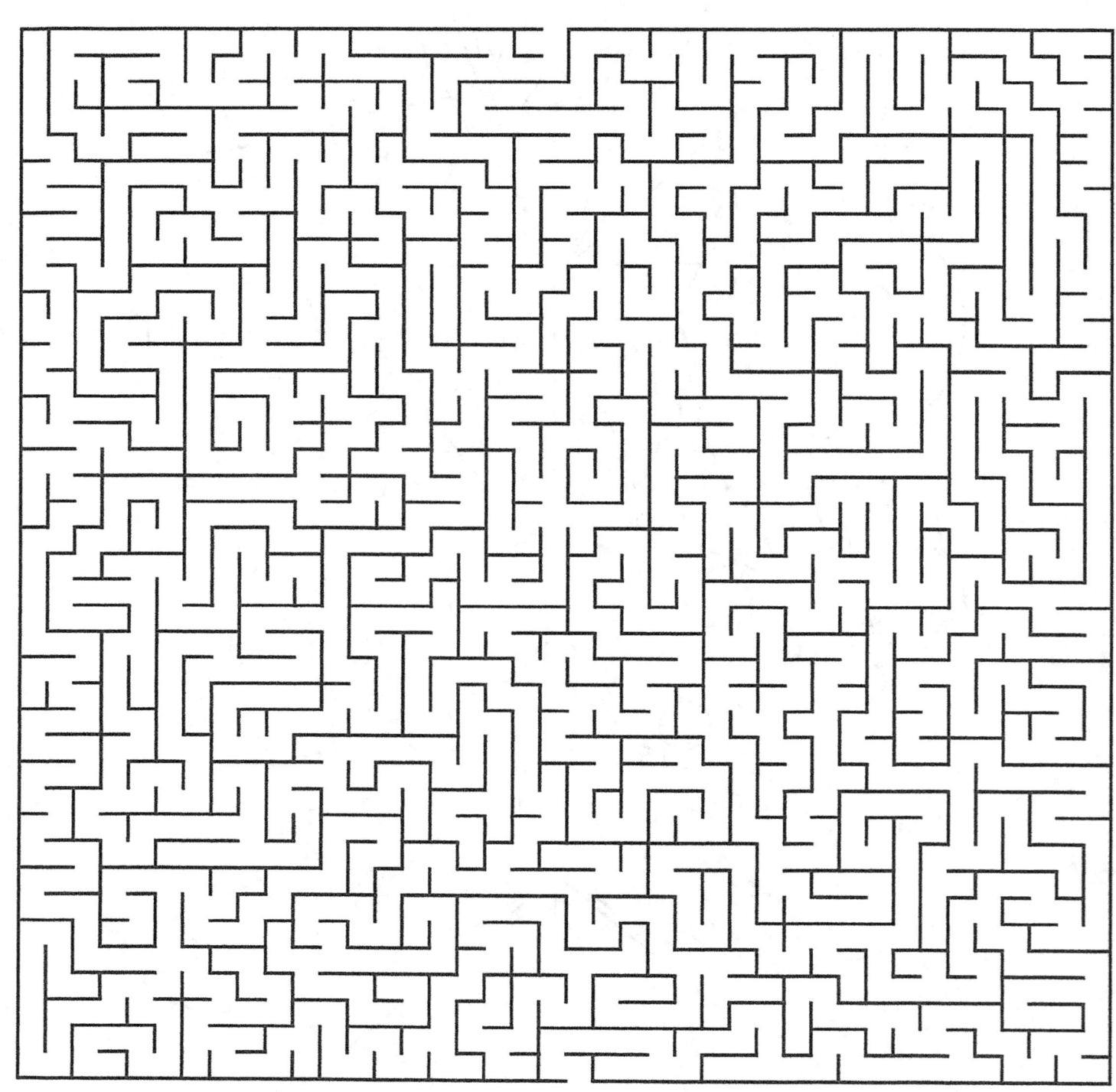

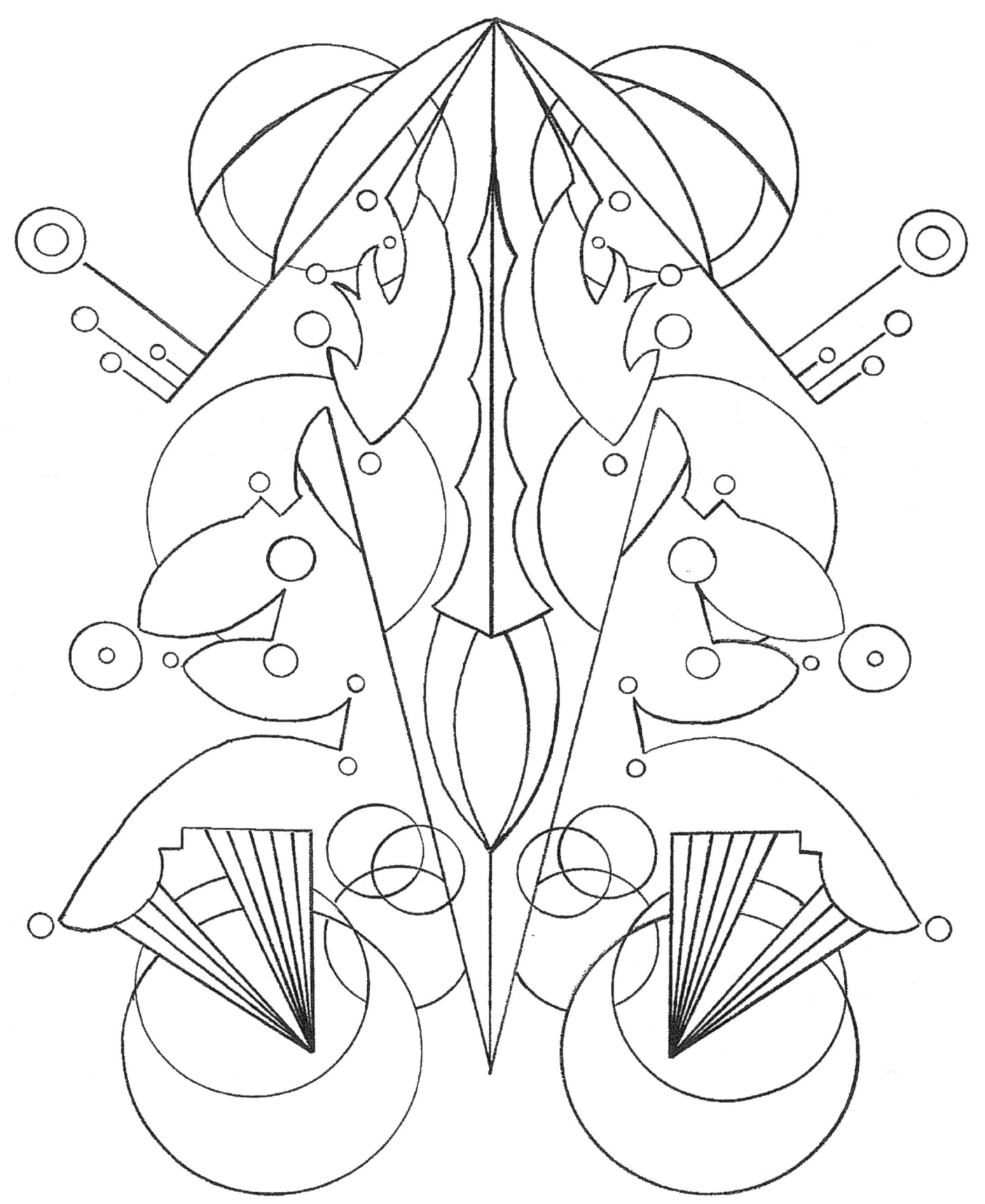

Our greatest weakness lies in giving up. The most certain way to succeed is always to try just one more time.

Thomas A. Edison

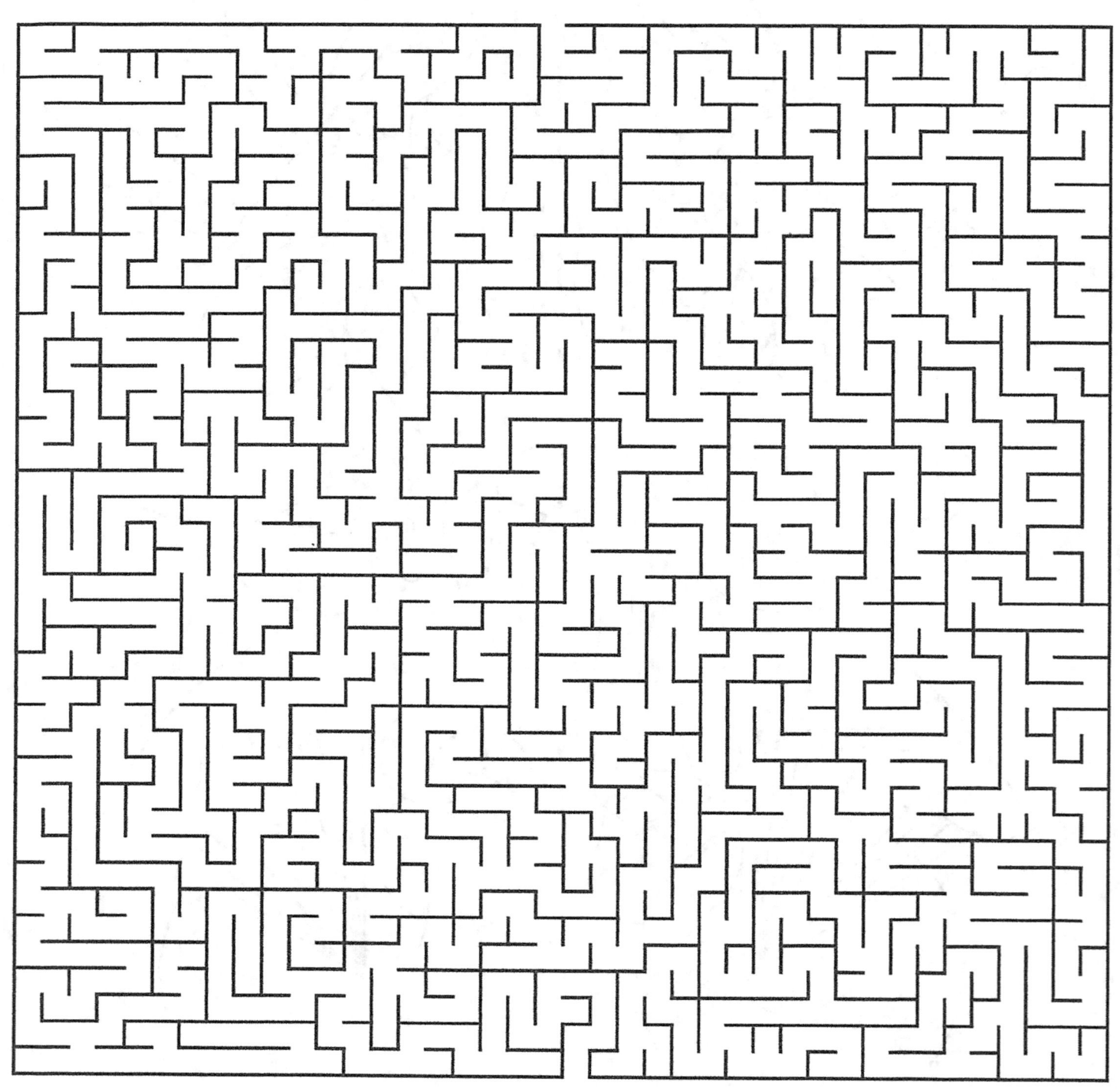

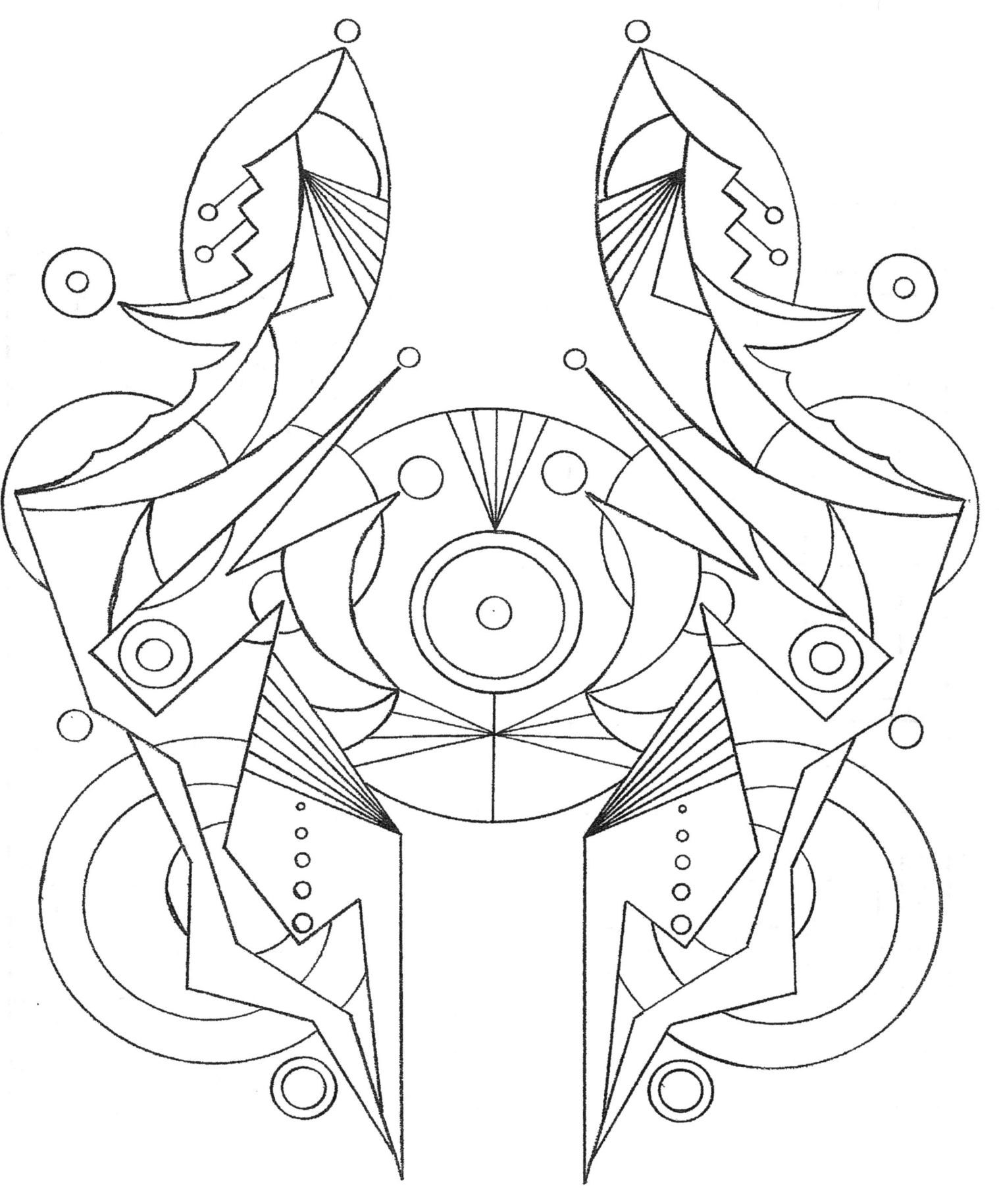

It always seems impossible until it's done.

Nelson Mandela

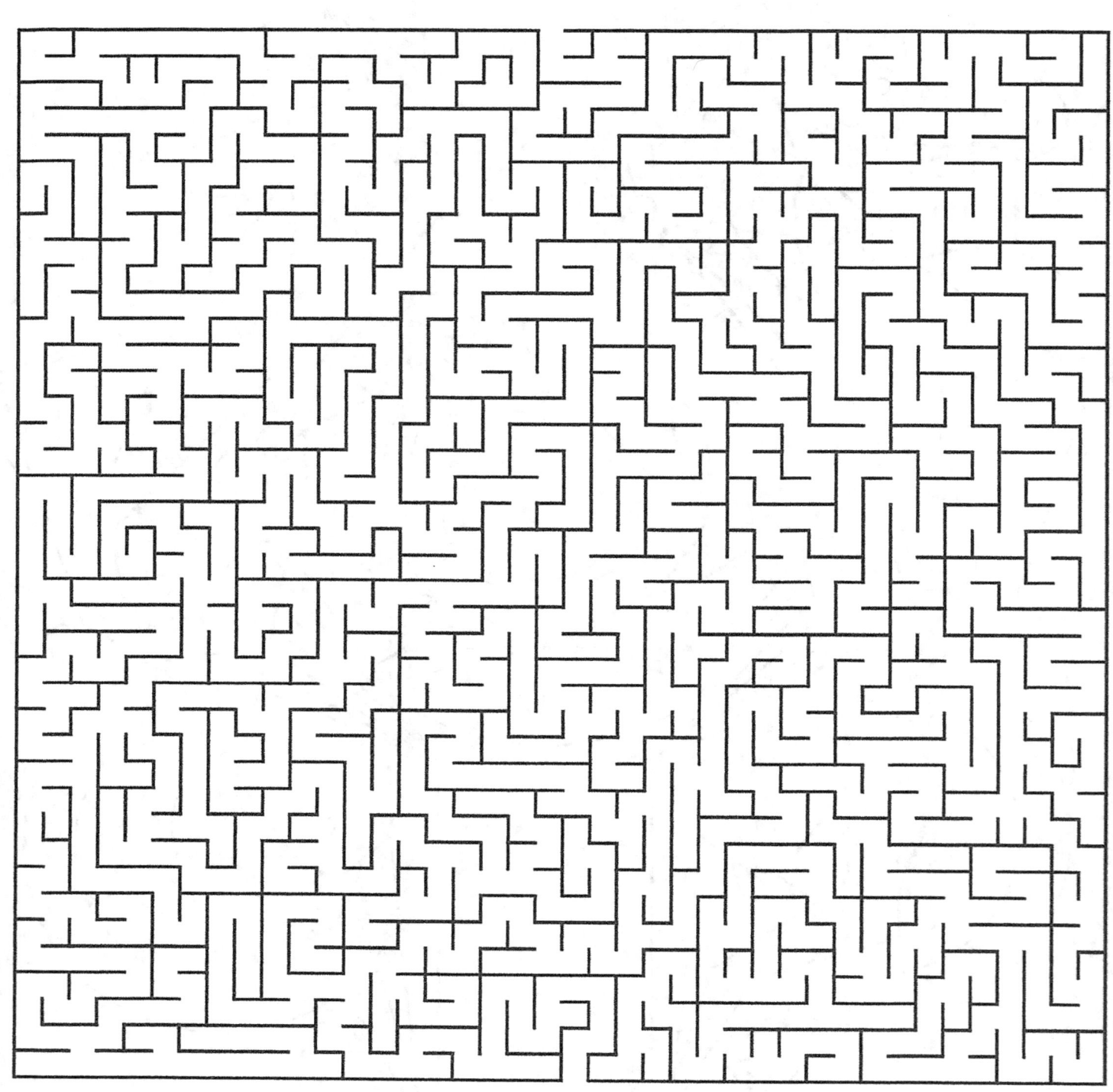

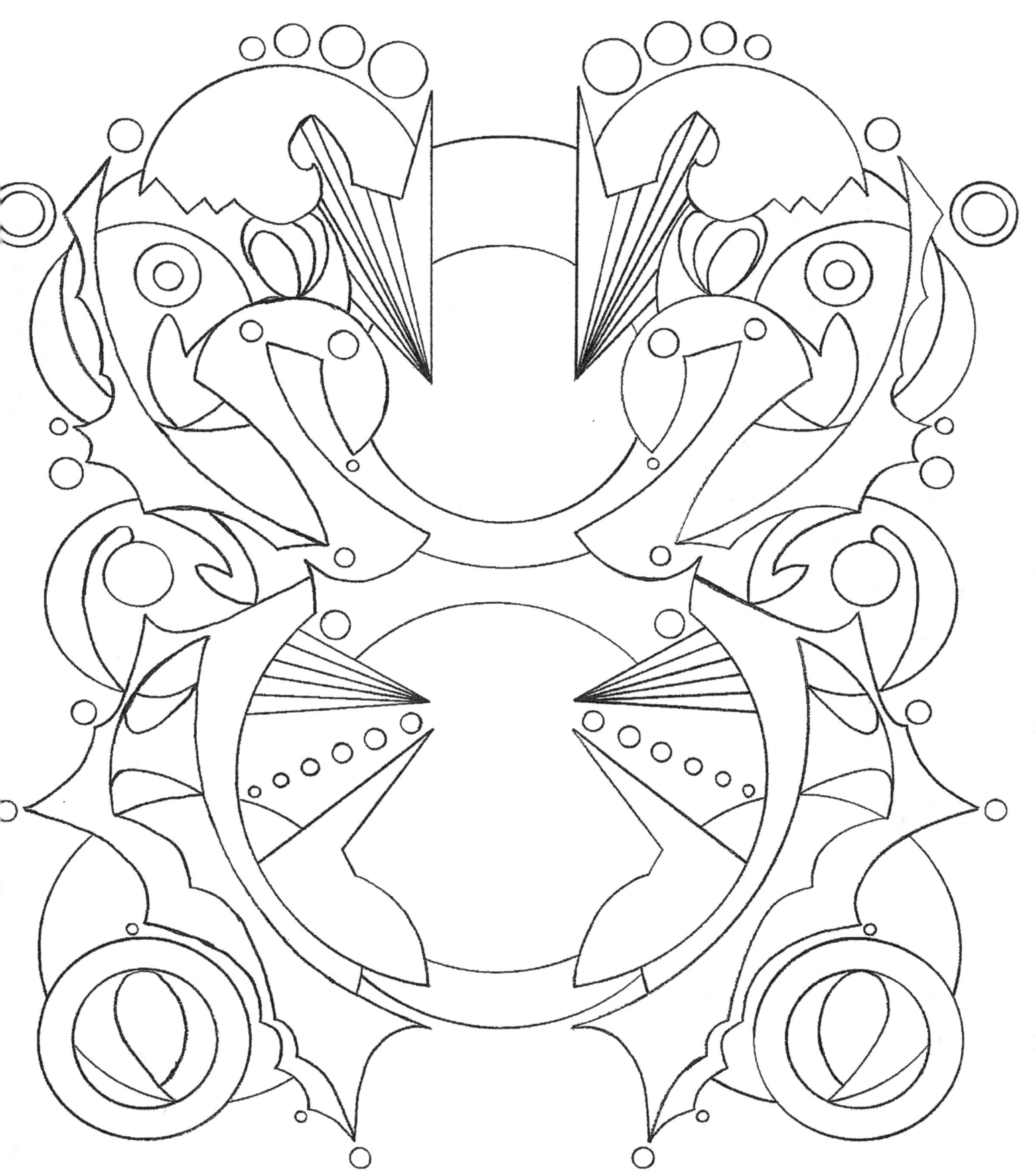

It does not matter how slowly you go as long as you do not stop.

Confucius

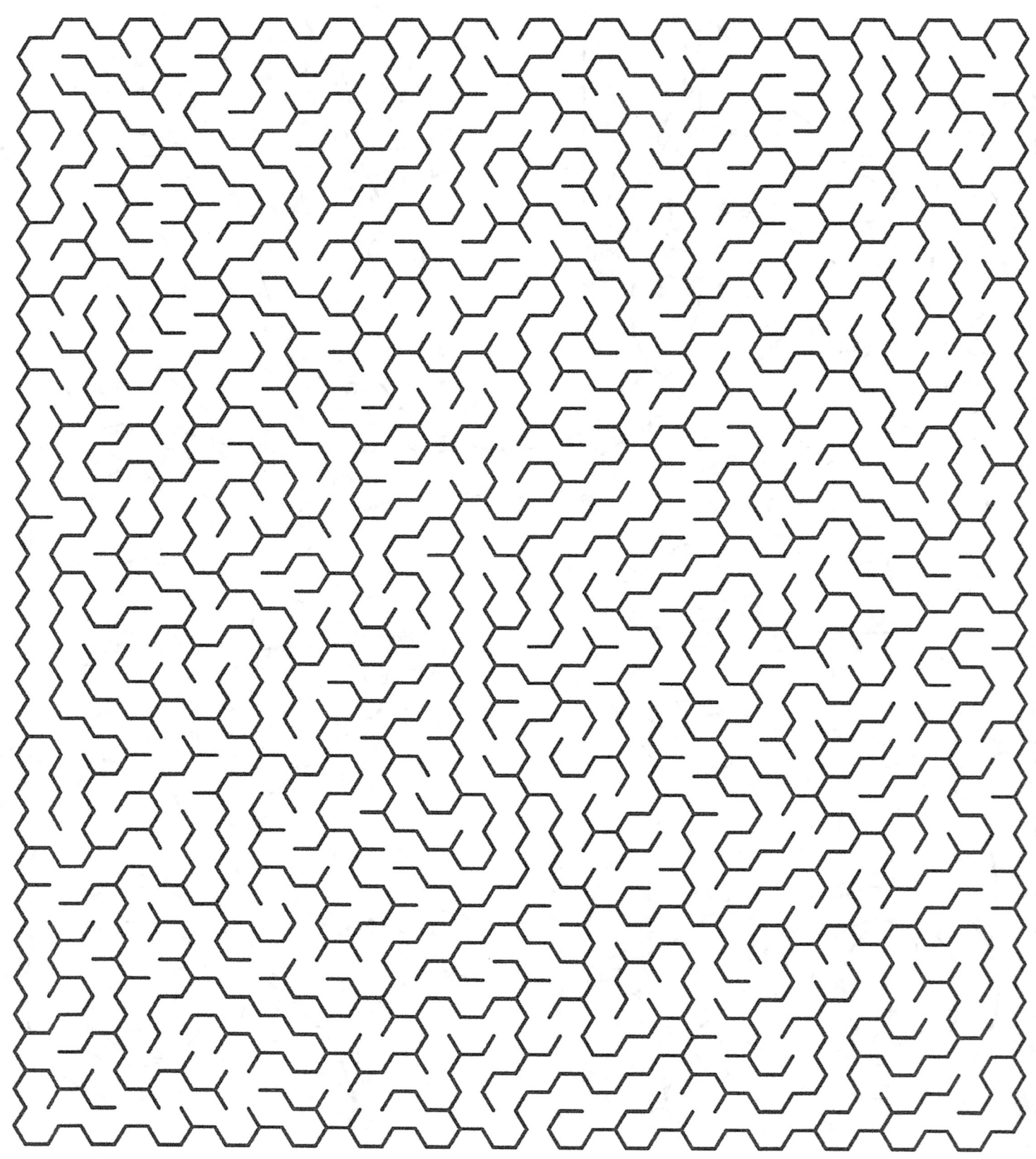

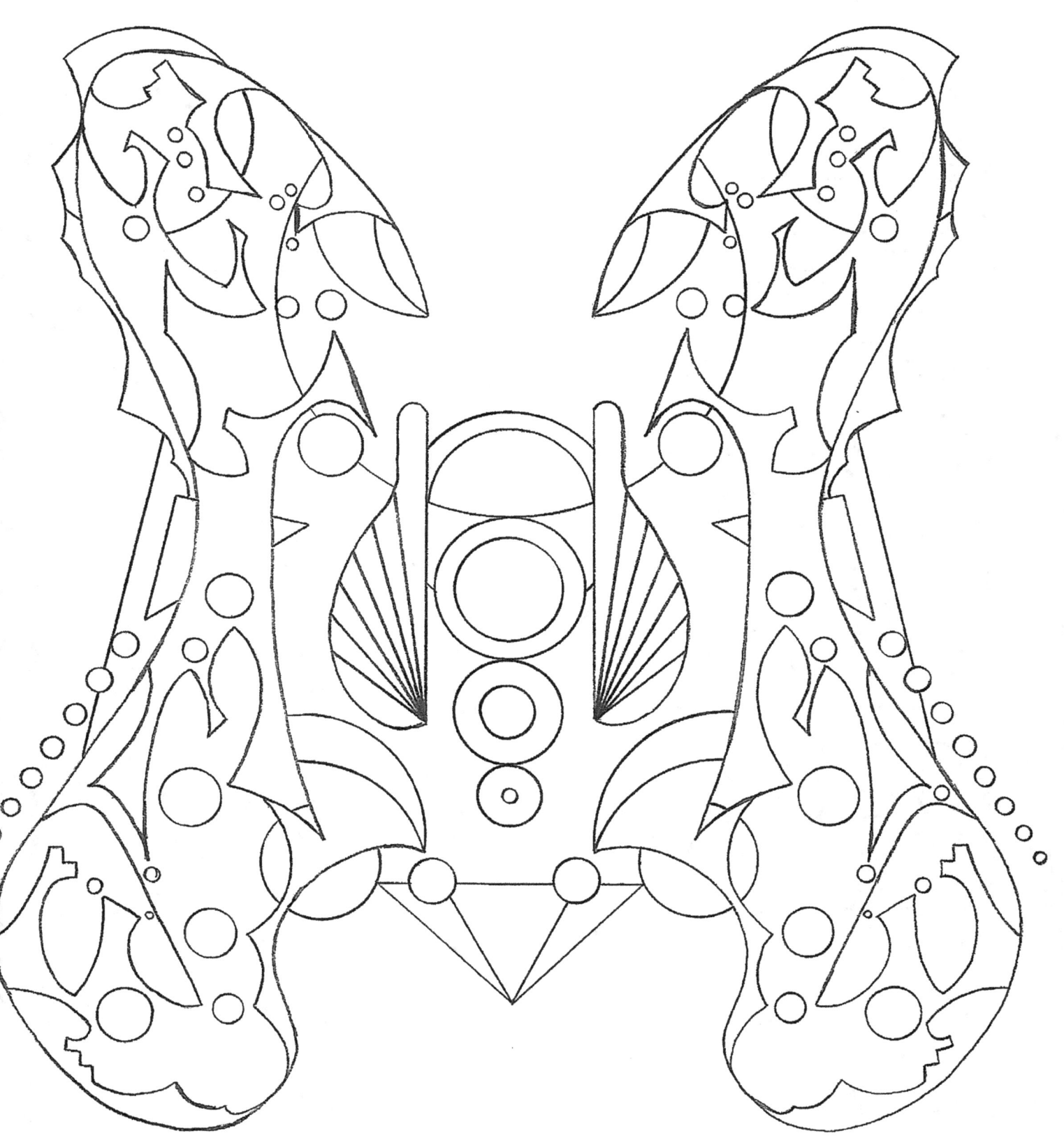

Setting goals is the first step in turning the invisible into the visible.

Tony Robbins

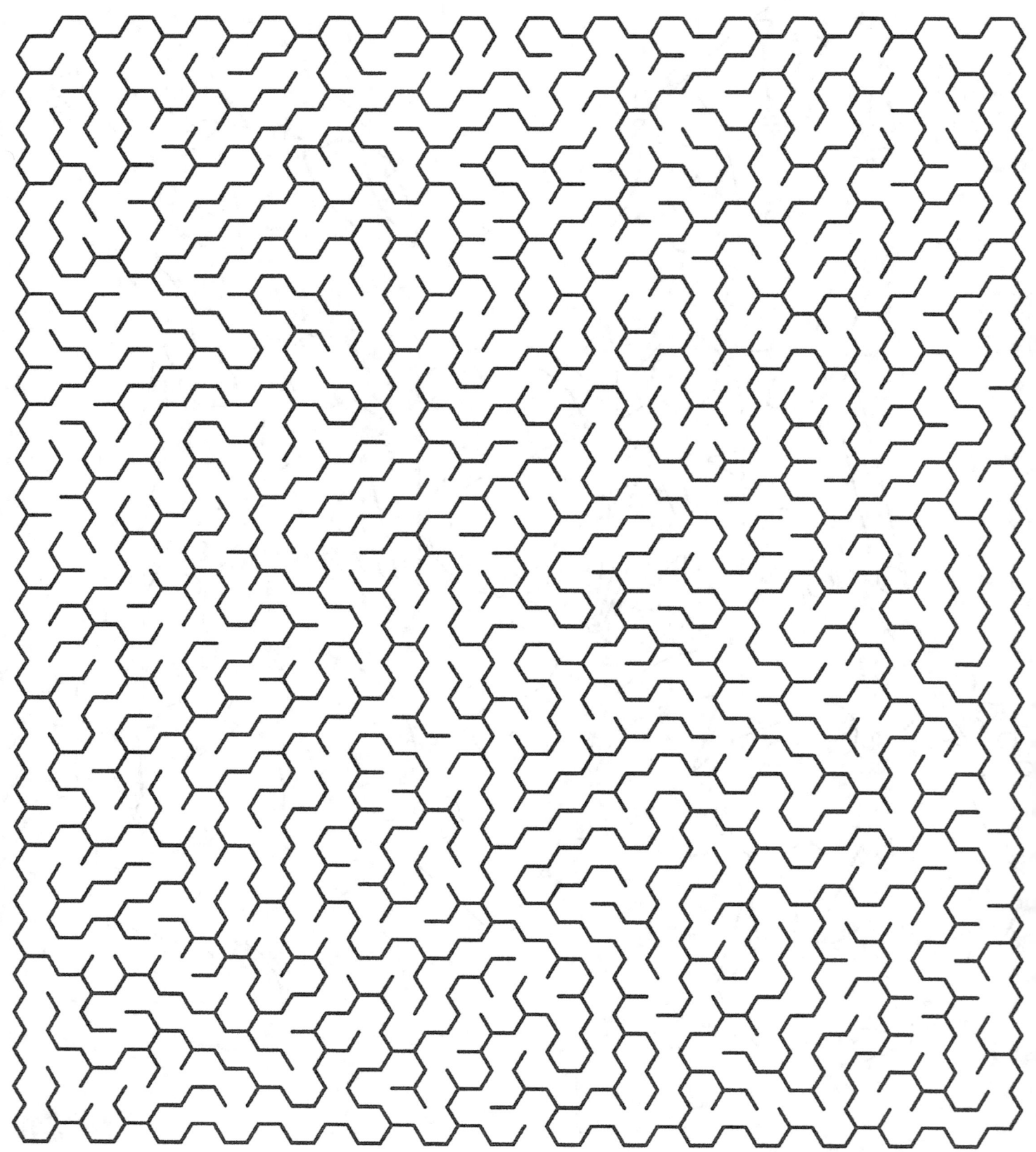

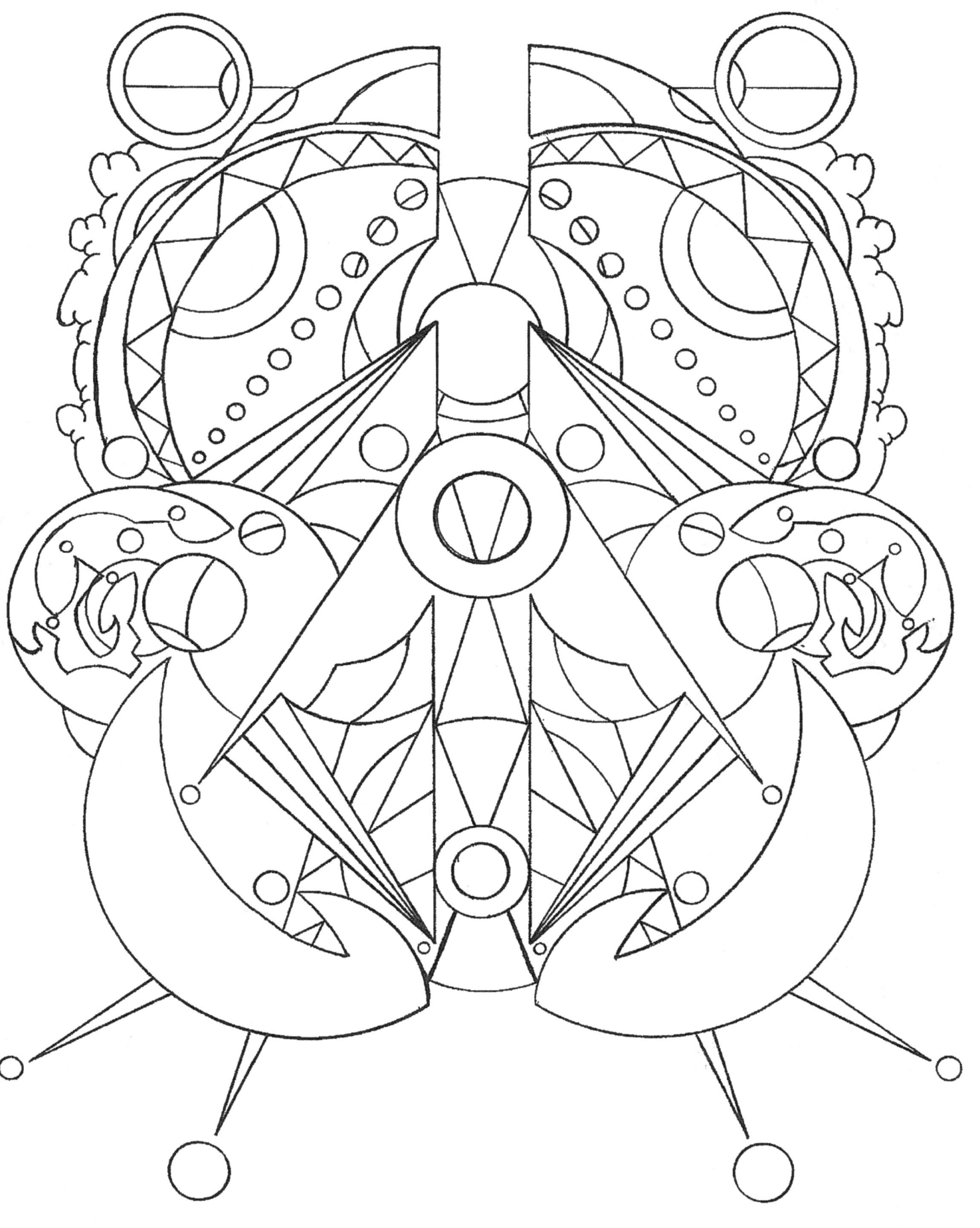

Keep your eyes on the stars, and your feet on the ground.

Theodore Roosevelt

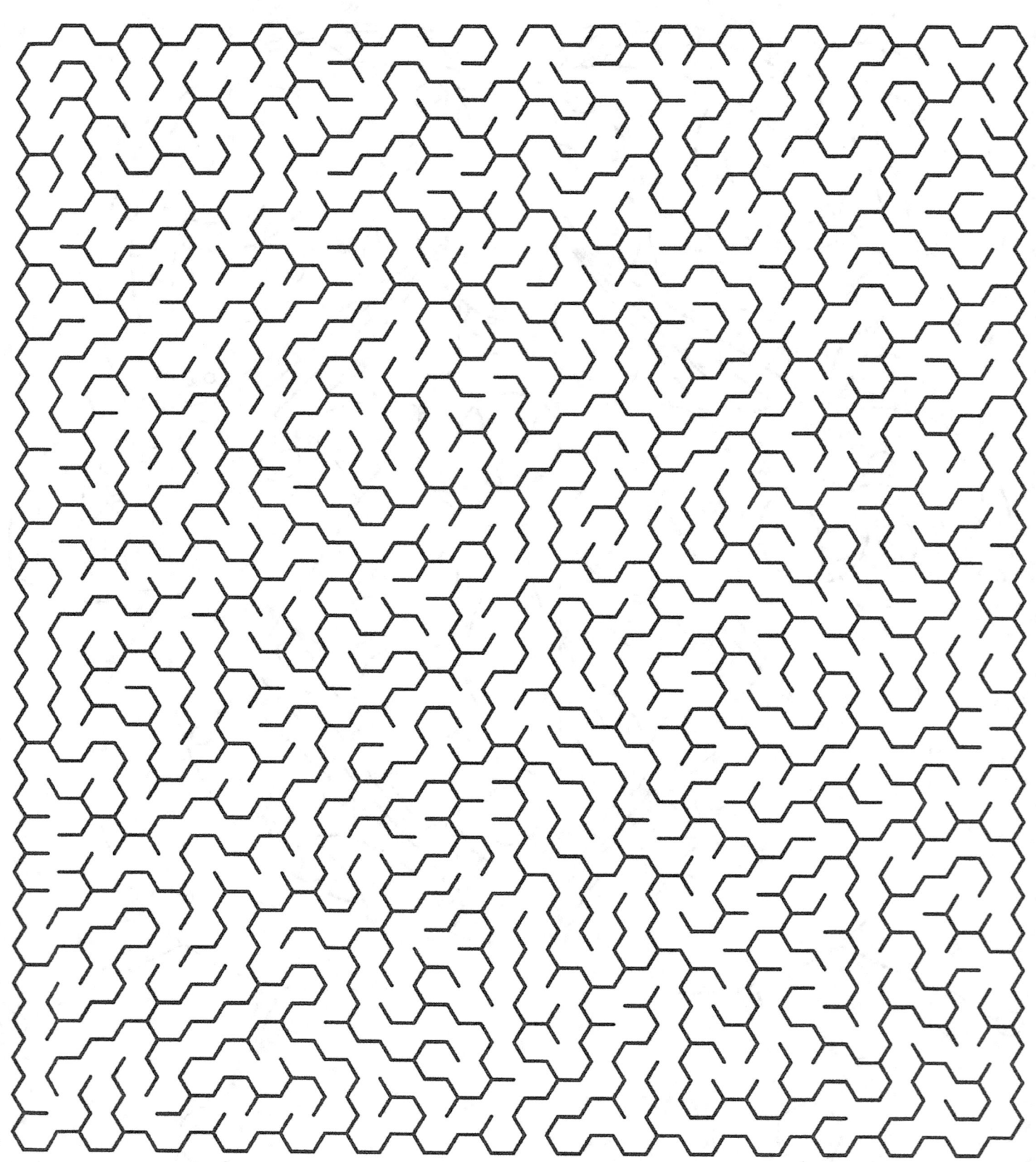

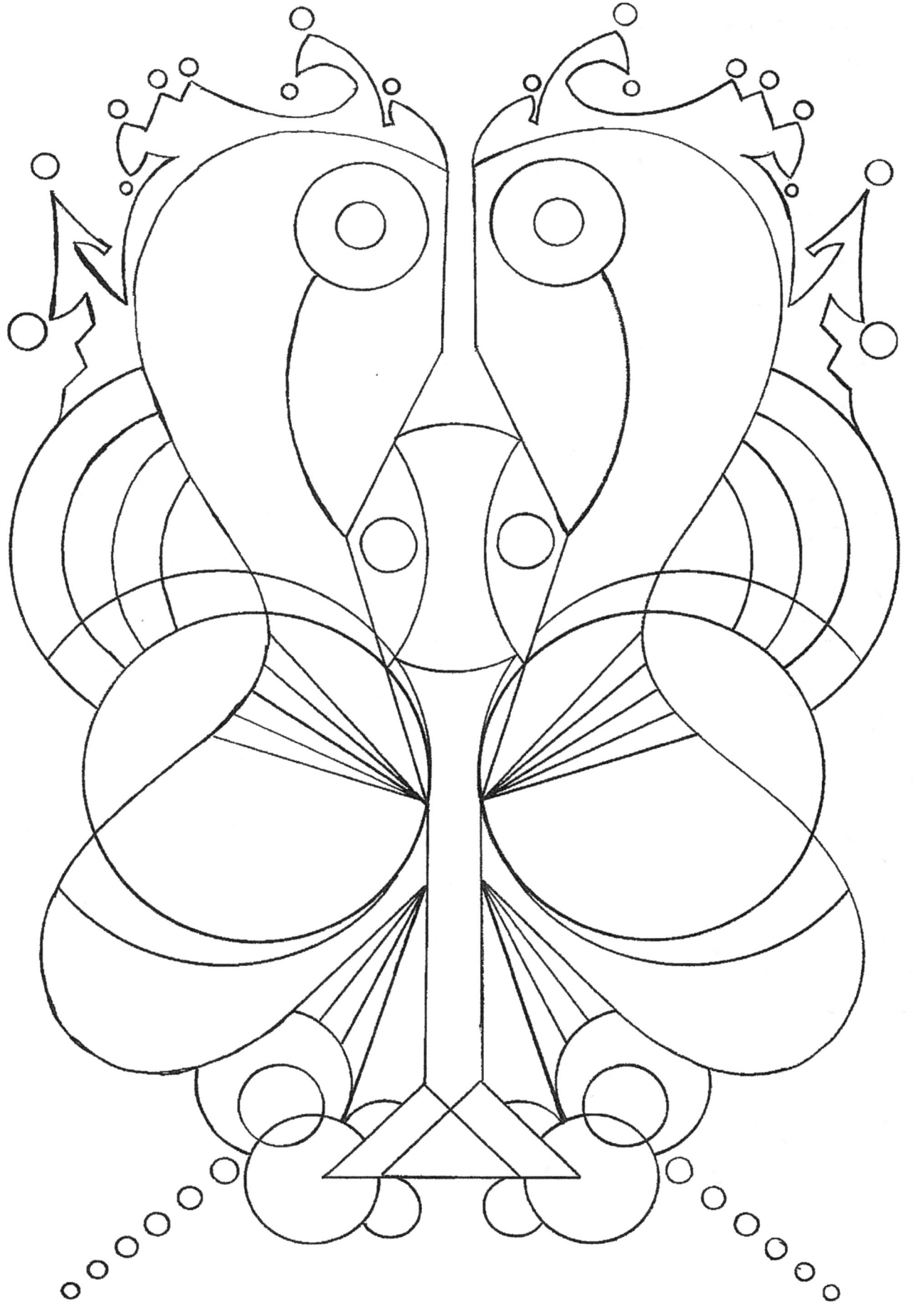

If you can dream it, you can do it.

Walt Disney

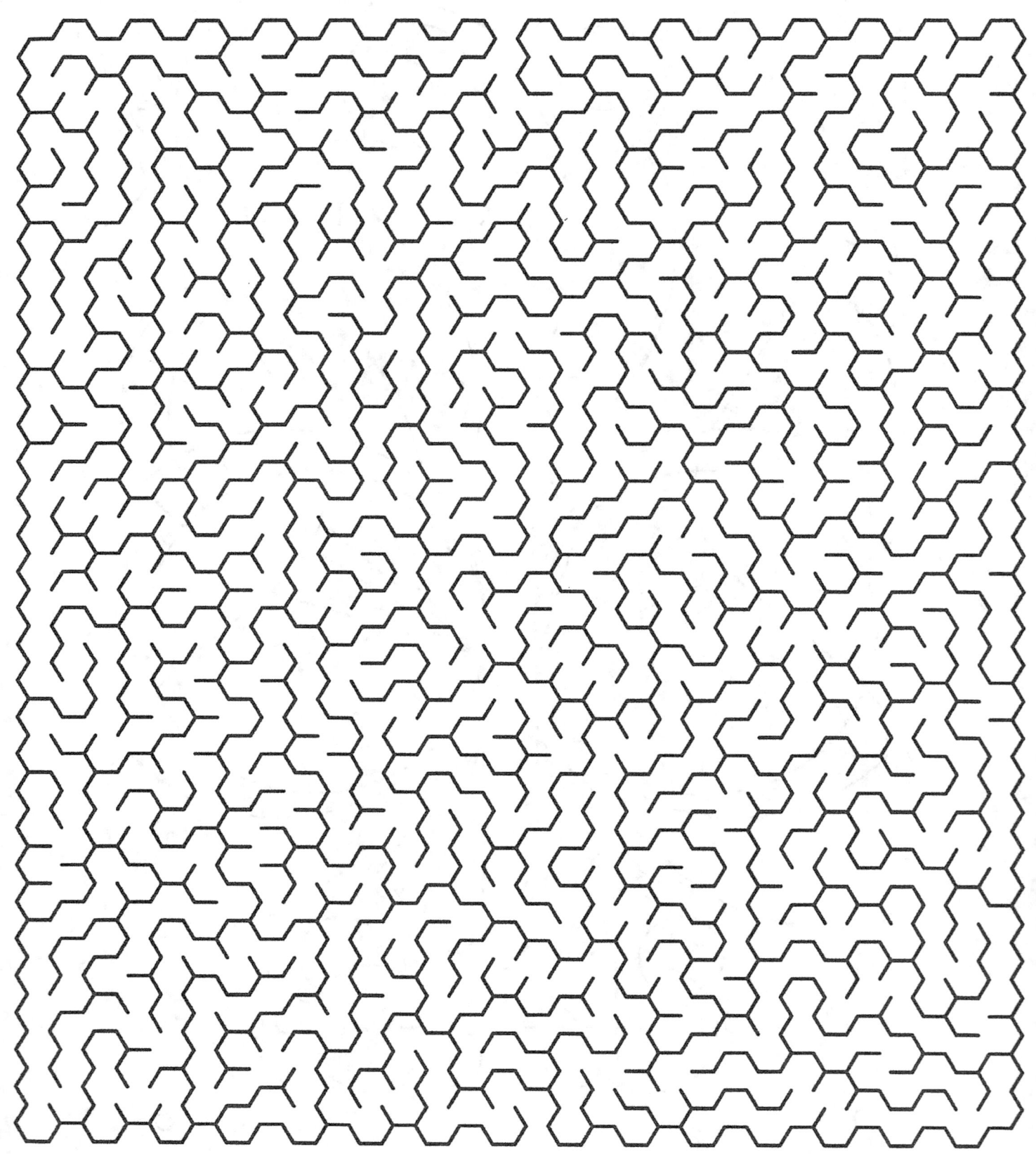

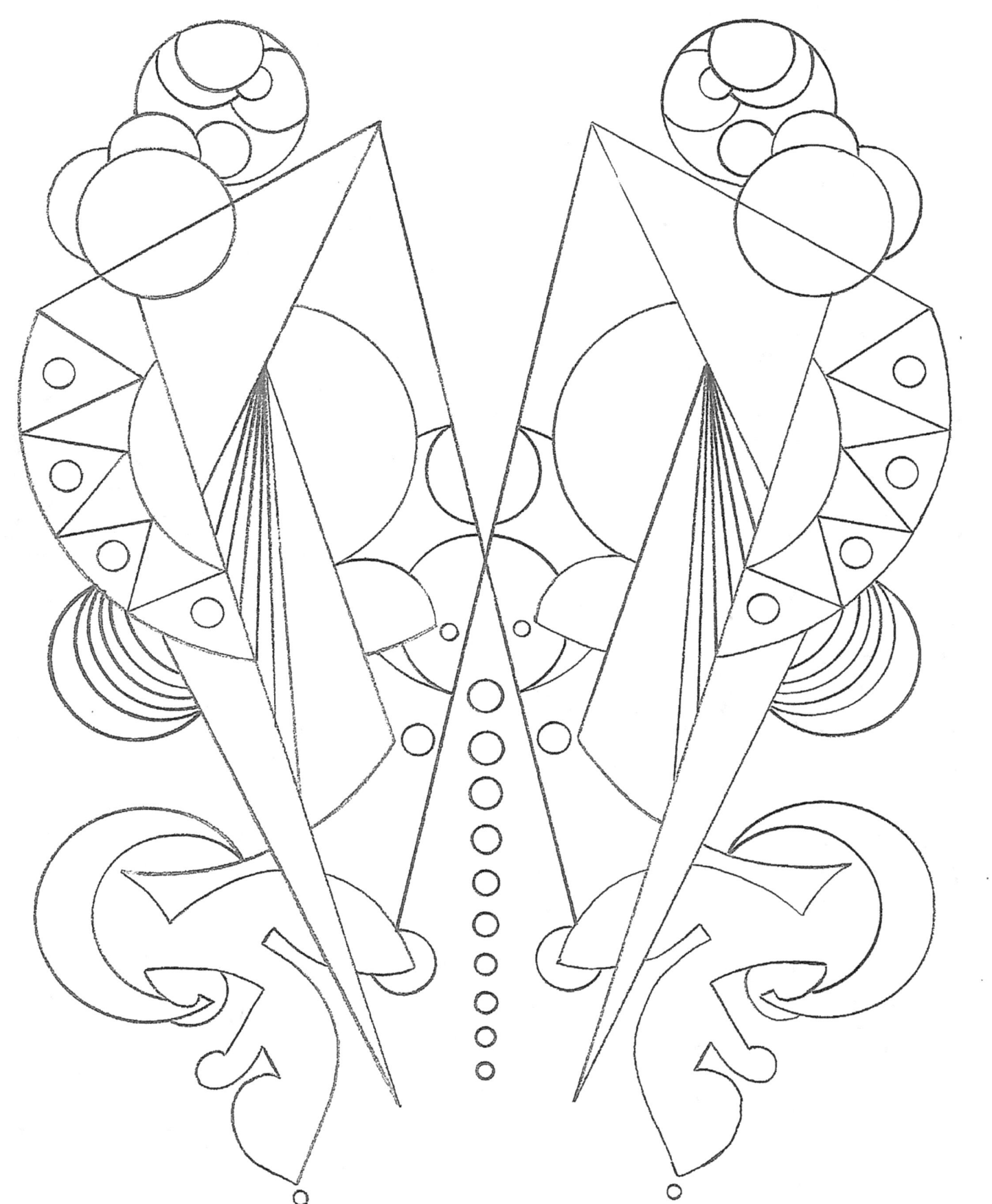

Your talent is God's gift to you. What you do with it is your gift back to God.

Leo Buscaglia

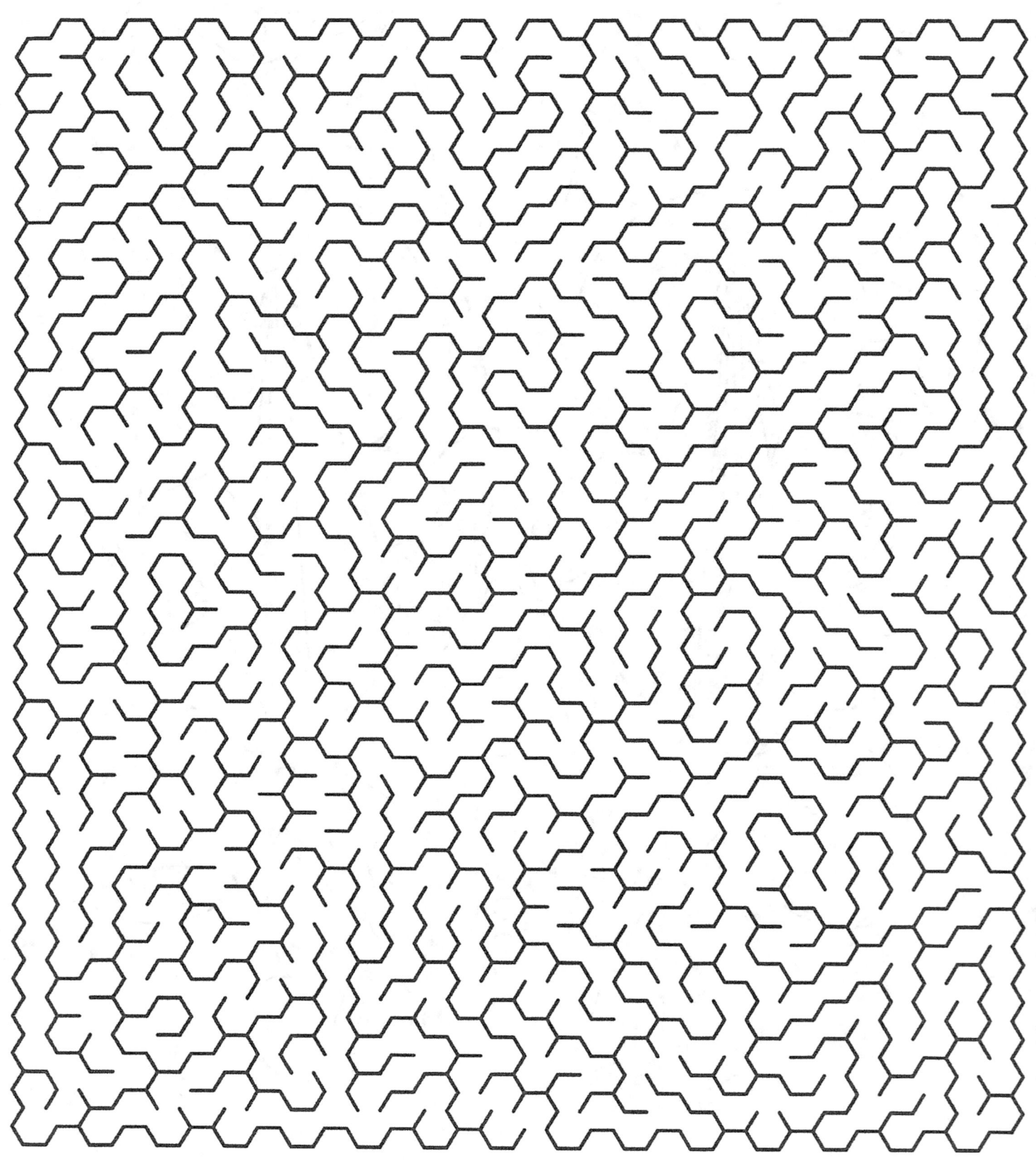

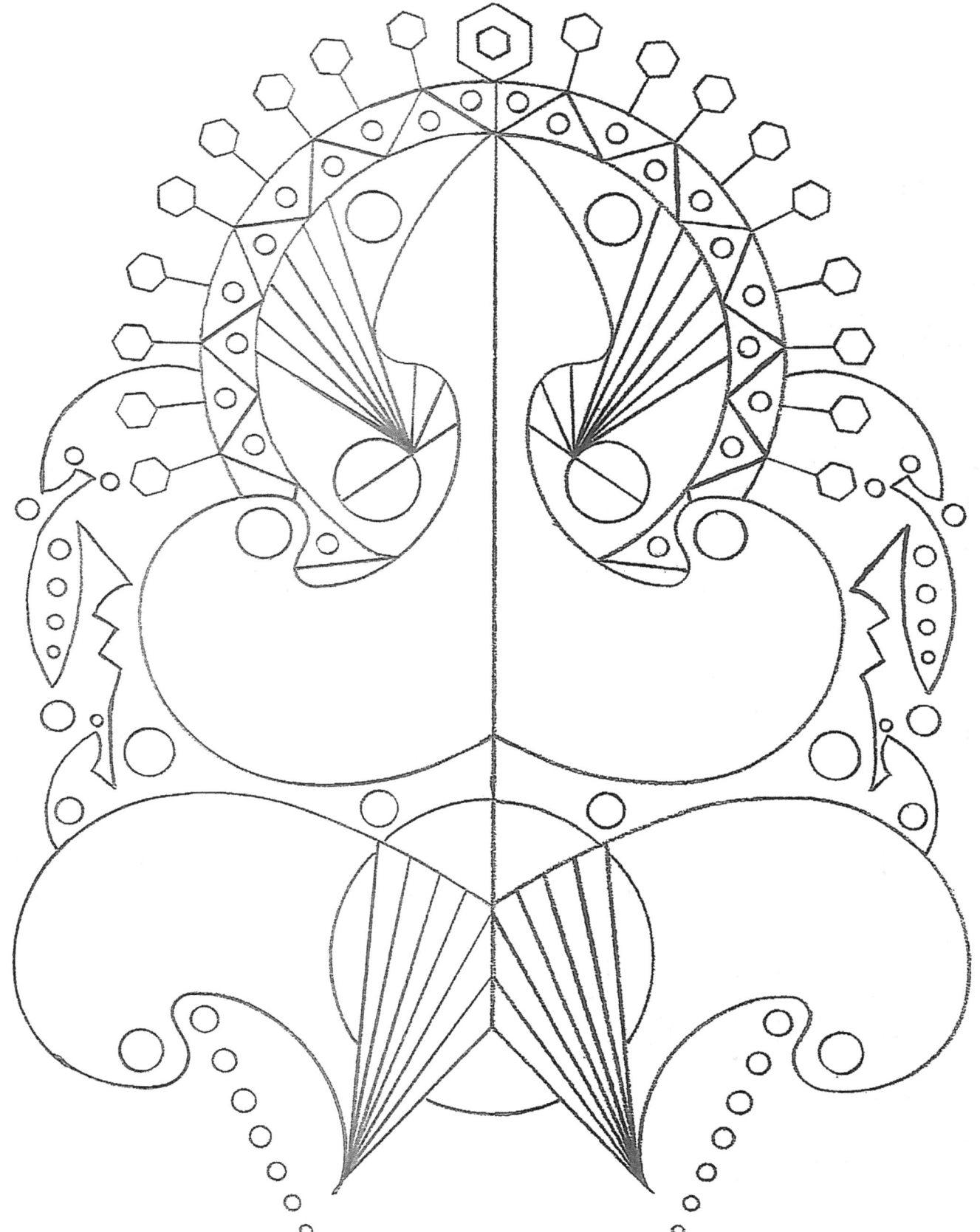

If you want to conquer fear, don't sit home and think about it. Go out and get busy.

Dale Carnegie

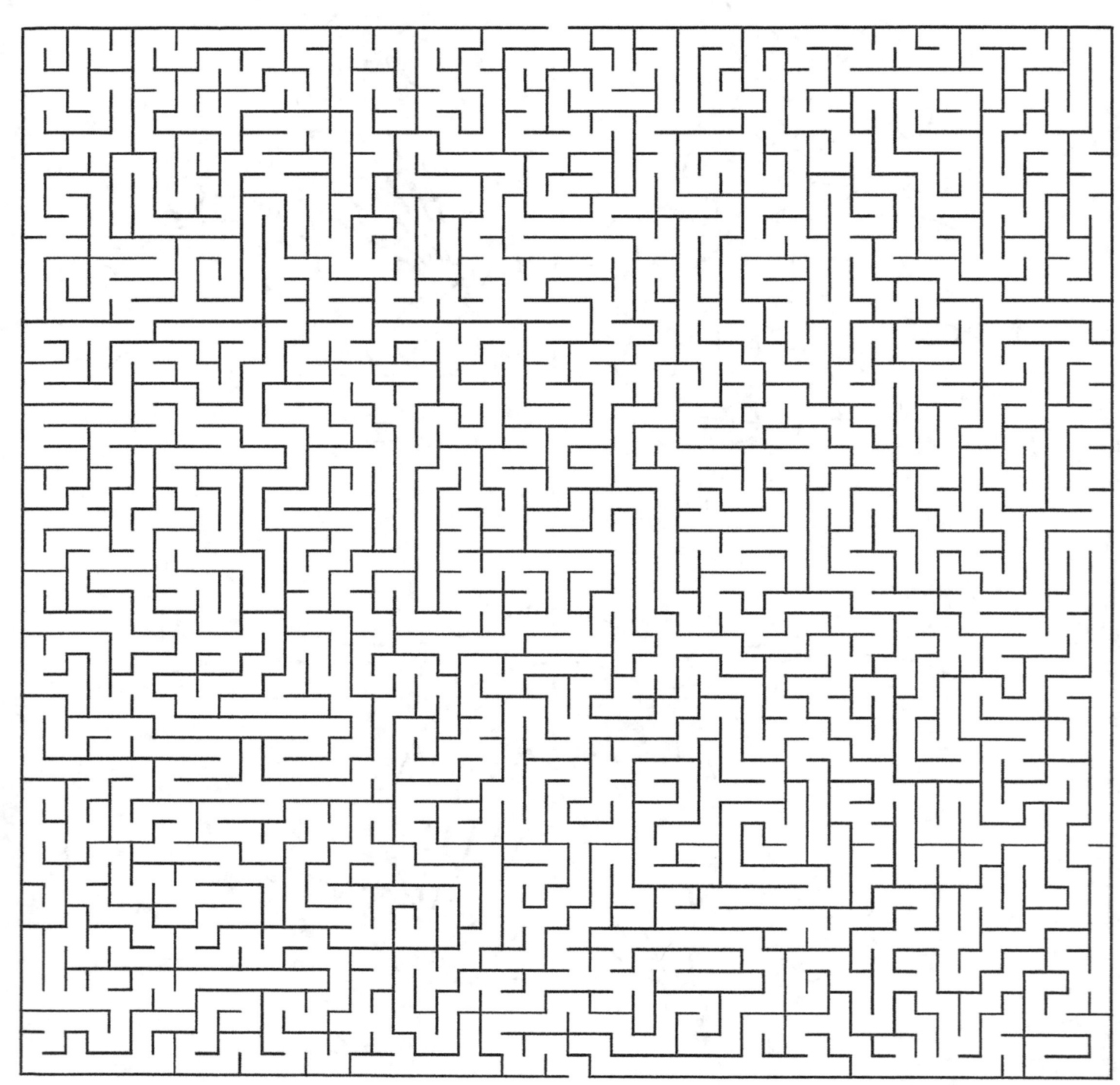

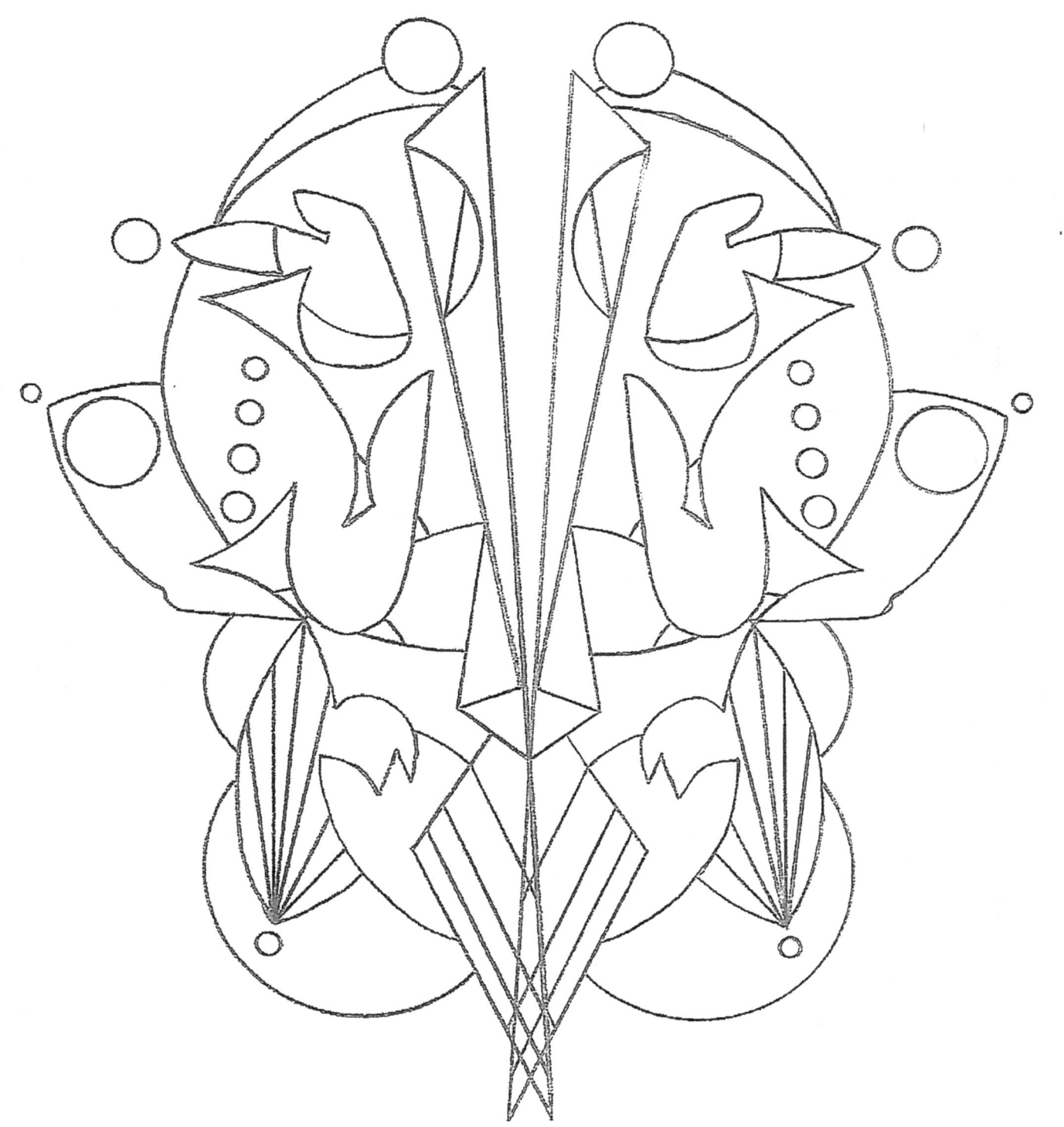

Accept the challenges so that you can feel the exhilaration of victory.

George S. Patton

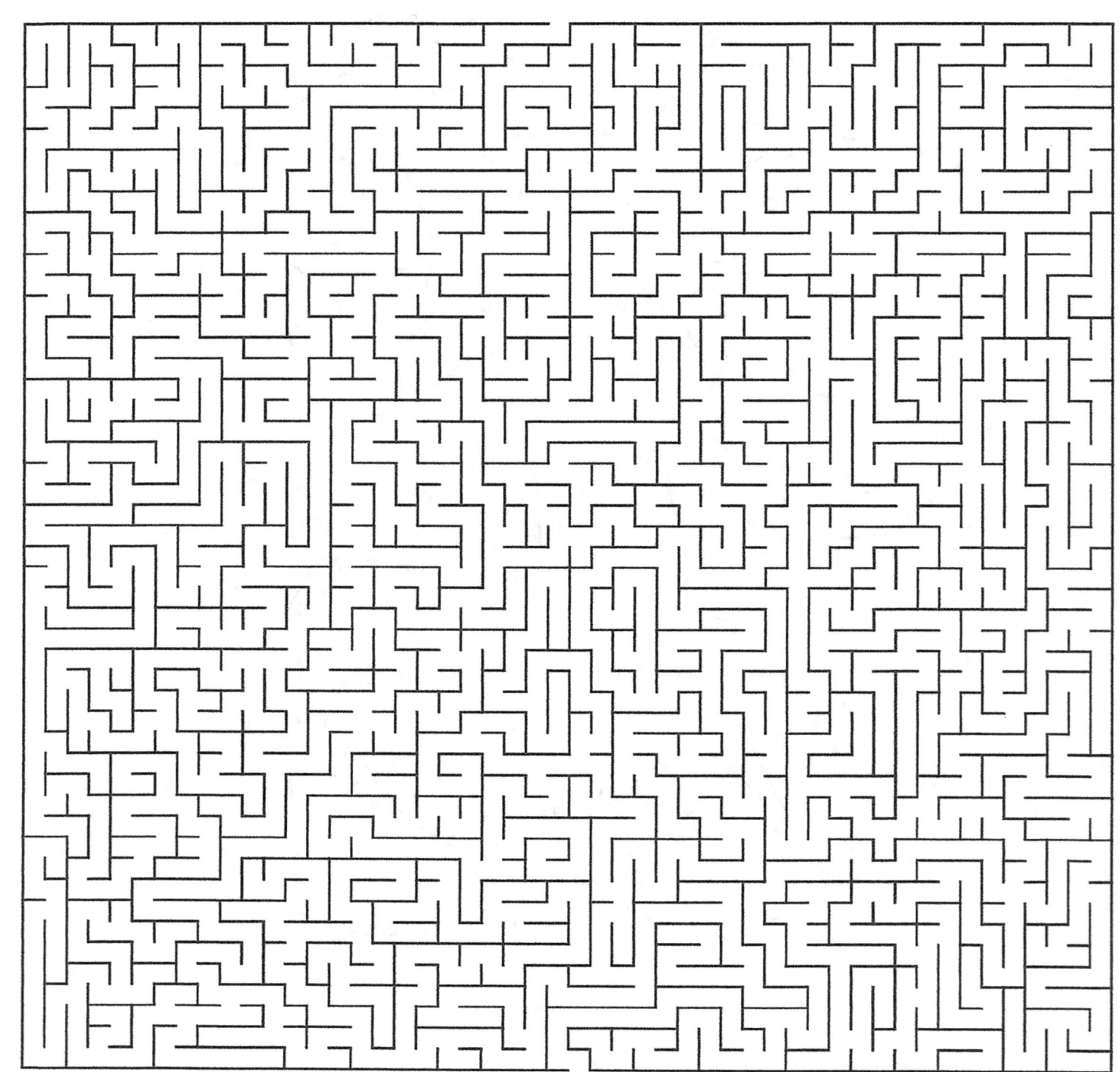

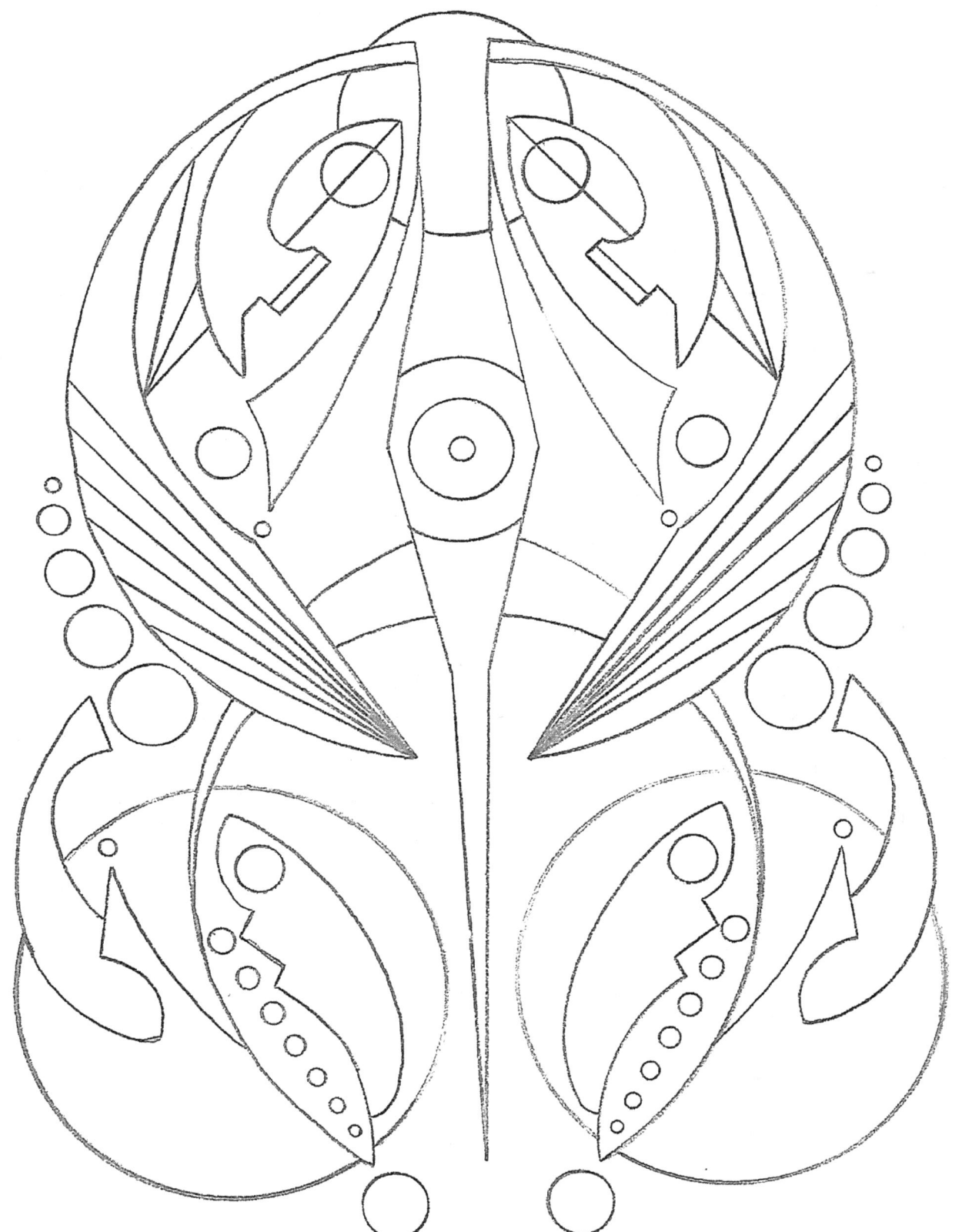

Accept the challenges so that you can feel the exhilaration of victory.

George S. Patton

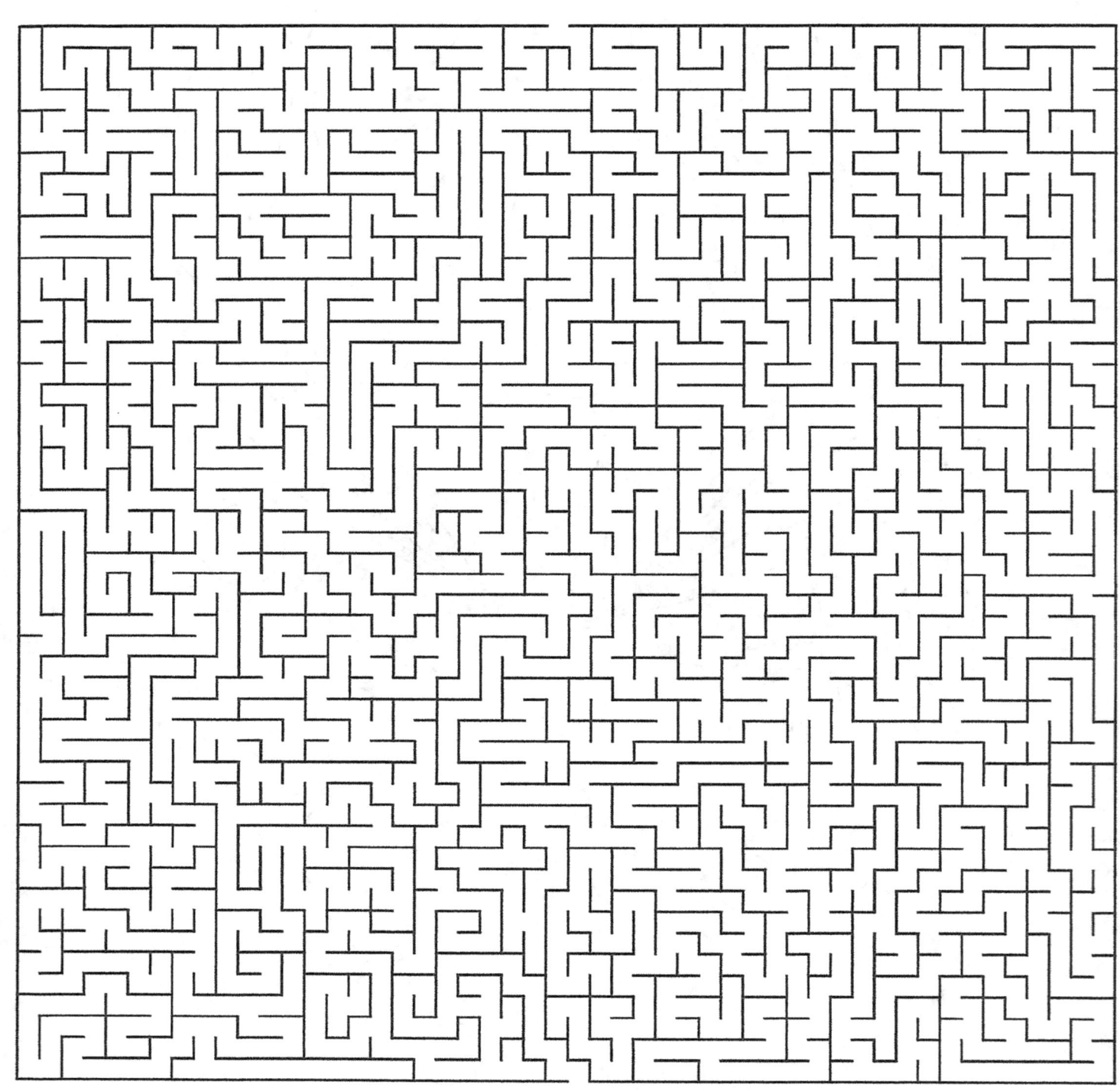

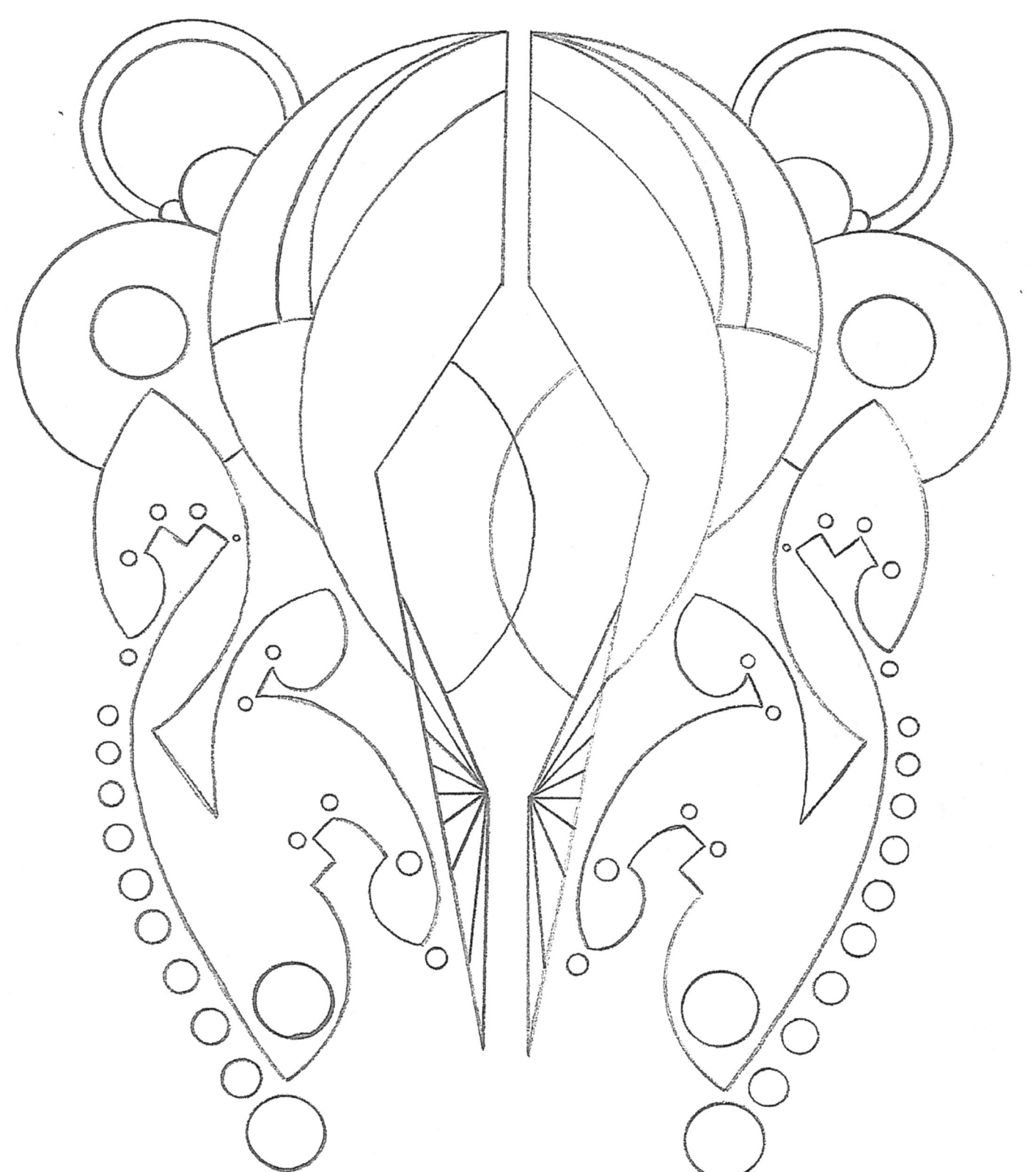

When something is important enough, you do it even if the odds are not in your favor.

Elon Musk

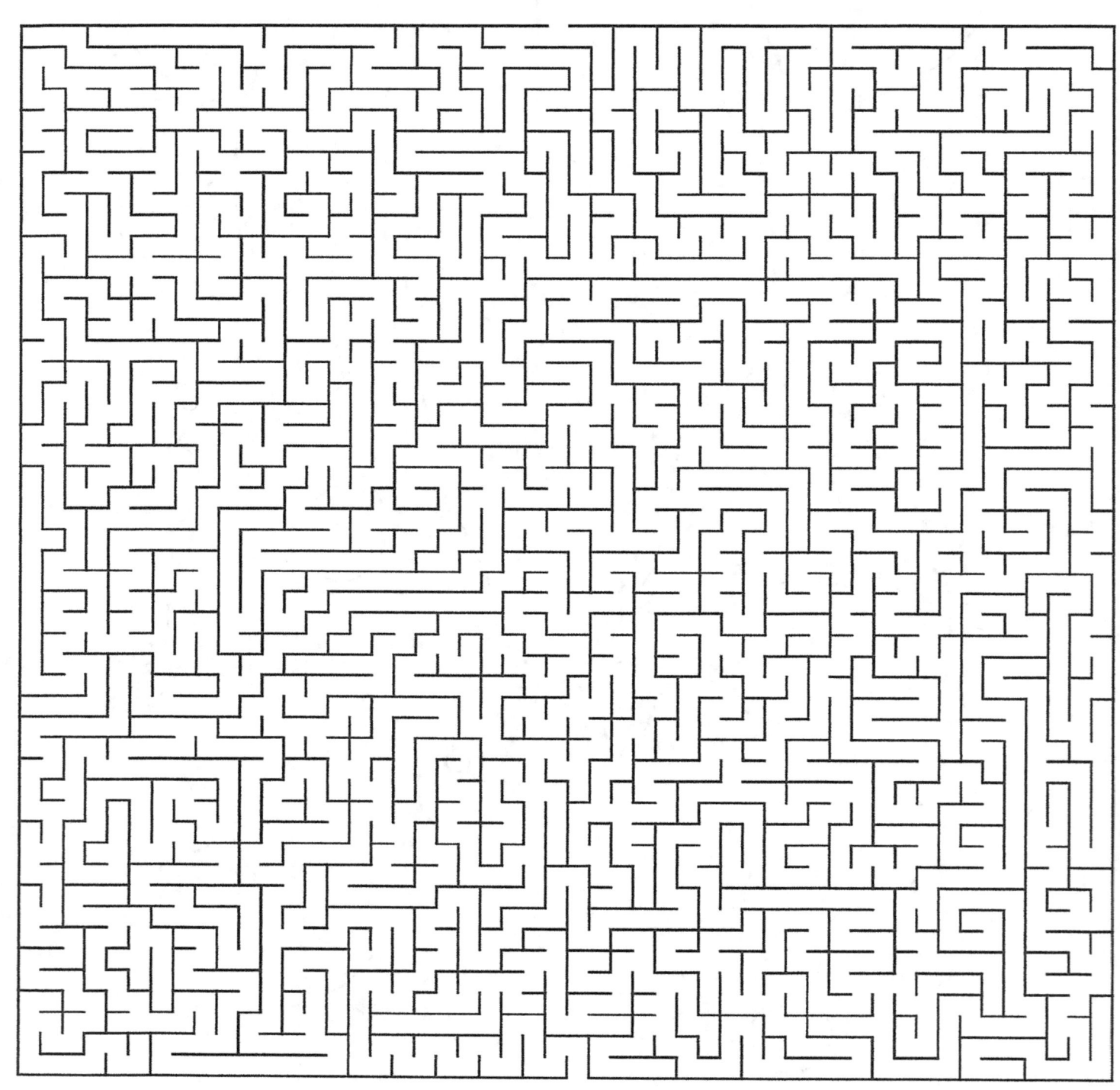

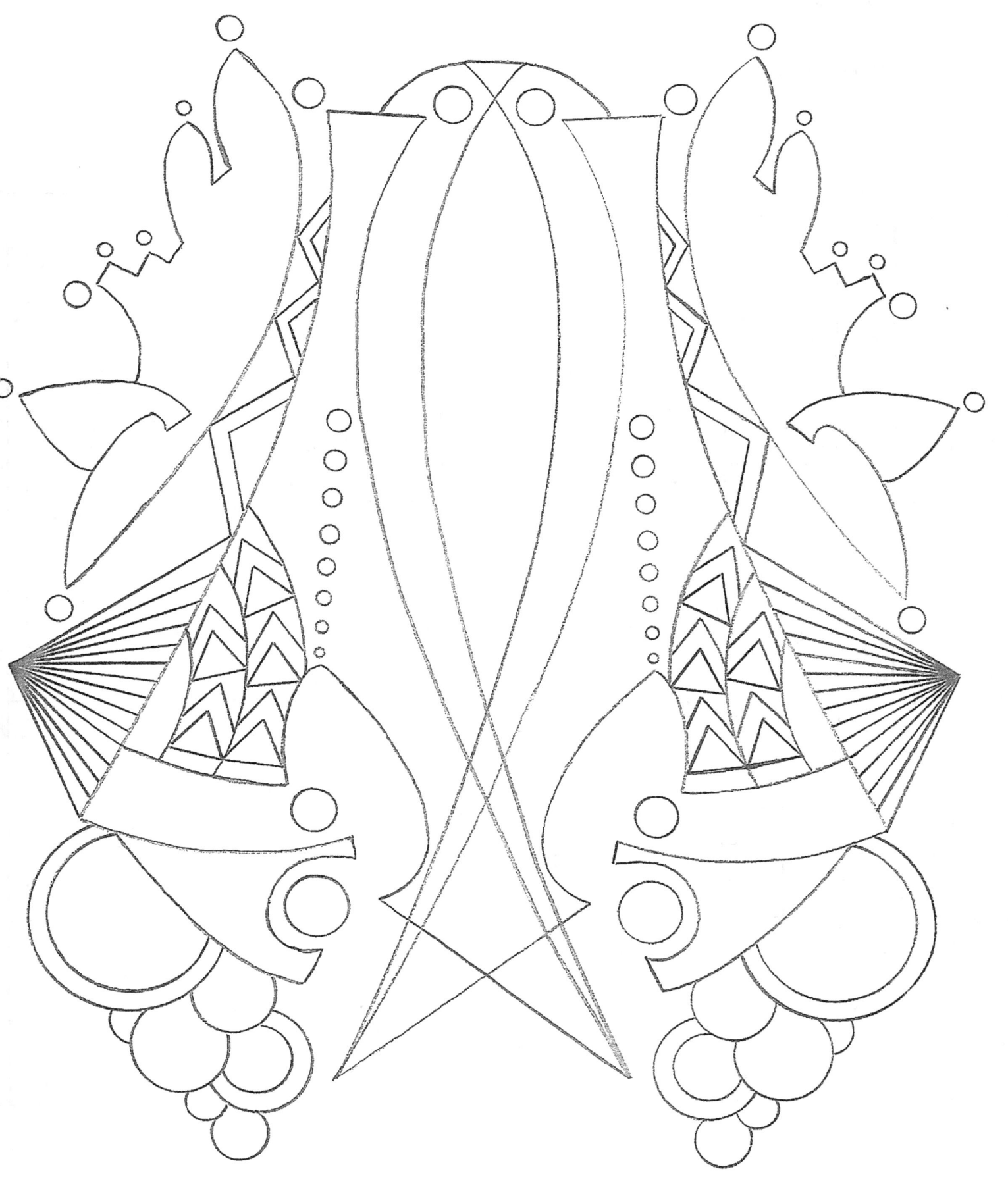

Success is not final, failure is not fatal: it is the courage to continue that counts.

Winston Churchill

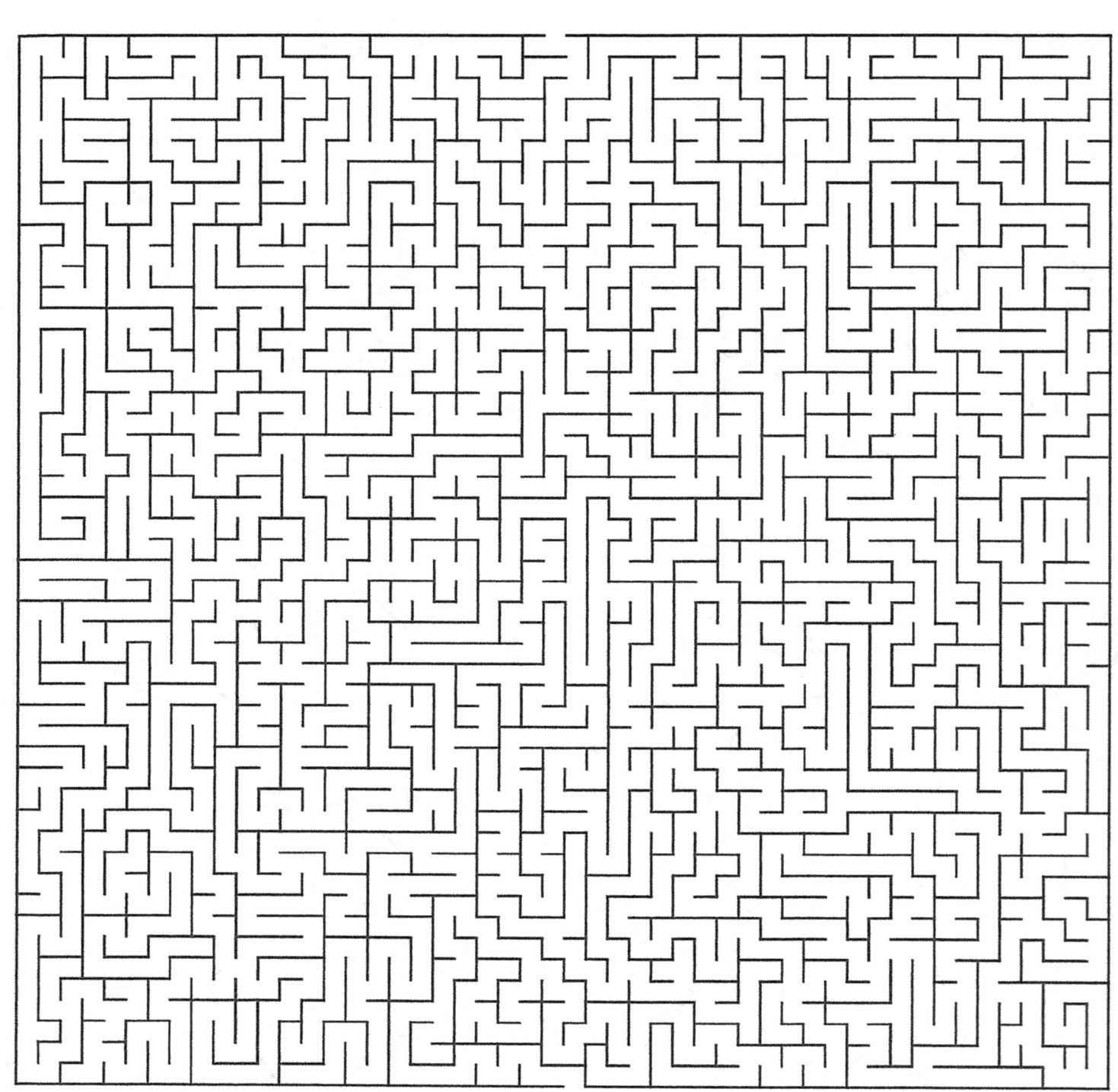

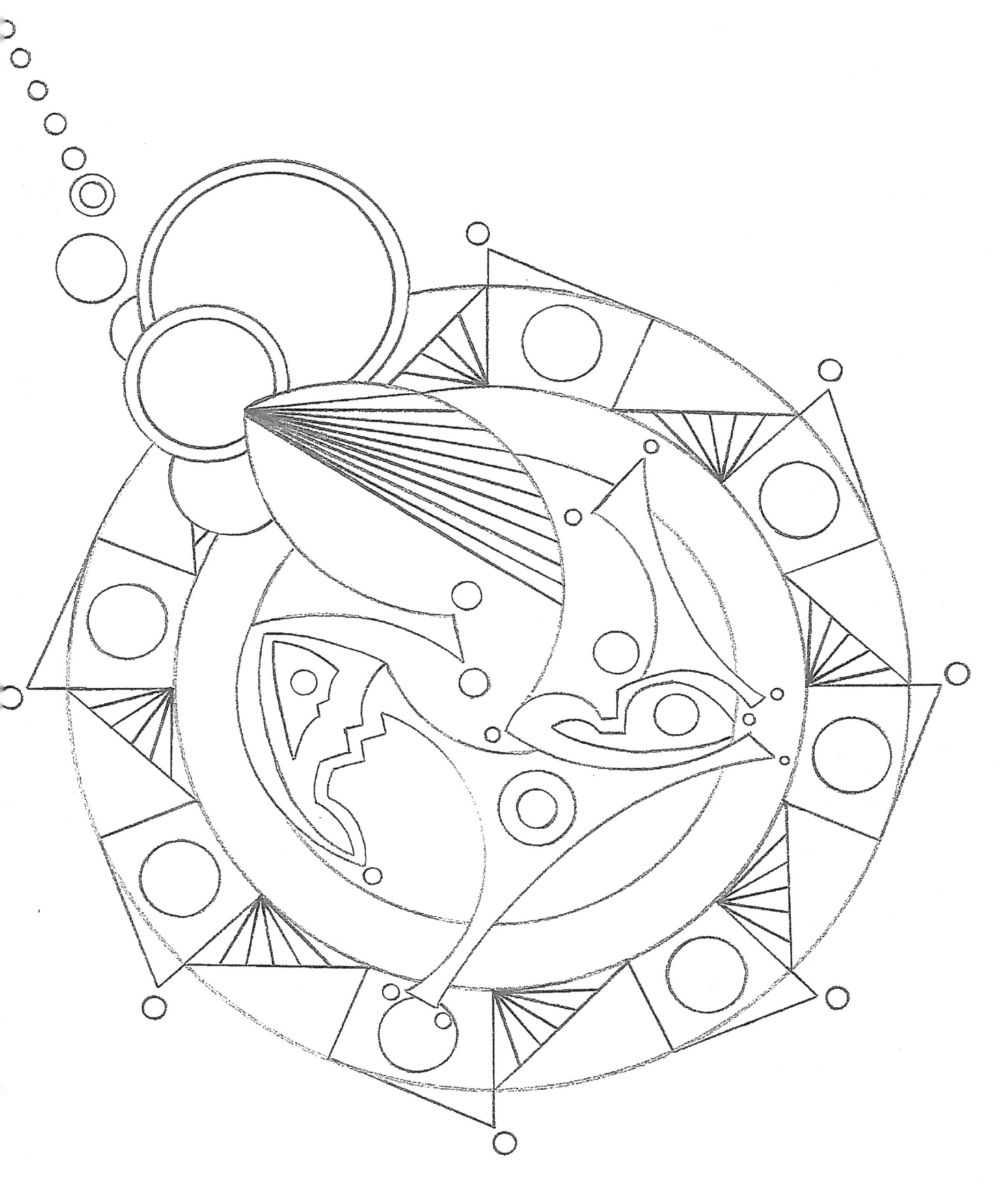

Coming together is a beginning; keeping together is progress; working together is success.

Henry Ford

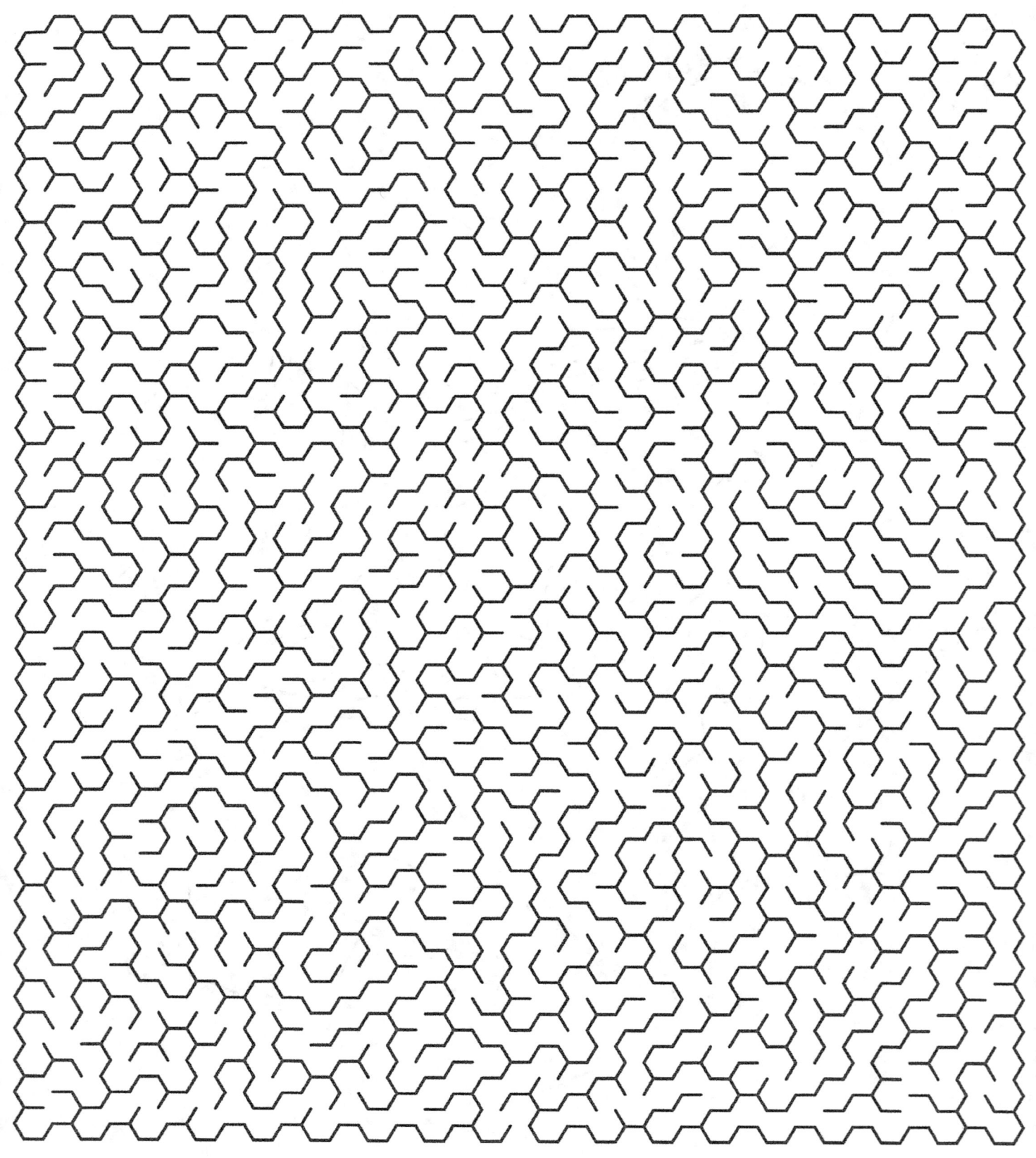

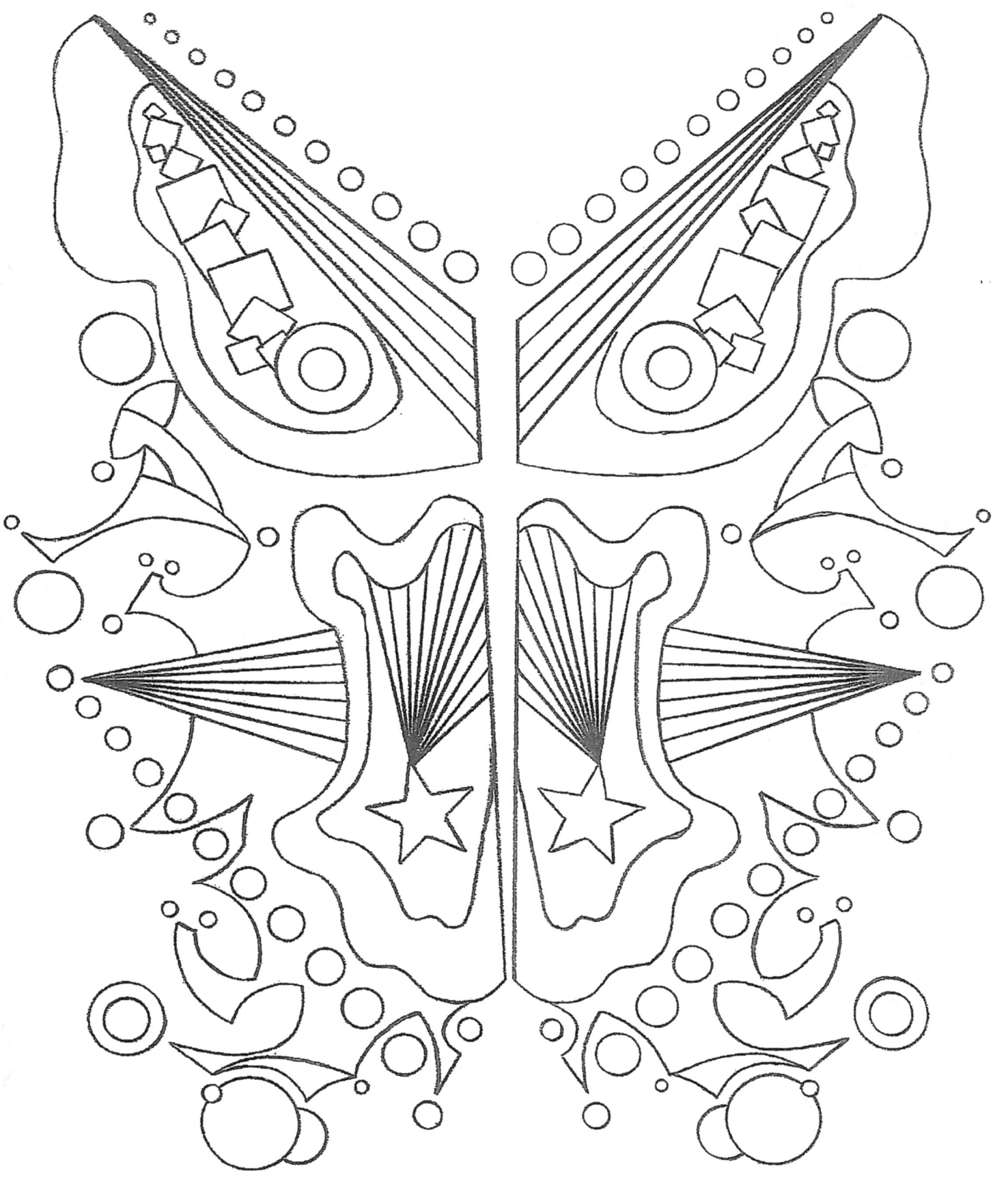

Always be yourself, express yourself, have faith in yourself, do not go out and look for a successful personality and duplicate it.

Bruce Lee

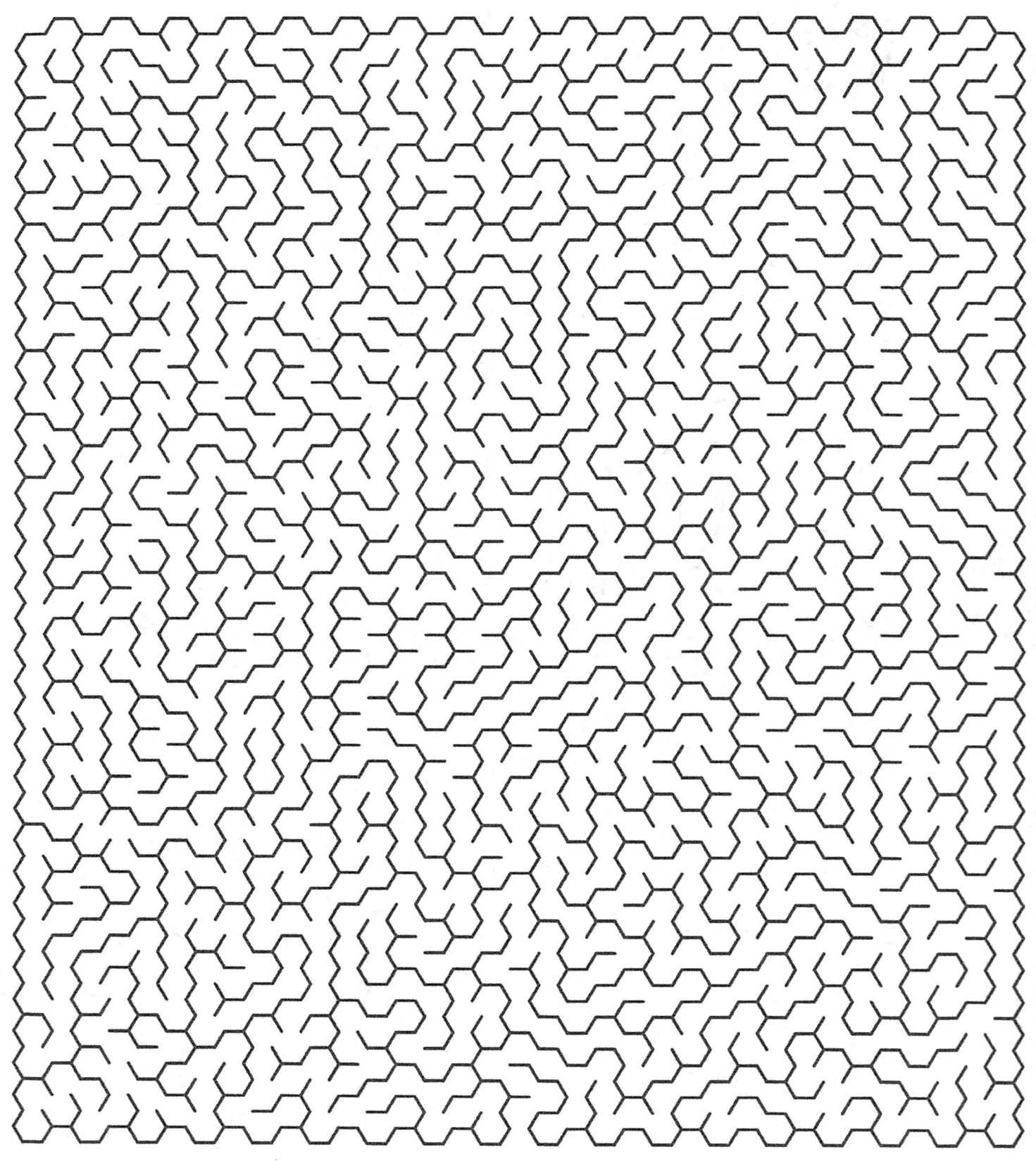

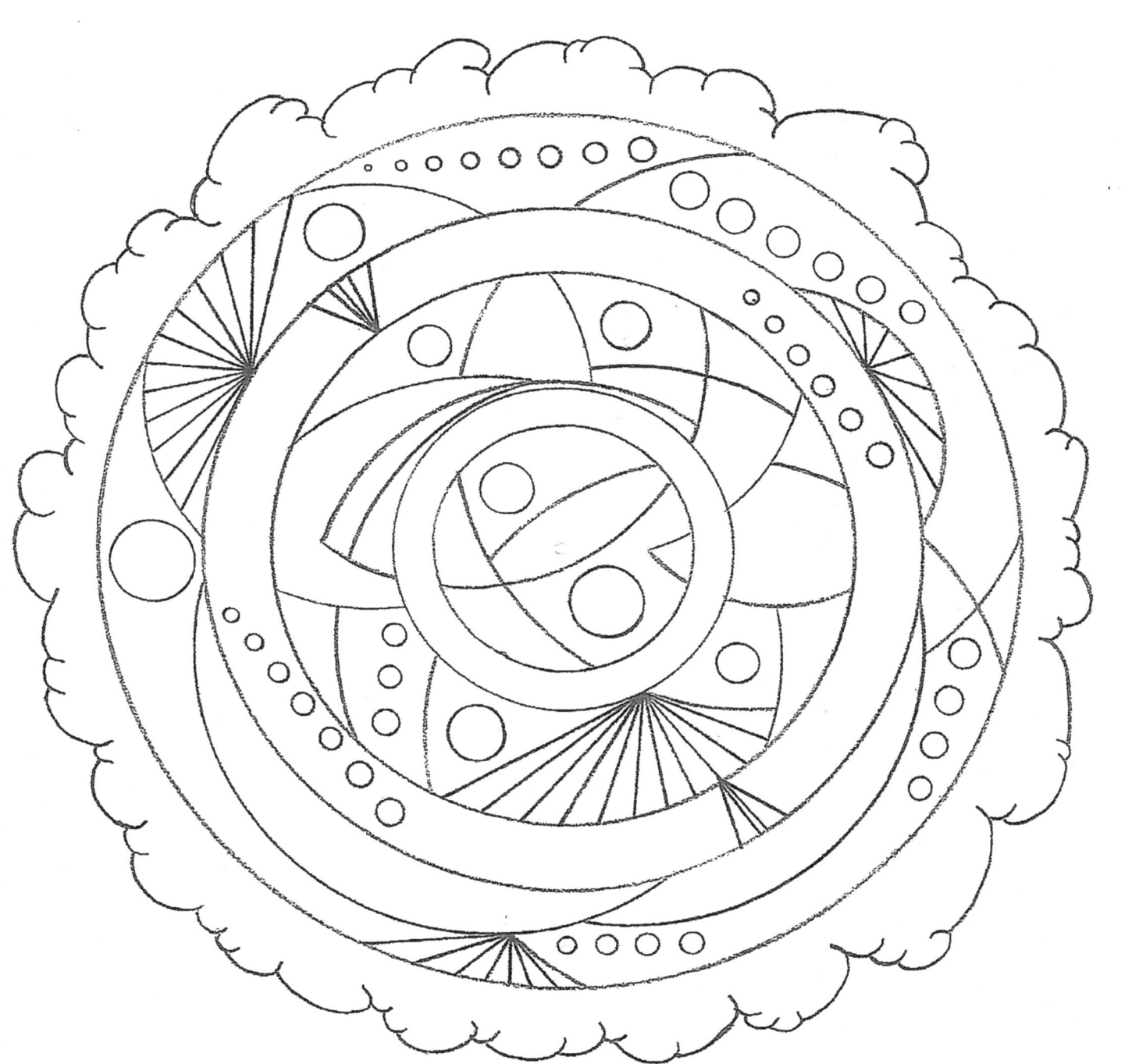

Success comes to those who dedicate everything to their passion in life. To be successful, it is also very important to be humble and never let fame or money travel to your head.

A. R. Rahman

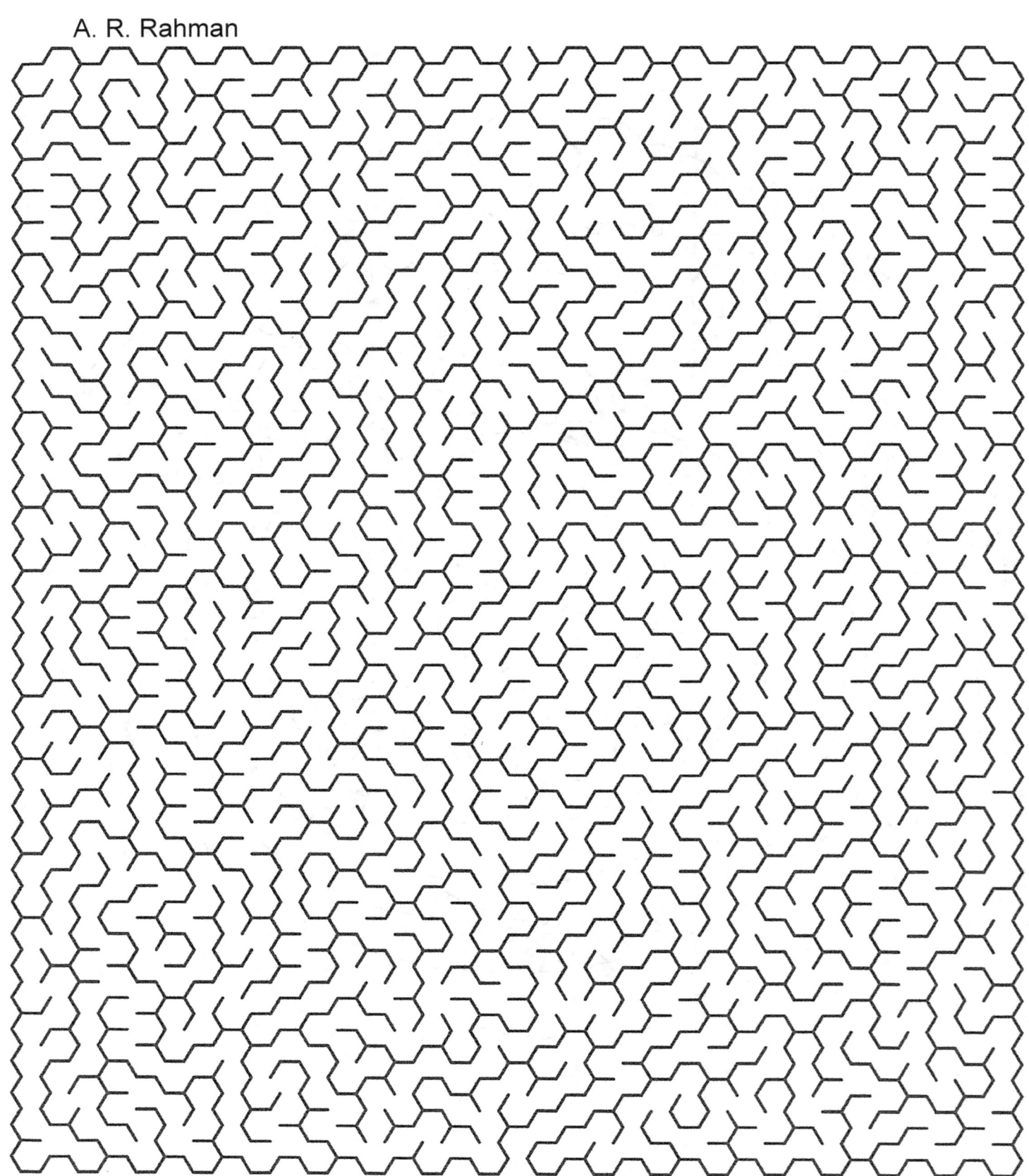

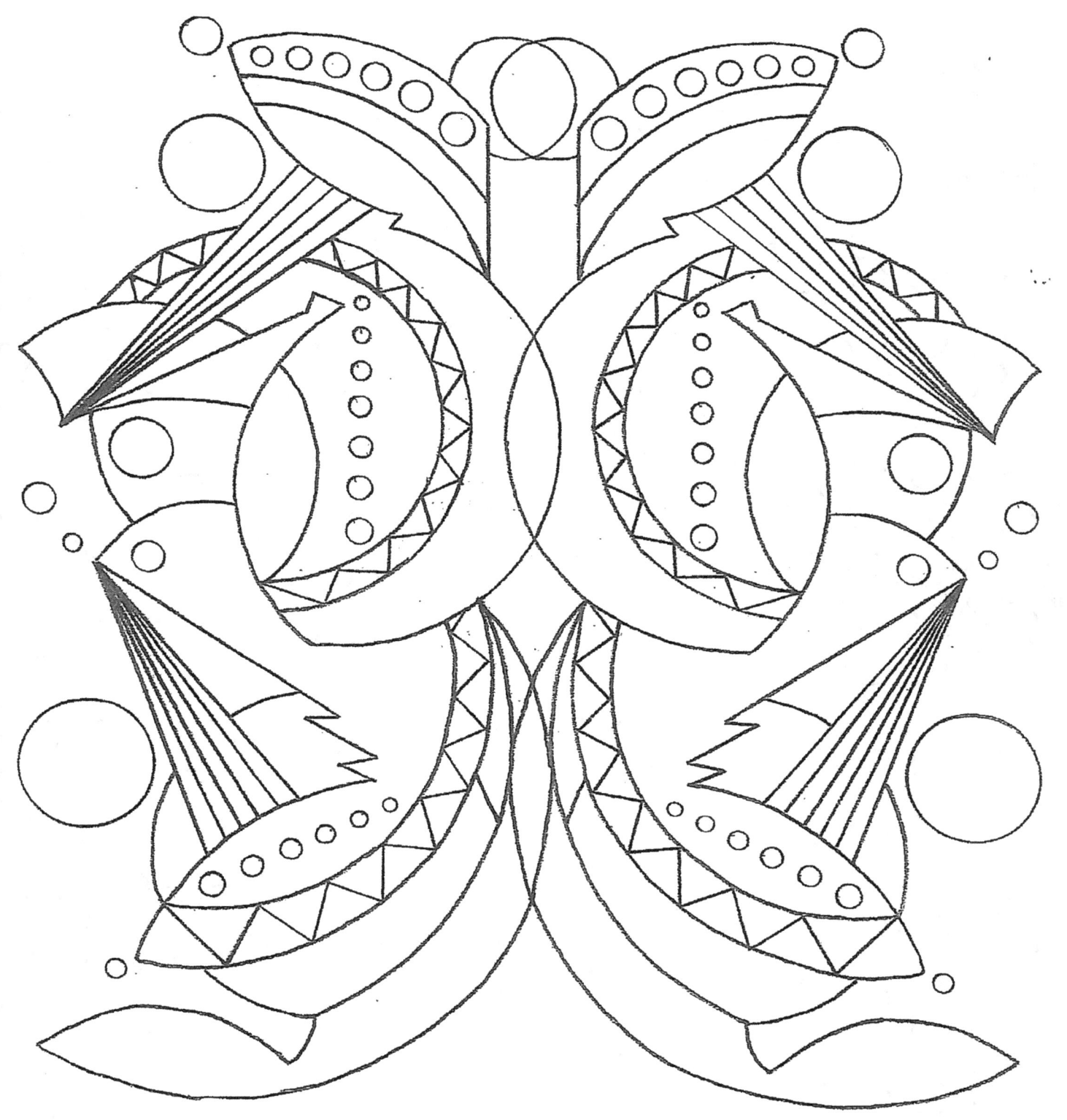

Success is where preparation and opportunity meet.

Bobby Unser

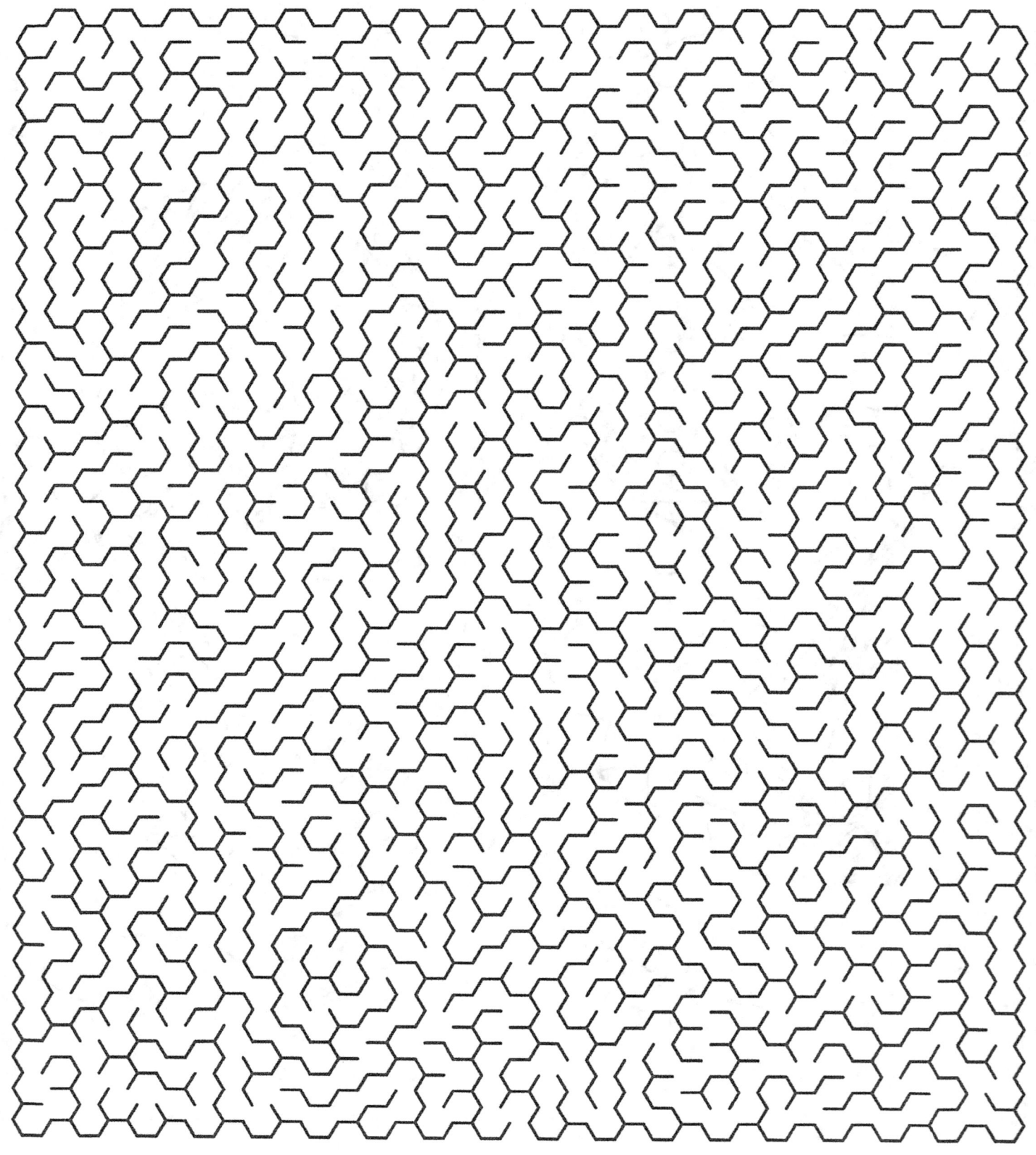

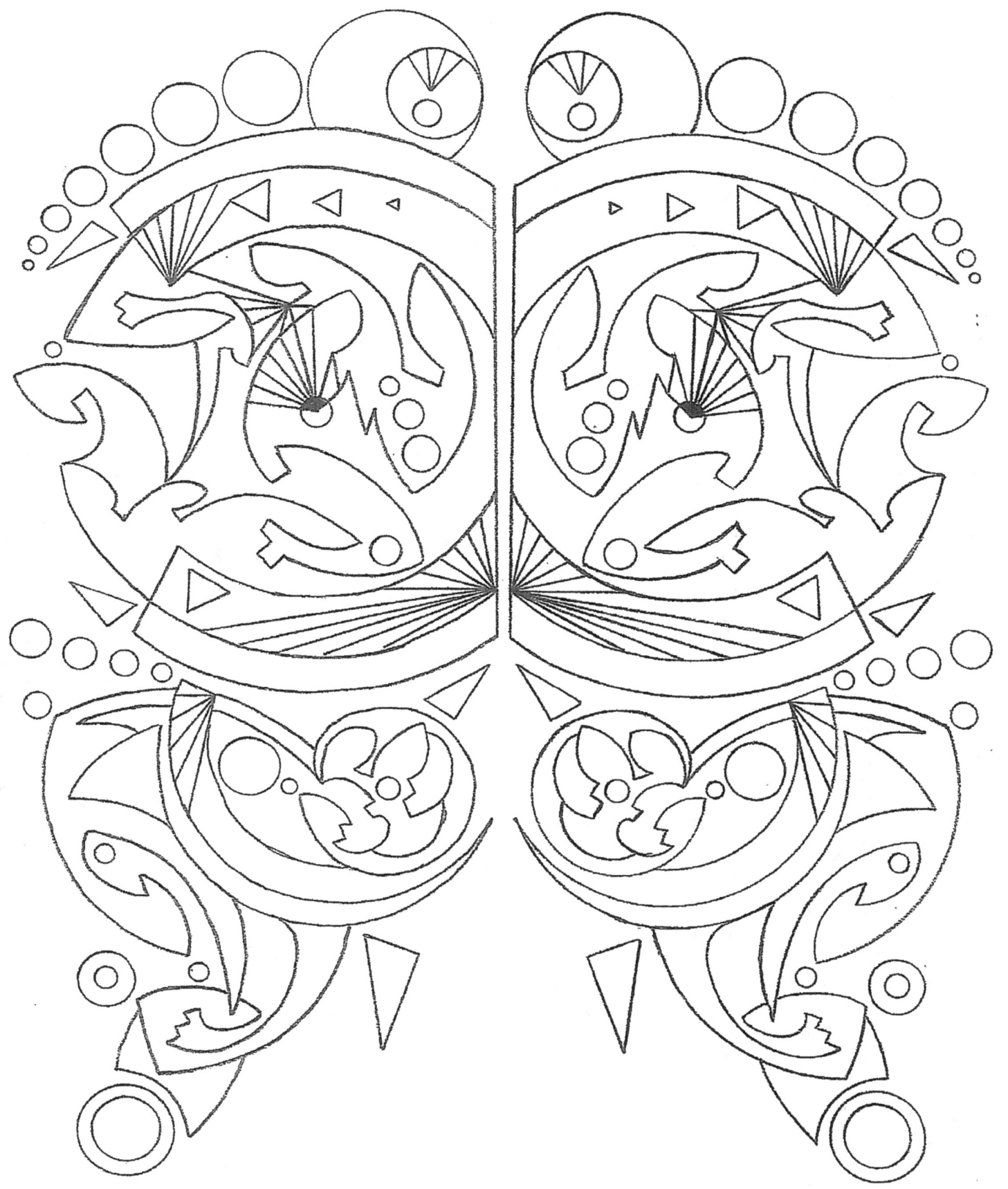

Character cannot be developed in ease and quiet. Only through experience of trial and suffering can the soul be strengthened, ambition inspired, and success achieved.

Helen Keller

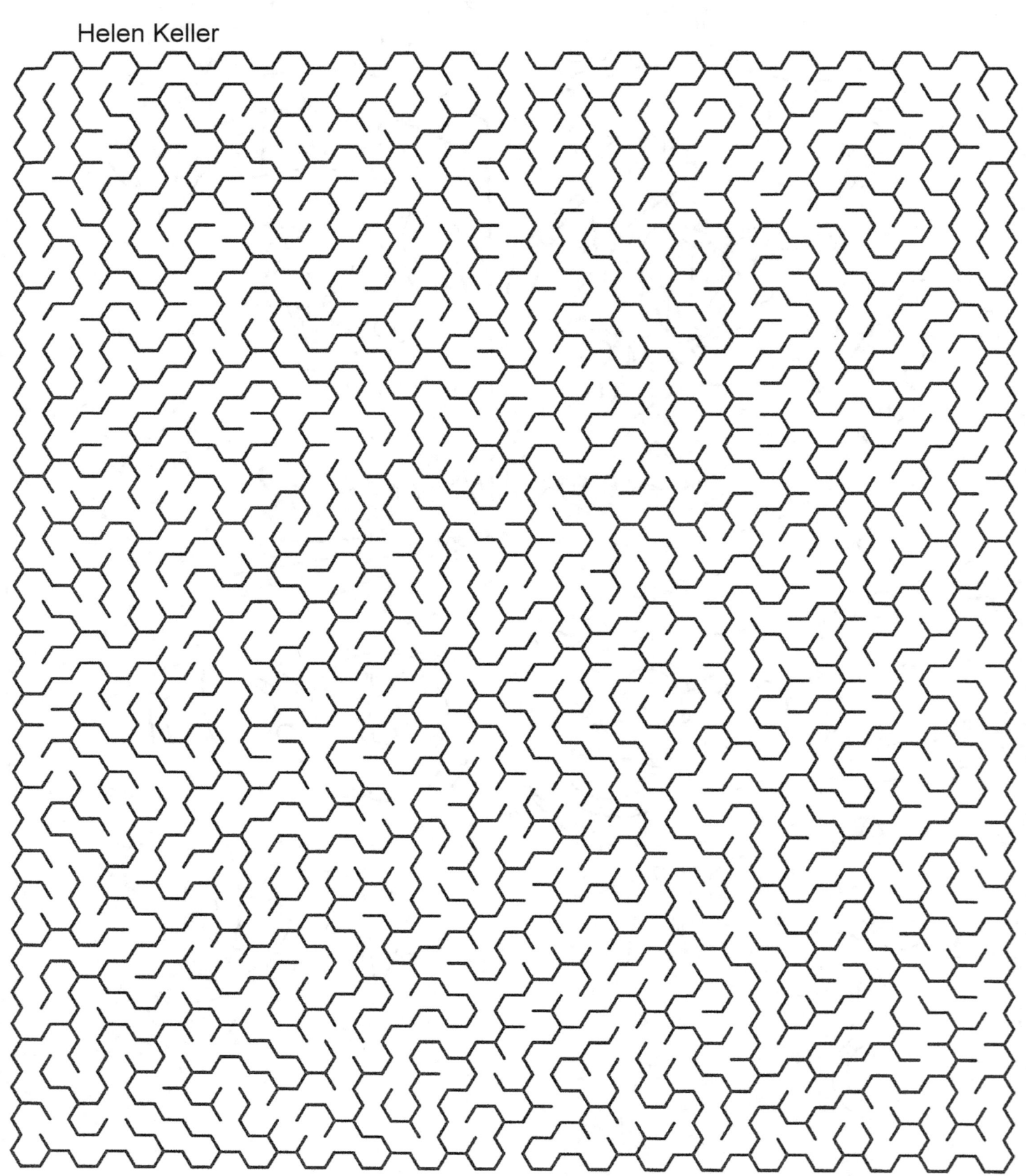

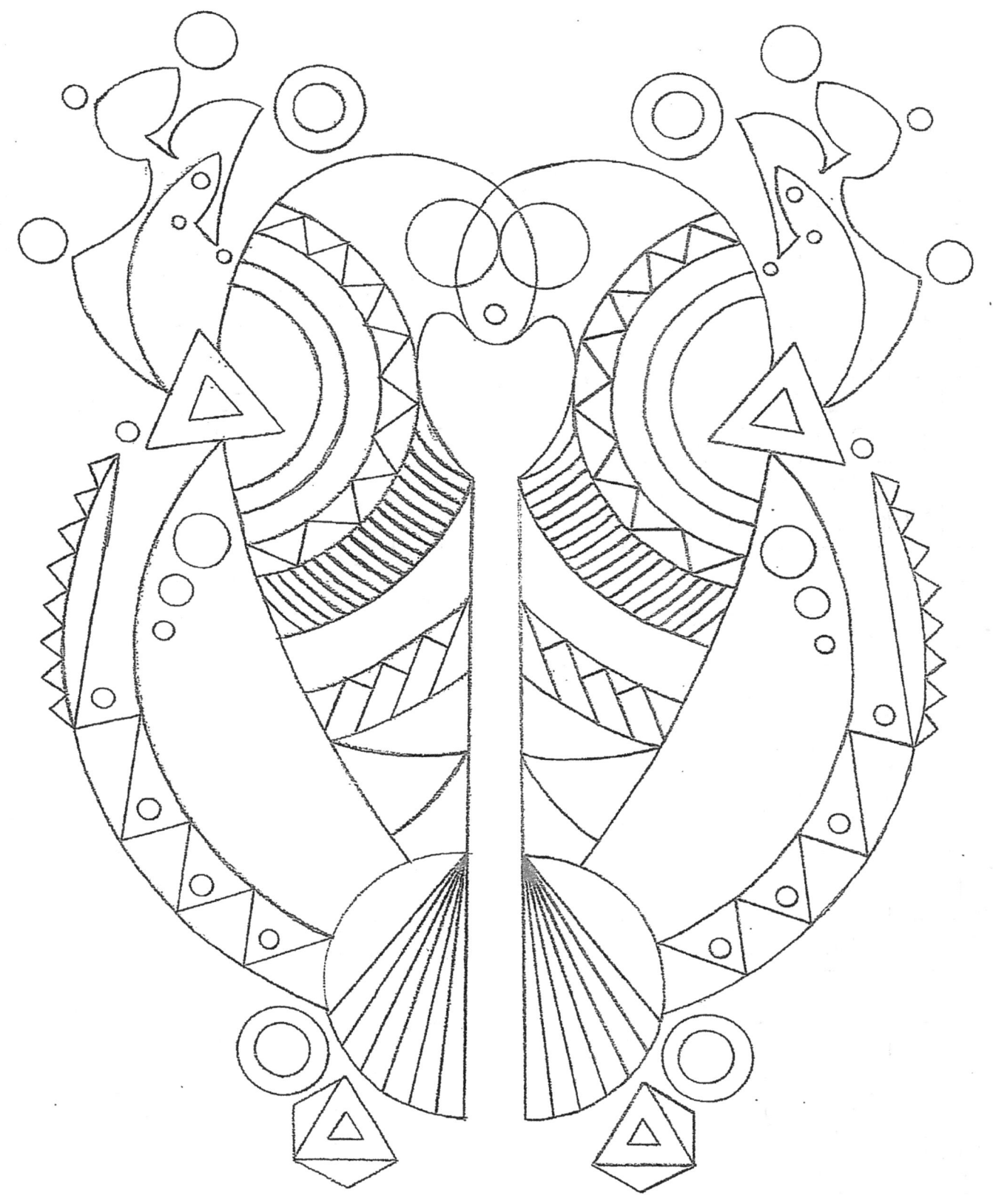

Patience, persistence and perspiration make an unbeatable combination for success.

Napoleon Hill

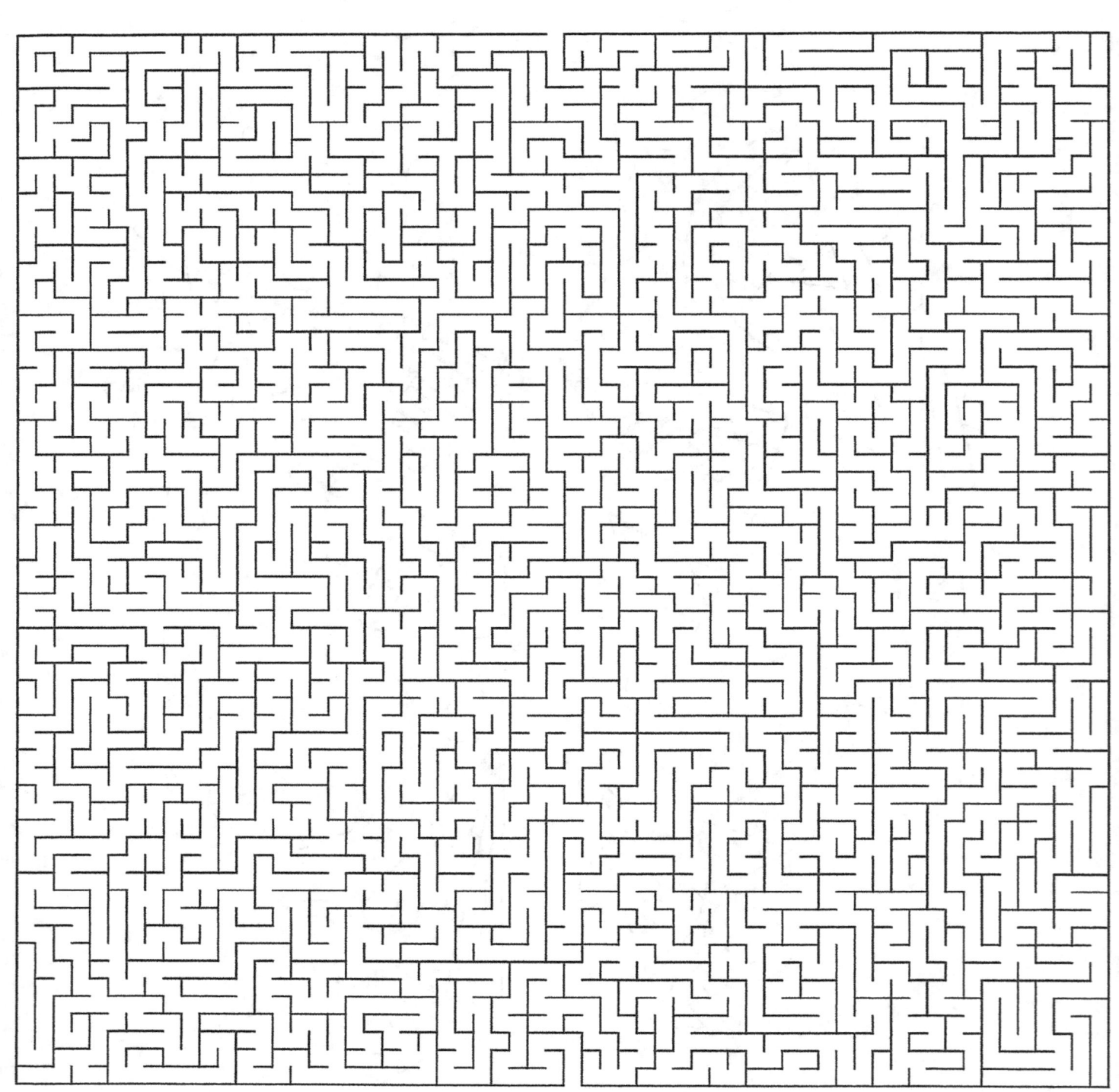

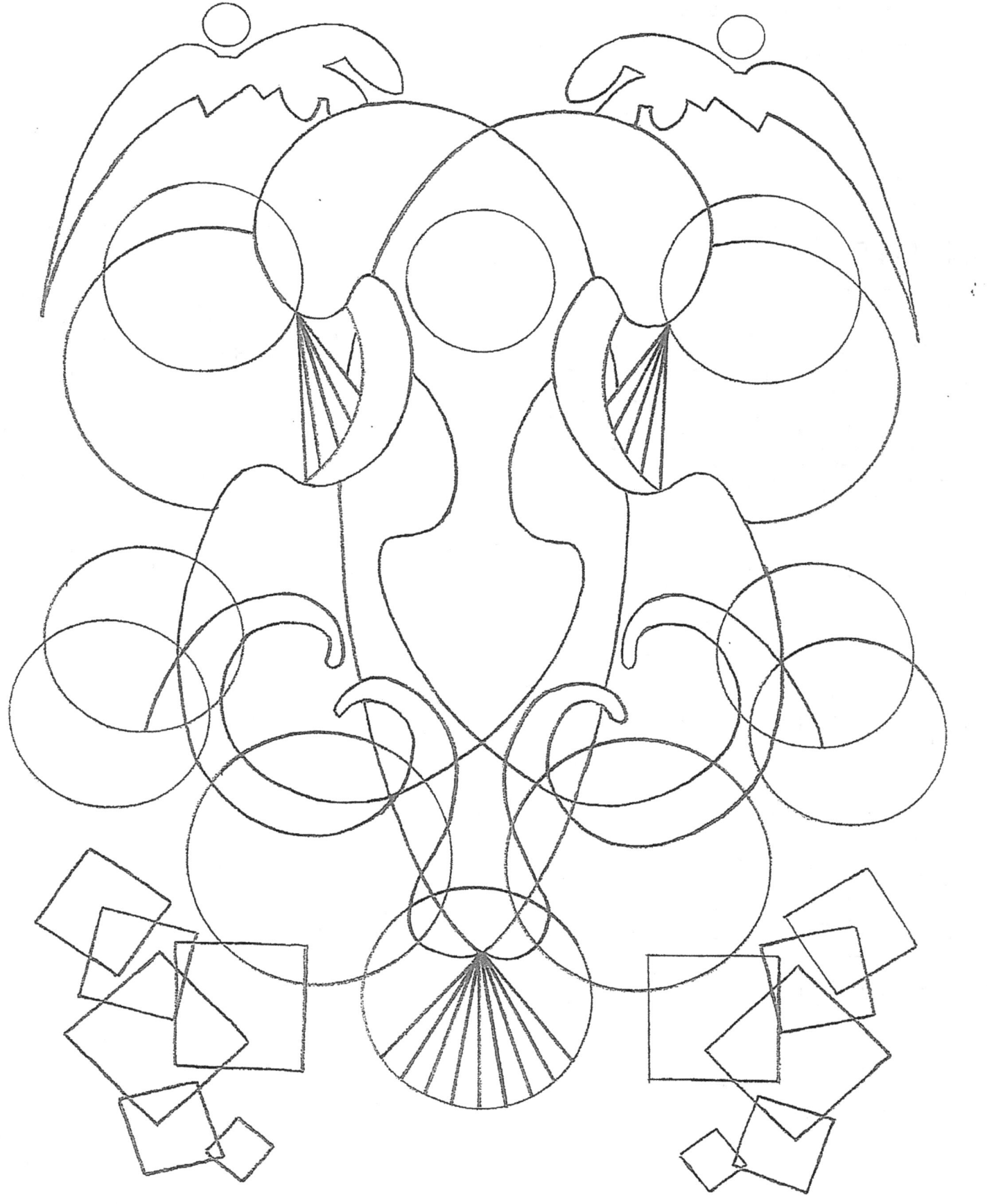

Success isn't always about greatness. It's about consistency. Consistent hard work leads to success. Greatness will come.

Dwayne Johnson

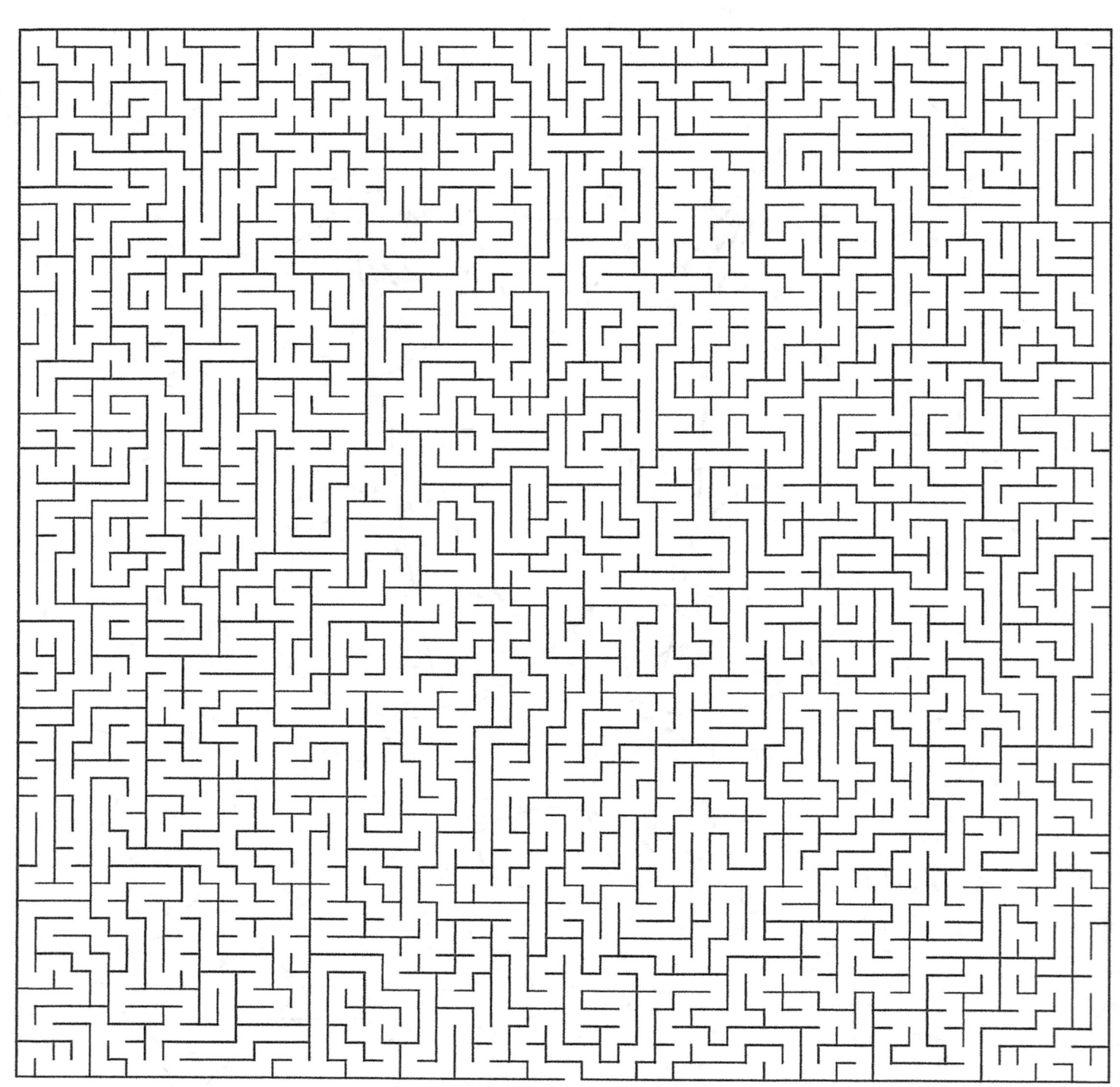

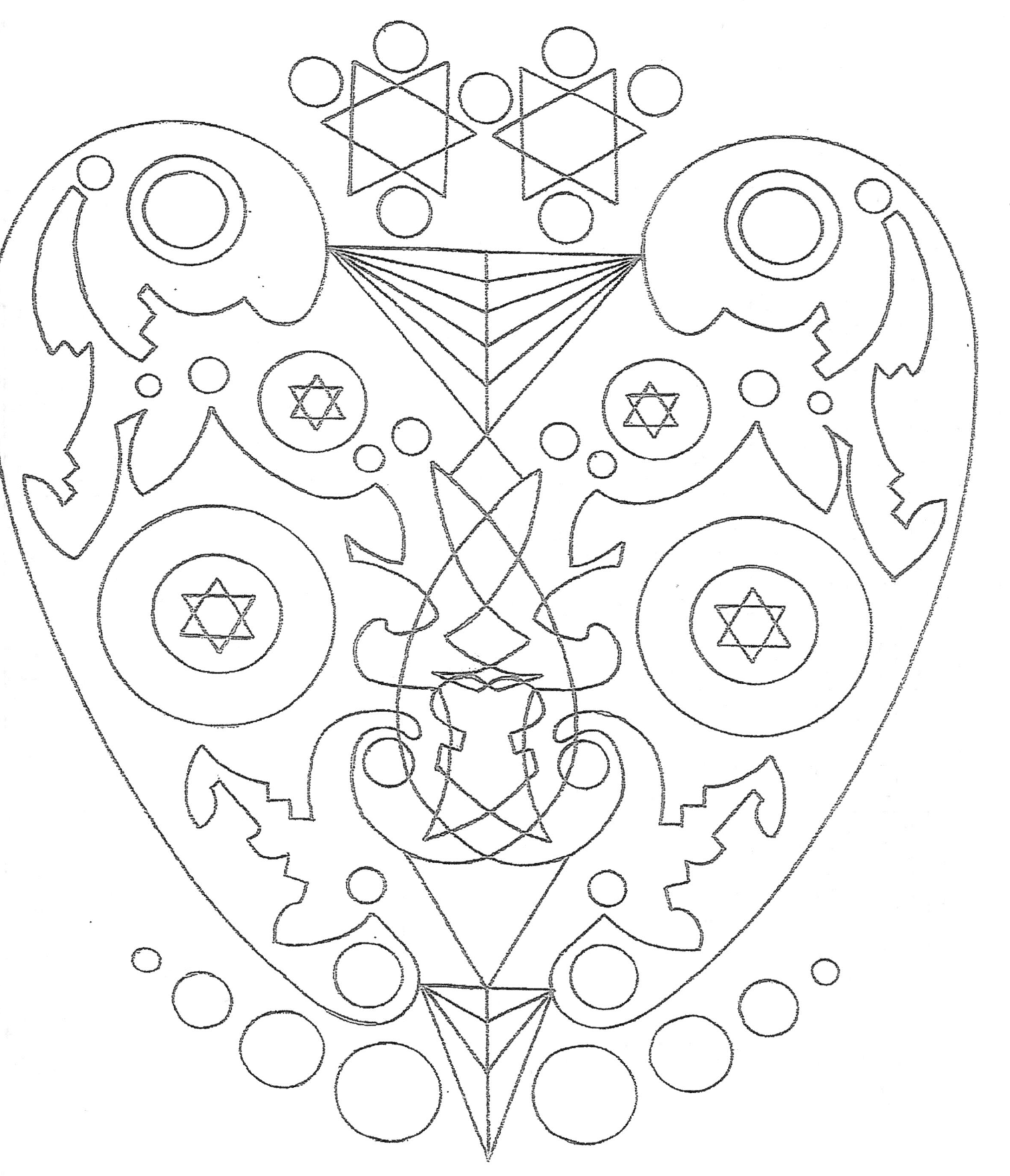

Success is a journey, not a destination. The doing is often more important than the outcome.

Arthur Ashe

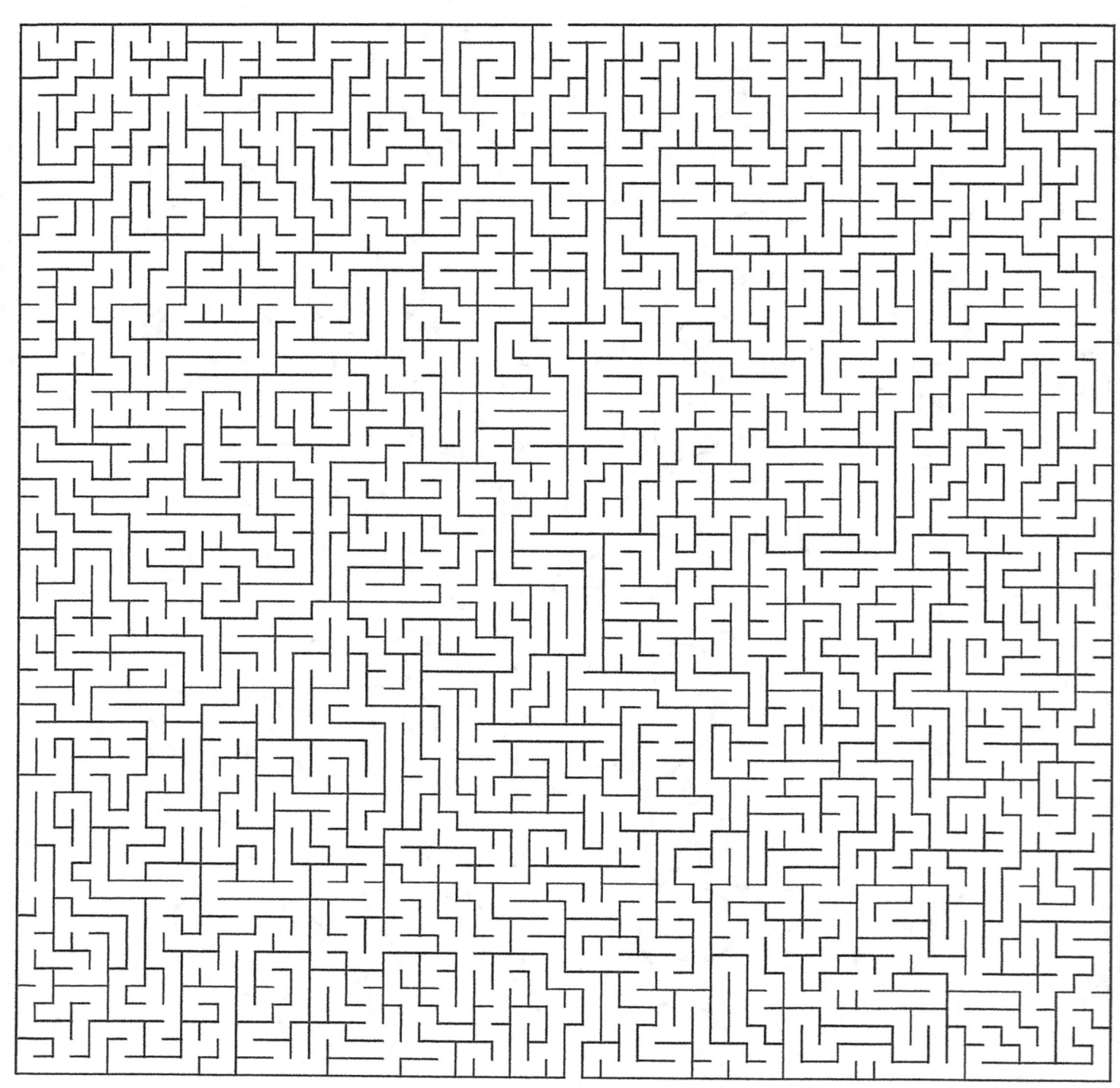

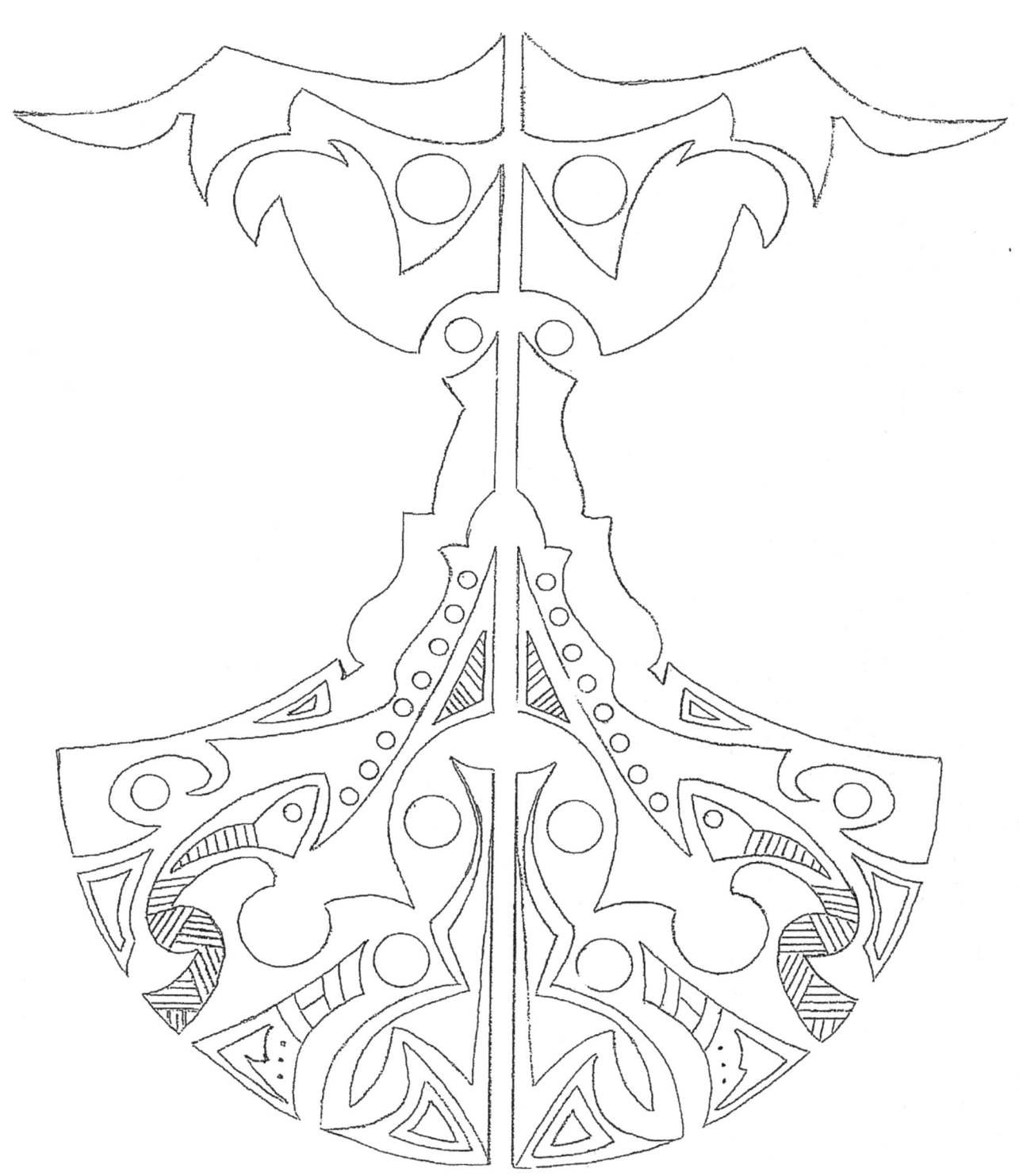

Ambition is the path to success. Persistence is the vehicle you arrive in.

Bill Bradley

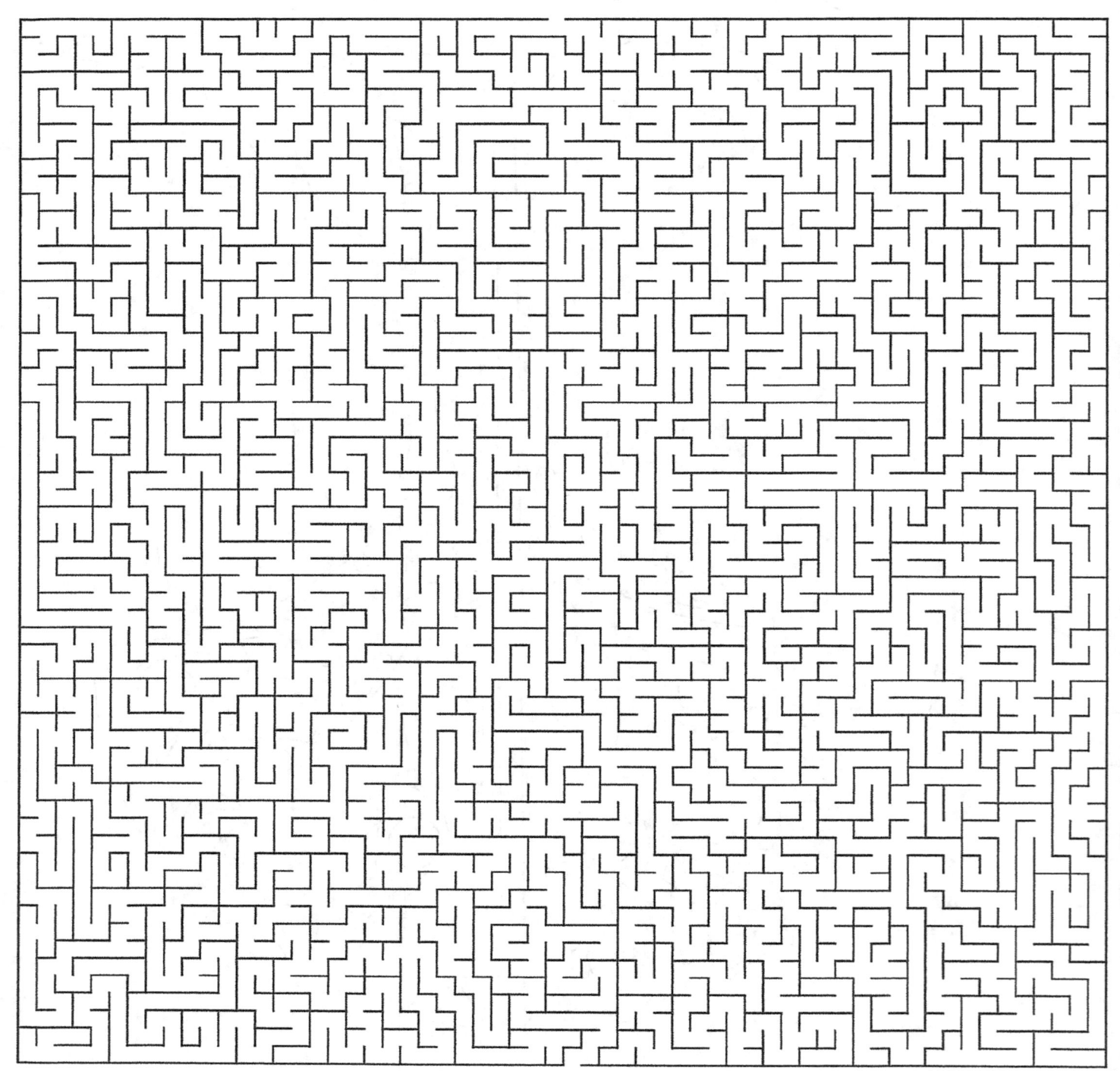

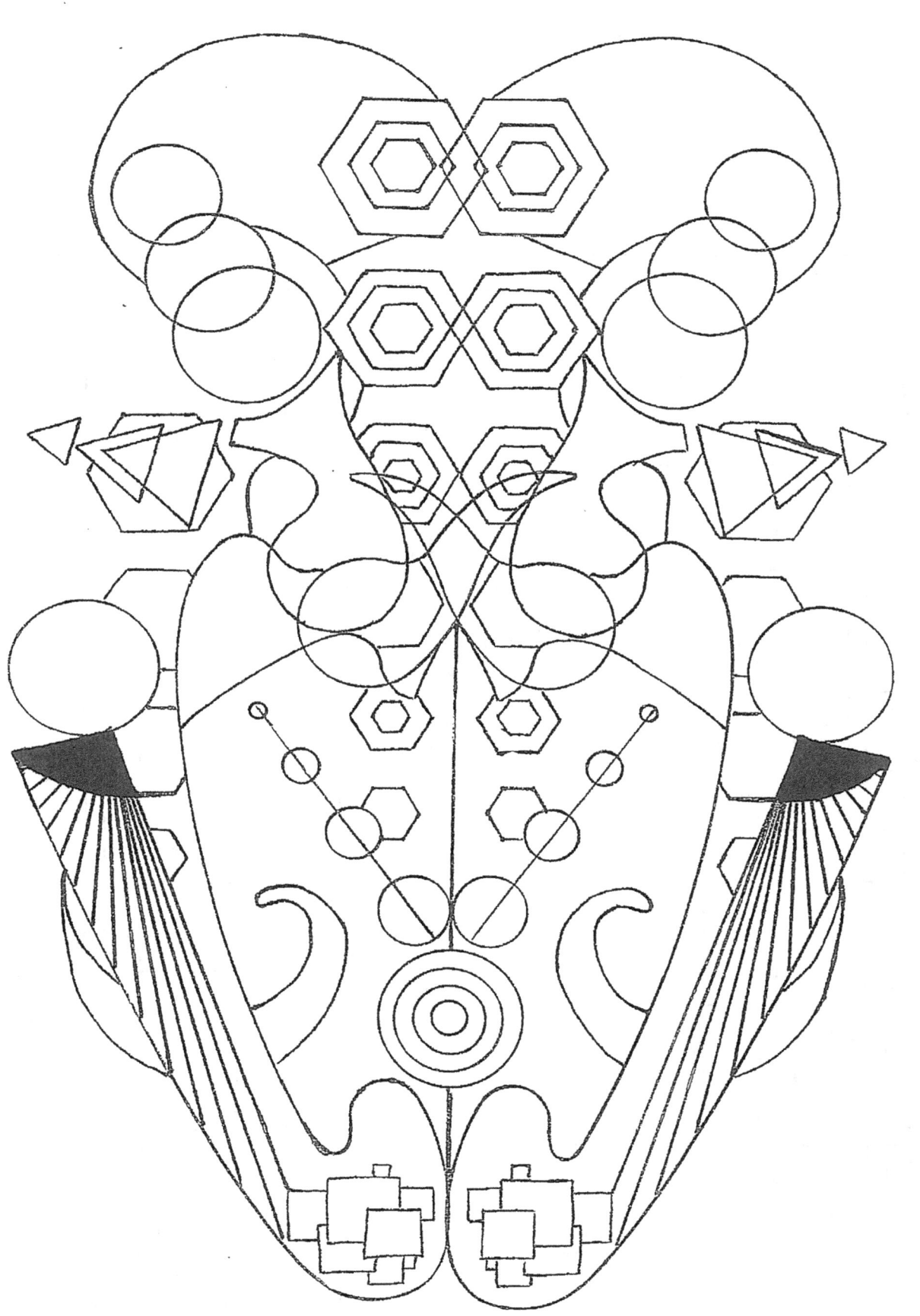

Think little goals and expect little achievements. Think big goals and win big success.

David Joseph Schwartz

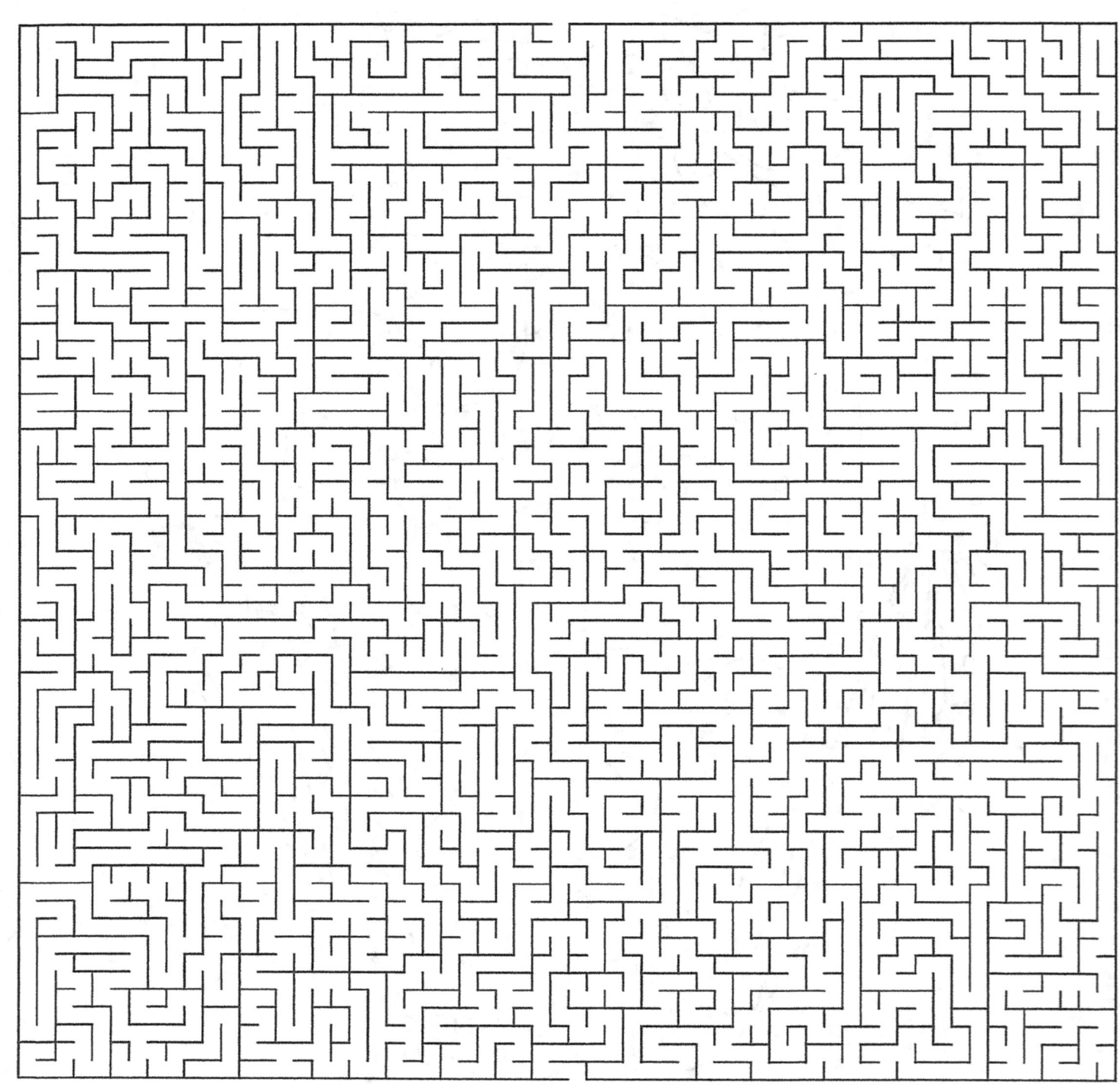

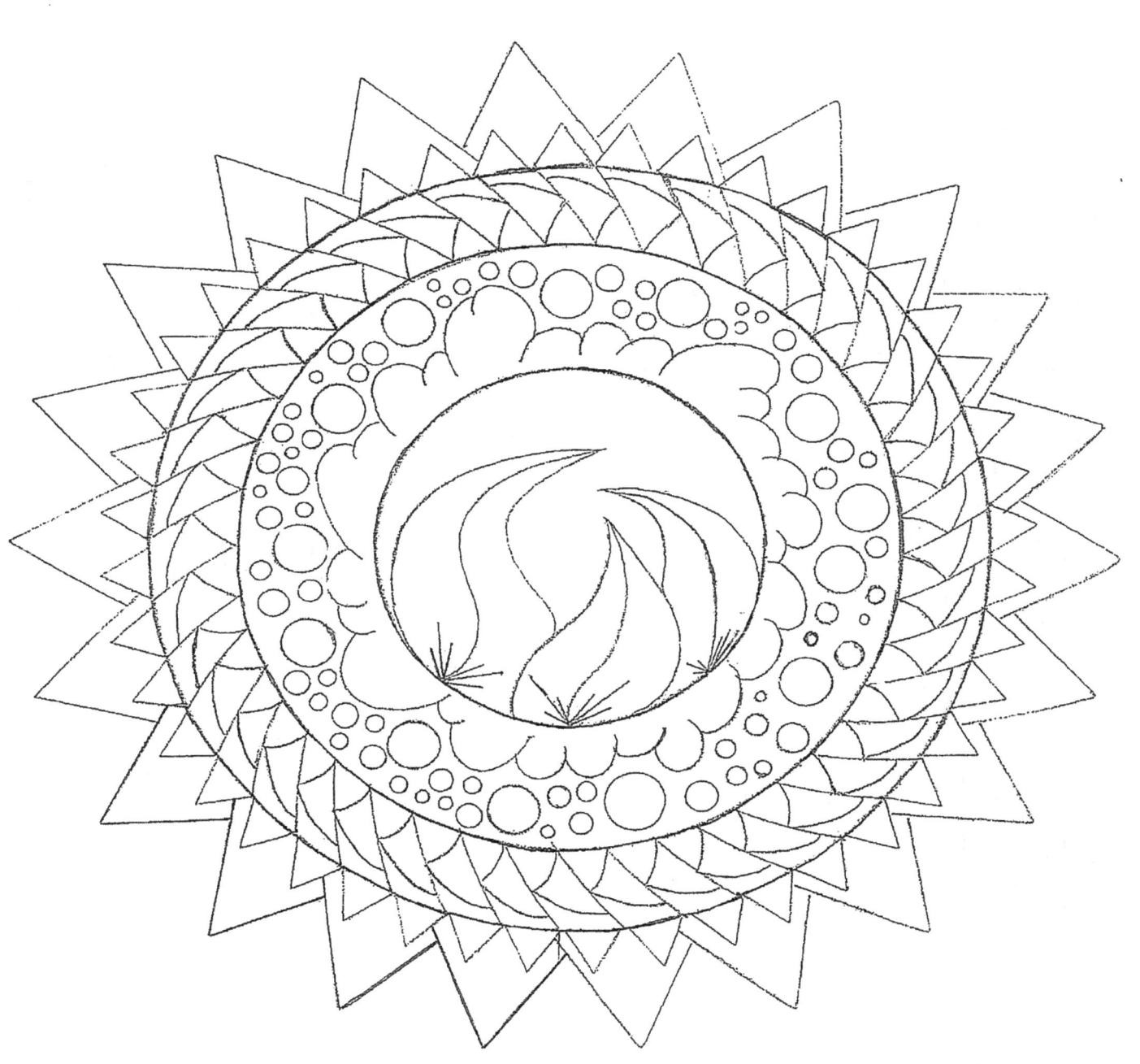

Discipline is the bridge between goals and accomplishment.

Jim Rohn

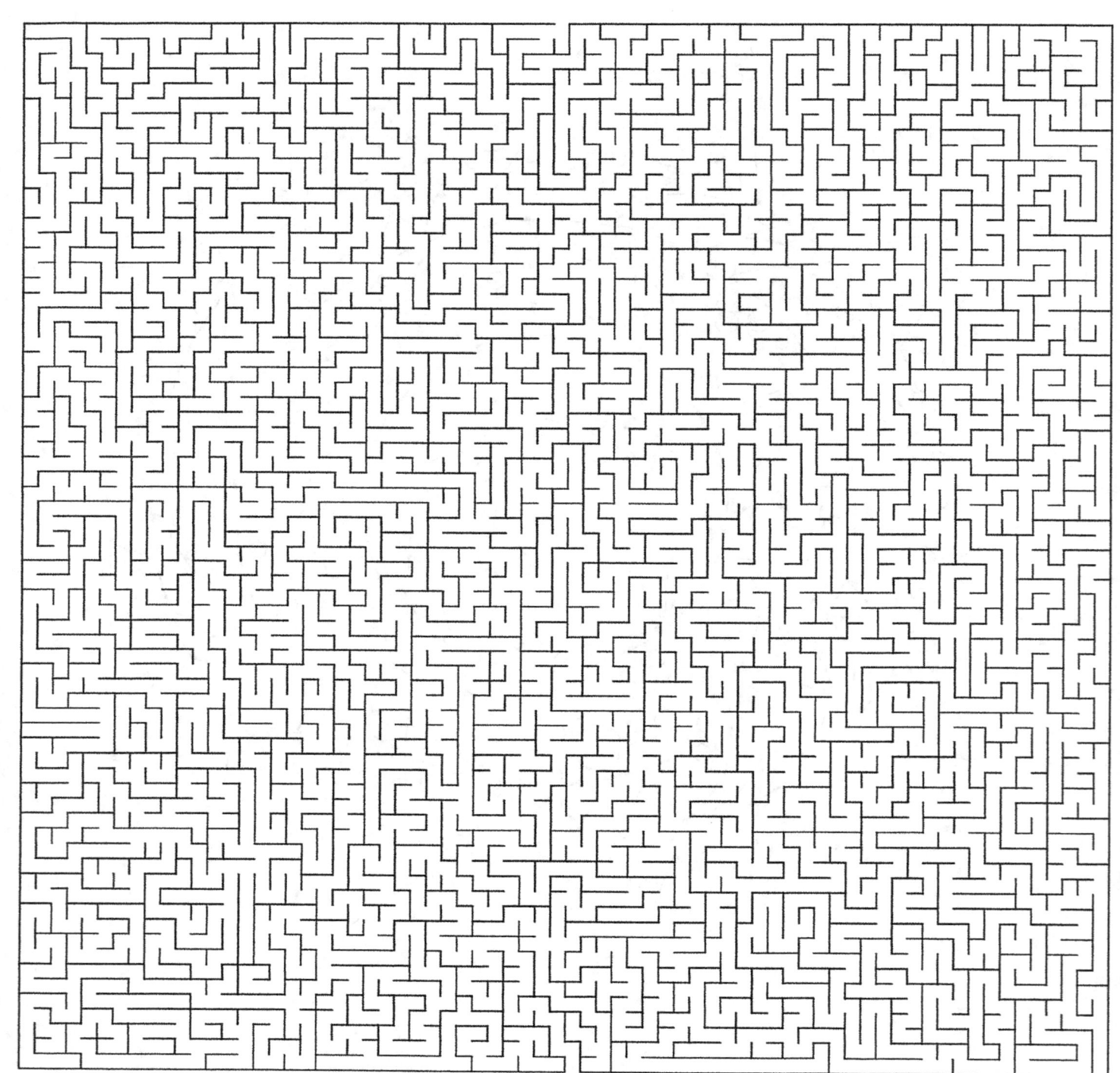

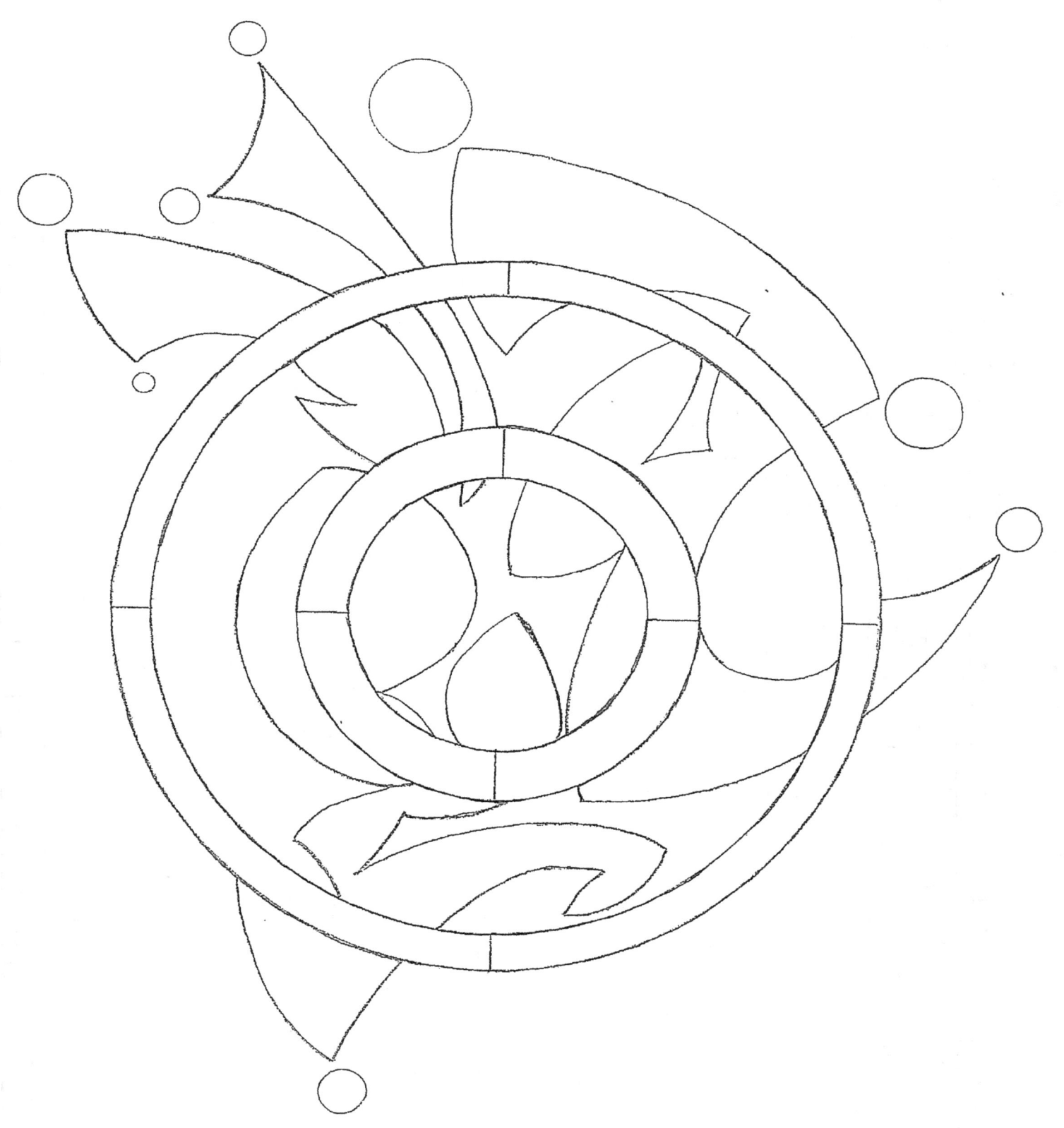

Work like you don't need the money. Love like you've never been hurt.
Dance like nobody's watching.

Satchel Paige

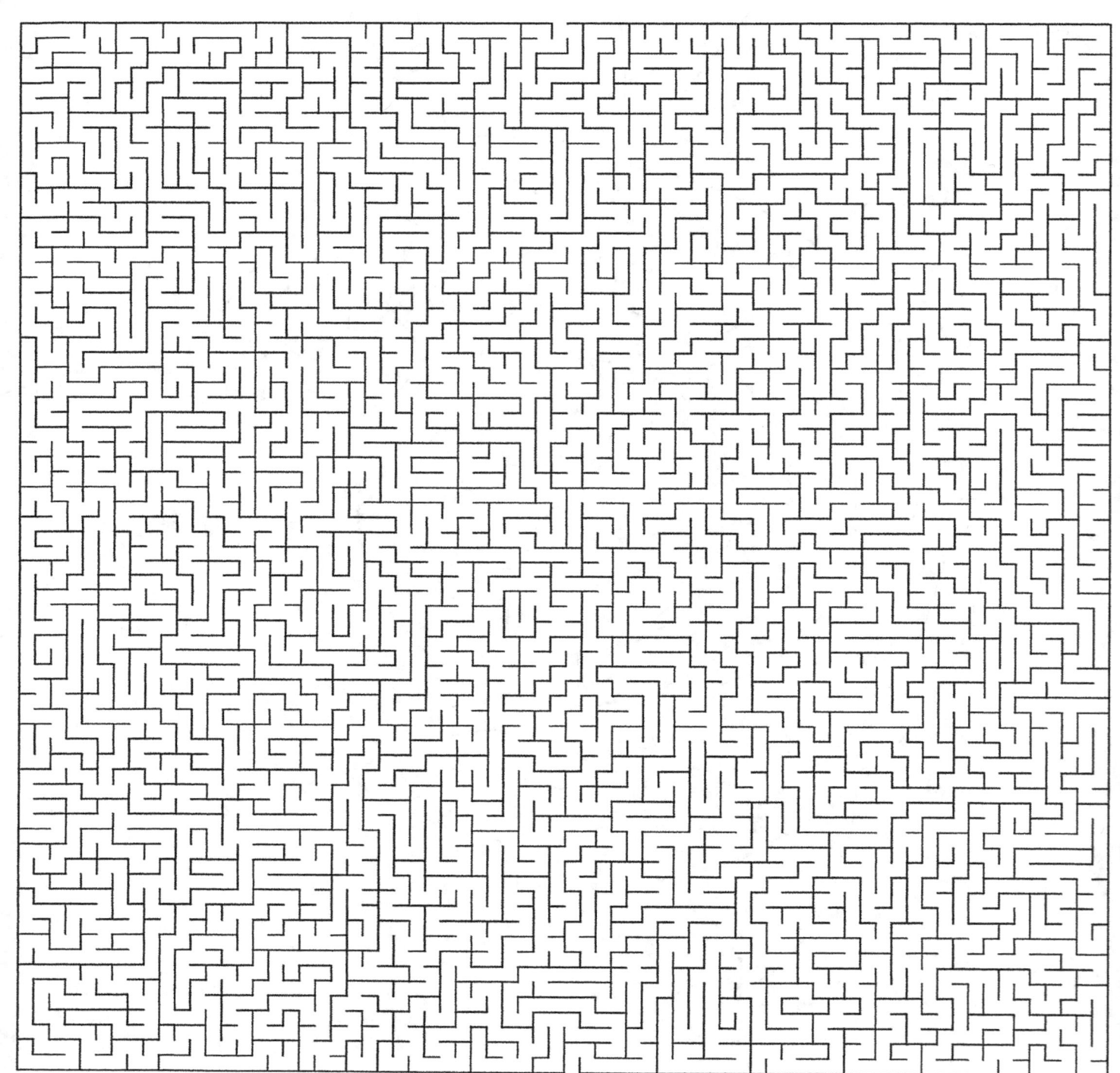

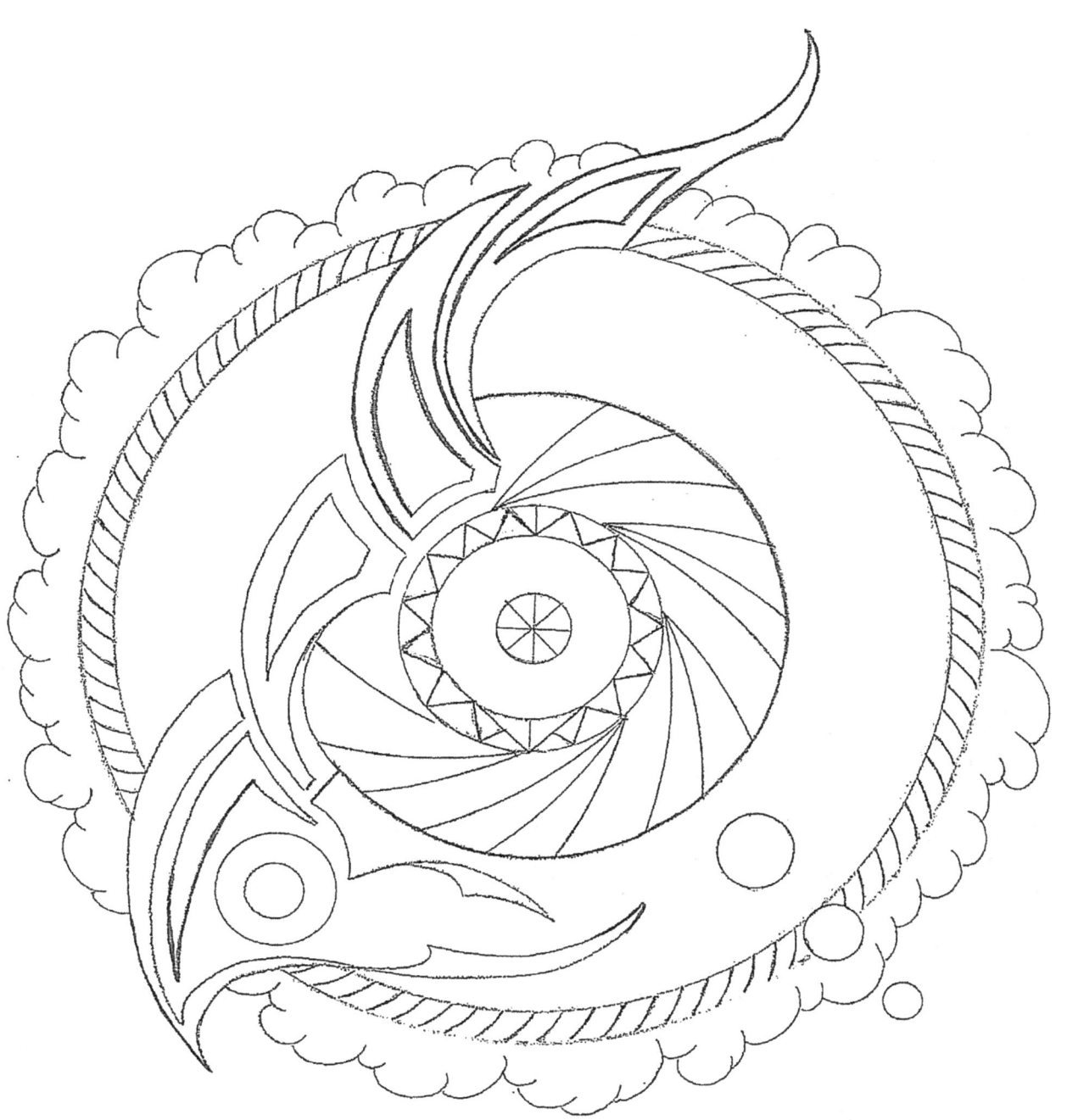

To enjoy good health, to bring true happiness to one's family, to bring peace to all, one must first discipline and control one's own mind. If a man can control his mind he can find the way to Enlightenment, and all wisdom and virtue will naturally come to him.

Buddha

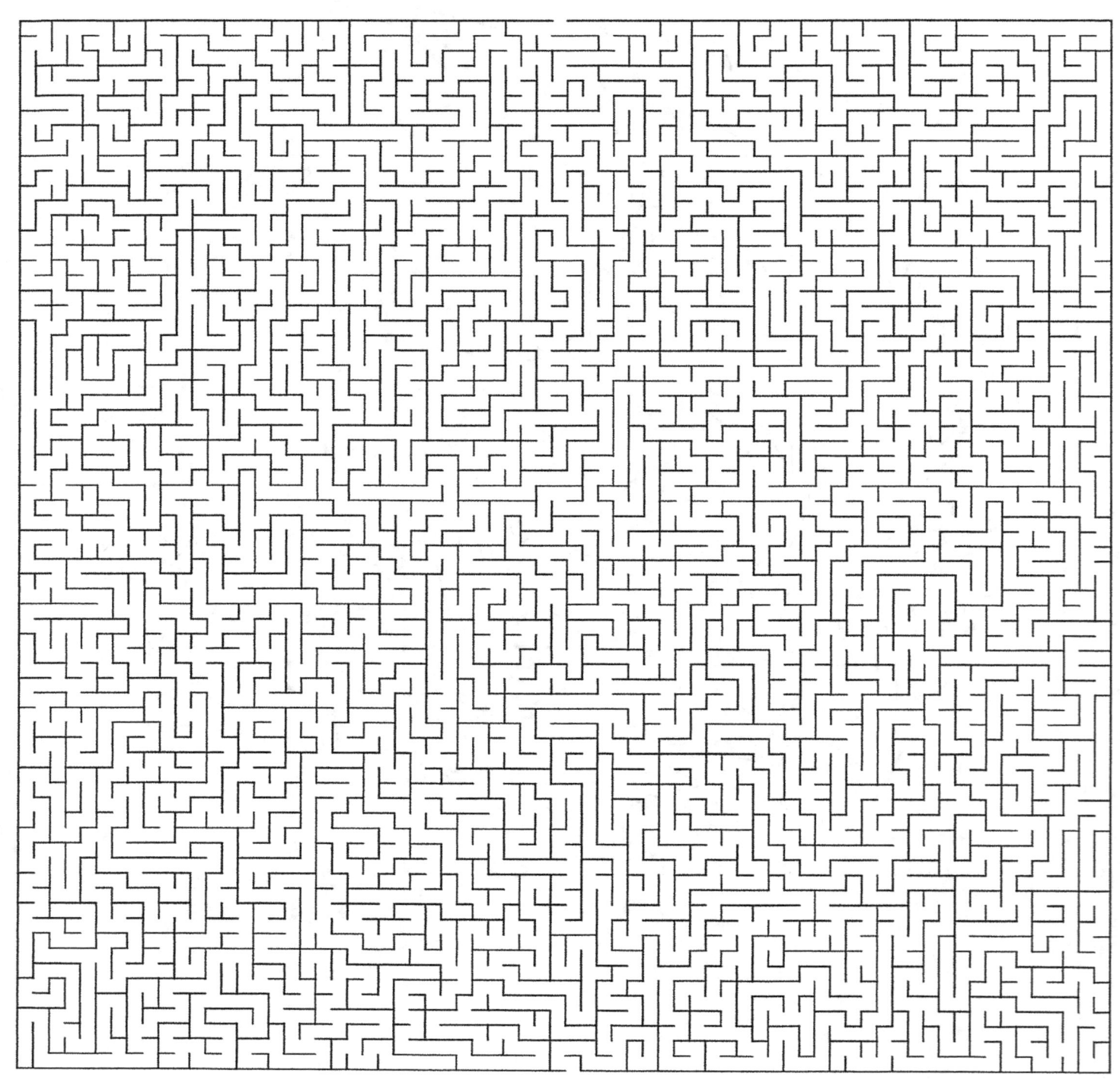

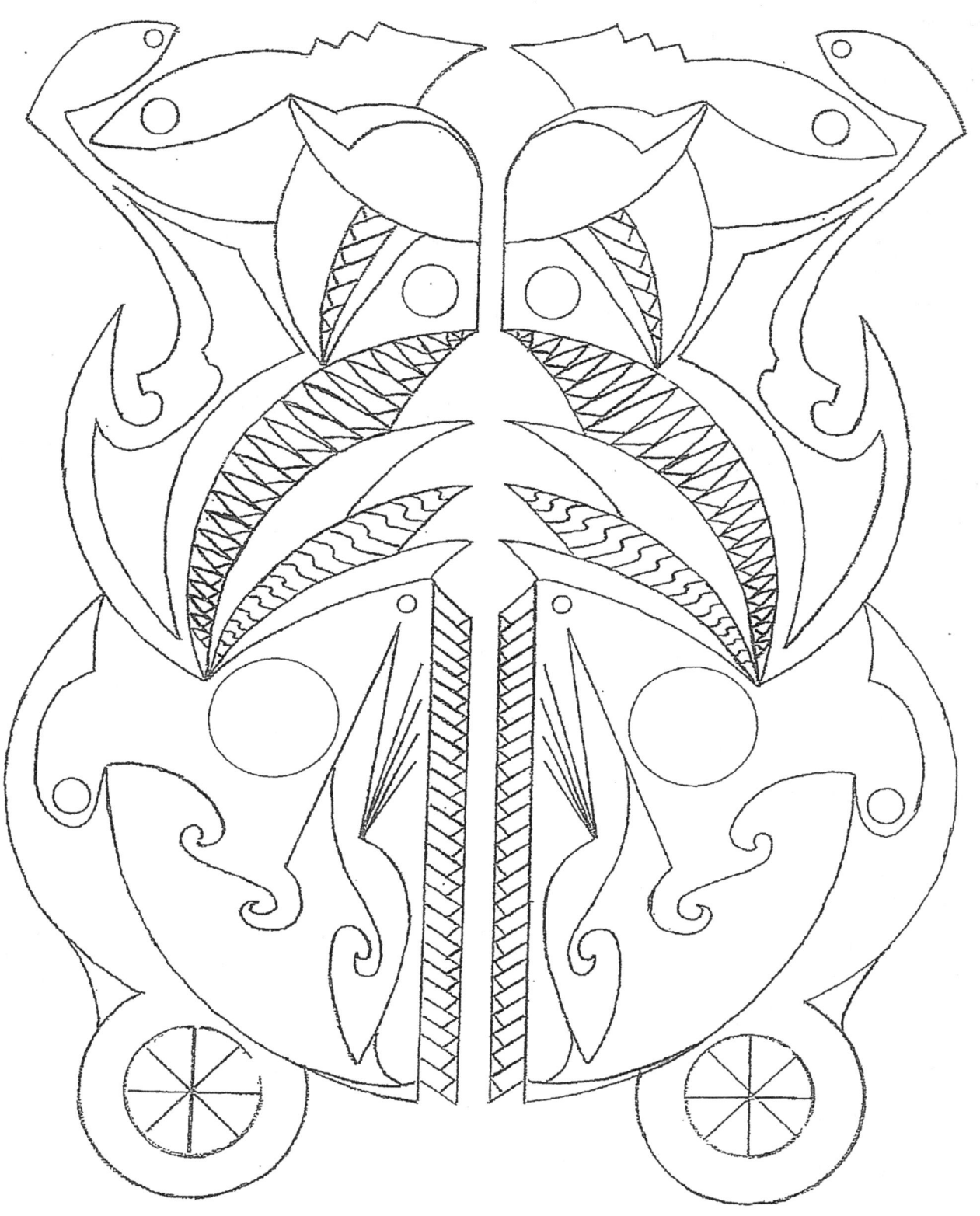

Do not go where the path may lead, go instead where there is no path and leave a trail.

Ralph Waldo Emerson

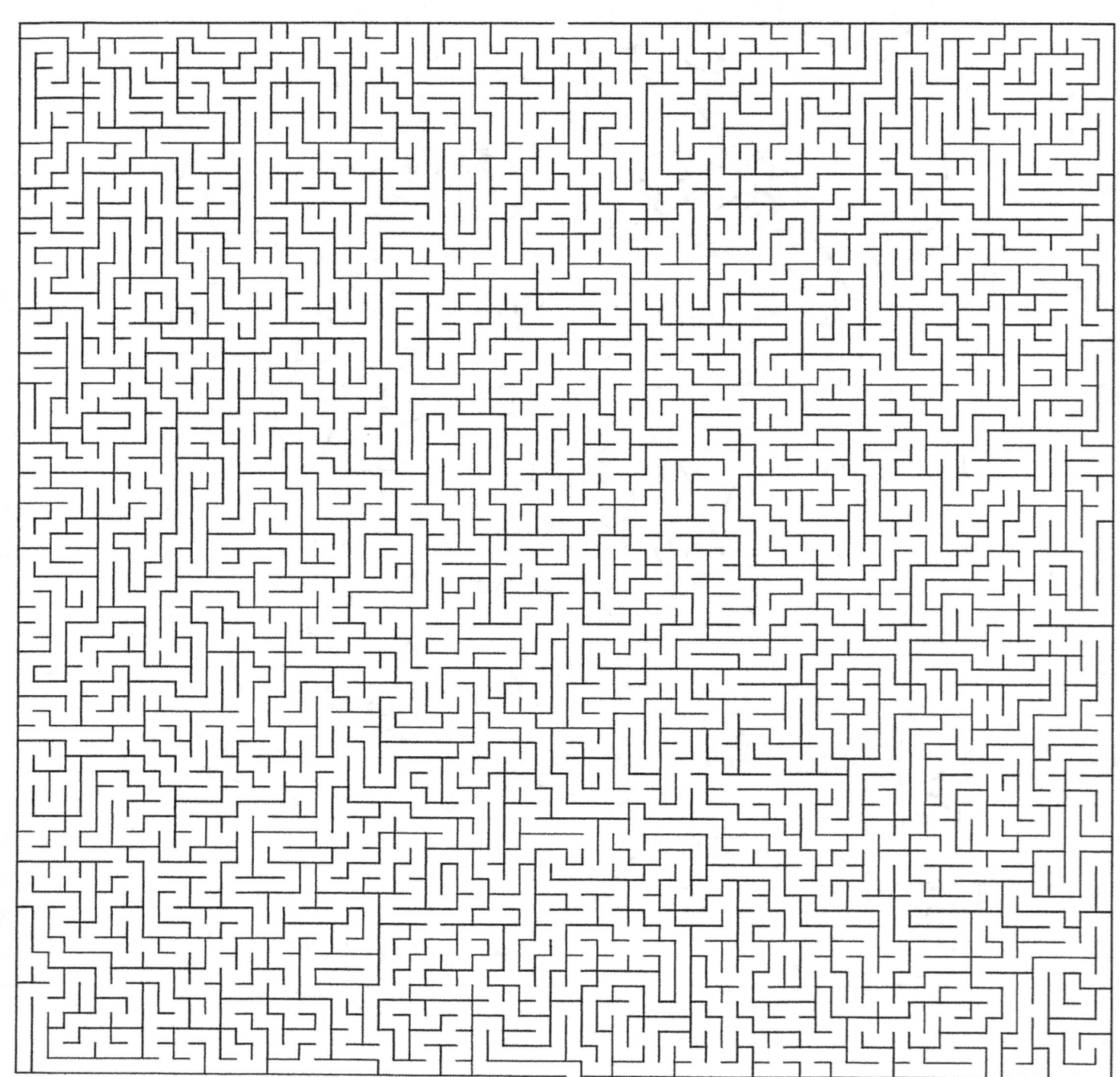

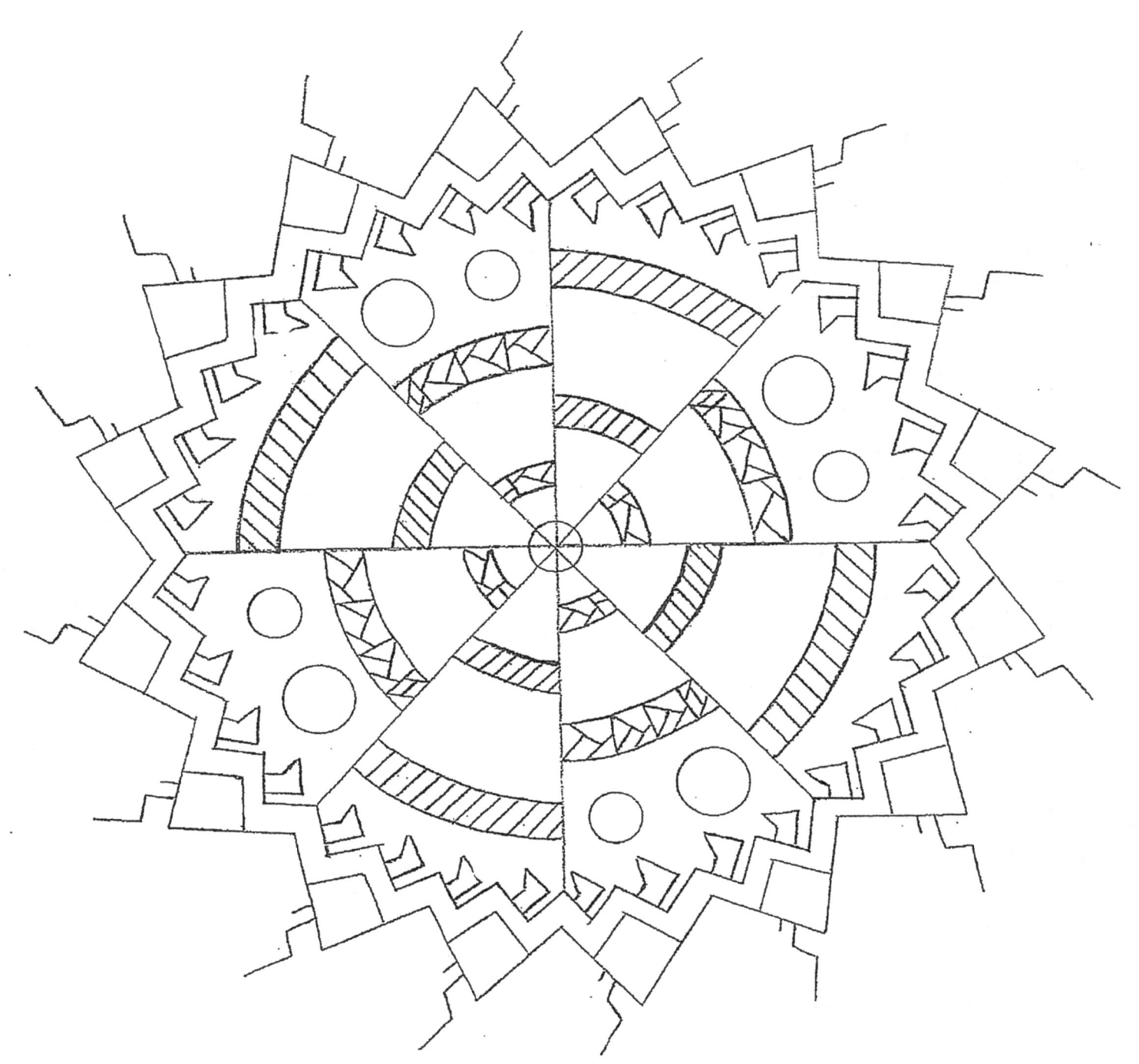

Don't wish it was easier, wish you were better. Don't wish for less problems, wish for more skills. Don't wish for less challenge, wish for more wisdom.

Jim Rohn

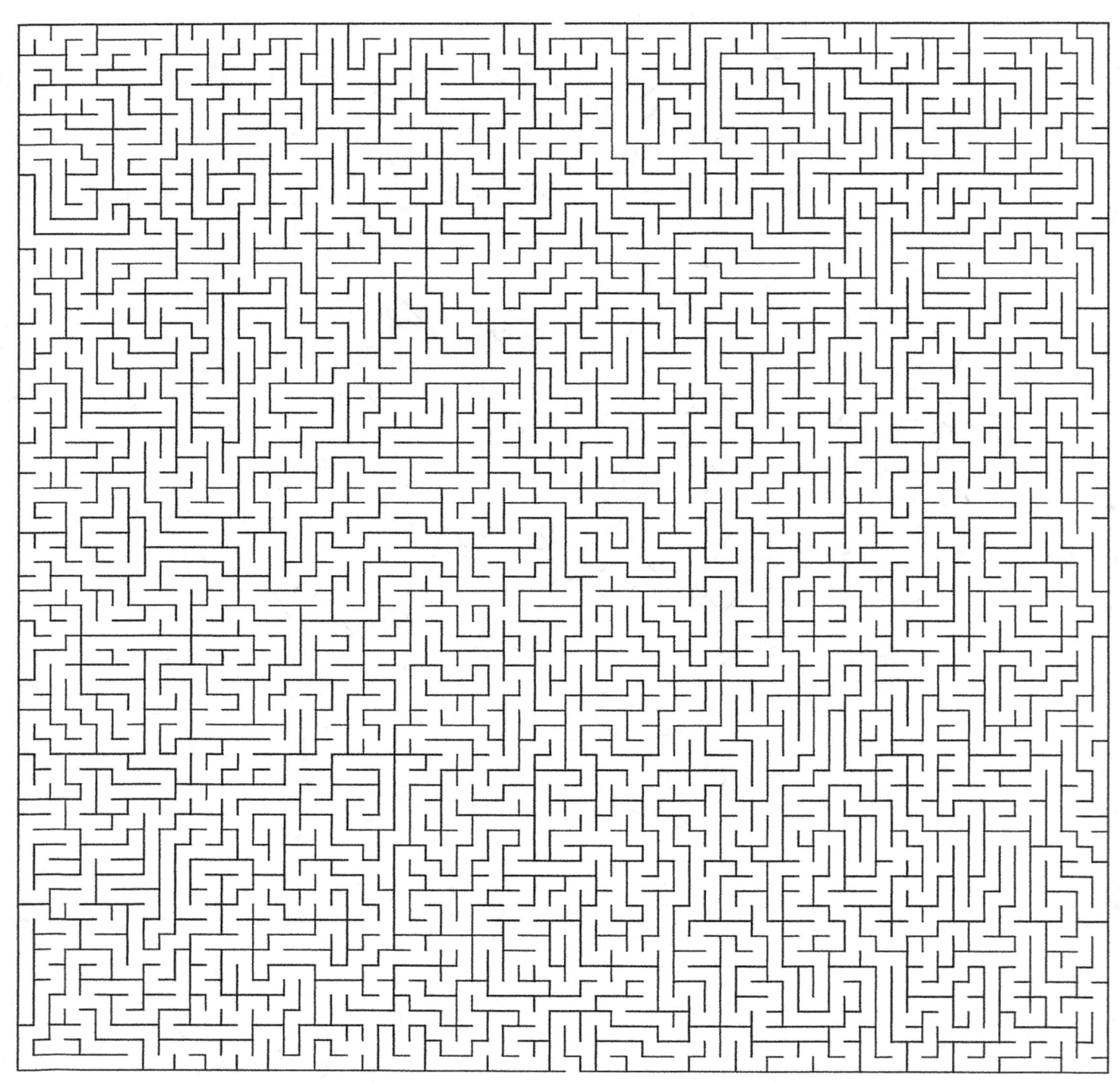

www.ingramcontent.com/pod-product-compliance
Lightning Source LLC
Chambersburg PA
CBHW081732220526

45468CB00008B/2071